ROSEDALE

ROSEDALE

Bess Hillery Crawford

The BOSTON MILLS PRESS

www.bostonmillspress.com

Canadian Cataloguing in Publication Data

Crawford, Bess, 1946–

Rosedale
Includes bibliographical references and index.

ISBN 1-55046-323-3

1. Rosedale (Toronto, Ont.) — History. 2. Toronto (Ont.) — History.
3. Rosedale (Toronto, Ont.) — History — Pictorial works.
4. Toronto (Ont.) — History — Pictorial works. I. Title.

FC3097.52.C72 2000   971.3'541   C00-9311821-6
F1059.5.T686R67 2000

04 03 02 01 00   1 2 3 4 5

Published in 2000 by
BOSTON MILLS PRESS
132 Main Street
Erin, Ontario N0B 1T0
Tel 519-833-2407
Fax 519-833-2195
e-mail books@bostonmillspress.com
www.bostonmillspress.com

Distributed in Canada by
GENERAL DISTRIBUTION SERVICES LIMITED
325 Humber College Boulevard
Toronto, Canada M9W 7C3
Orders 1-800-387-0141 Ontario & Quebec
Orders 1-800-387-0172 NW Ontario & other provinces
e-mail cservice@genpub.com

An affiliate of
STODDART PUBLISHING CO. LIMITED
34 Lesmill Road
Toronto, Ontario, Canada
M3B 2T6
Tel 416-445-3333
Fax 416-445-5967
e-mail gdsinc@genpub.com

Distributed in the United States by
GENERAL DISTRIBUTION SERVICES INC.
PMB 128, 4500 Witmer Industrial Estates
Niagara Falls, New York 14305-1386
Toll-free 1-800-805-1083
Toll-free fax 1-800-481-6207
e-mail gdsinc@genpub.com
www.genpub.com

OVERLEAF: *Rosedale House,* circa 1832. Watercolour by James W. Hamilton
Alden G. Meredith, *Mary's Rosedale and Gossip of Little York,* Toronto Reference Library

Text design by Bess Hillery Crawford and Gill Stead
Jacket design by Gill Stead
Printed and bound in Canada by Friesen Printers

THE CANADA COUNCIL | LE CONSEIL DES ARTS
FOR THE ARTS | DU CANADA
SINCE 1957 | DEPUIS 1957

*We acknowledge for their financial support of our
publishing program the Canada Council, the Ontario Arts Council,
and the Government of Canada through the Book Publishing
Industry Development Program (BPIDP).*

Dedicated to

Anna Ellen Stockdale Hillery

Rosedale Ravine, circa 1900.
Toronto Reference Library 968-12-568

Acknowledgments

Most of the material for this book was found at the Metropolitan Toronto Reference Library. Anyone who is not familiar with that library is missing a wealth of information about almost any topic imaginable. My research started as a purely casual exercise and gradually developed into an all-out foray for information about Toronto in its early days and specifically information pertaining to Rosedale. My thanks go to all the authors both living and dead who, through their writing, got me interested in the history of Toronto. The staff at the library have acquired a vast reservoir of material about Toronto, past and present. Toronto owes a huge debt of gratitude to men like Henry Scadding and John Ross Robertson, who left a gold mine of information. Also, our collective thanks should go to all the private individuals and families who have over the years given letters, photo albums, diaries and other memorabilia; their donations are a tremendous asset to the library. Did they imagine the thrill that could be generated by reading the actual letters written by Samuel Peters Jarvis, ink blots and all, sealing wax still present on the outside sheet? Such an experience tends to move one's imagination into high gear.

My twin brother, John Hillery, and my long-time friend Jon Maxim were probably the two people most instrumental in spurring me into action. Their encouraging words, when I first hatched the idea for this book, gave me the confidence to begin. My daughter, Melissa, helped solve the myriad computer problems encountered along the way. My husband, Roger, took many of the photographs, edited the first draft, and bought me the much-needed laser printer. My brother-in-law, Carter Crawford, from Houston, Texas gave an outsider's perspective on the first draft. Mario Angastiniotis produced great pictures, provided photographic advice and let me borrow his camera.

Special thanks go to Bronwen Ledger for editing the first drafts. I could never have done this without her professional input. Bill Greer's comments were also especially helpful. His vast knowledge of old Toronto buildings and architectural details provided welcome contributions.

CONTENTS

Introduction	9
The Story of Rosedale	13
Early Beginnings	25
The Era of Subdividing	33
Rosedale Plans of Subdivision 1854-1910	34
Chronology of Development 1854-1890	35
Rosedale and the Jarvis Family	39
William Botsford Jarvis	39
Samuel Peters Jarvis	53
Edgar John Jarvis	59
Setting the Scene	65
Milestones 1840-1900	66
A Bird's-Eye View of Rosedale by Street, 1890	69
A Who's Who of Rosedale's First Century	81
Street Names: Their Origin and Evolution	88
The First Landowners	84
The Original Rosedale Estates	95
Architecture of Rosedale Homes	97
Rosedale House 1824	102
Drumsnab 1834	104

Chestnut Park 1850-55	106
Caverhill 1855	110
Idlewold 1859	112
The Dale 1862	114
Denbrae 1876	116
Lorne Hall 1876	118
Hollydene 1876-1880	120
The Thom House 1881	122
Guiseley House 1885	124
North Rosedale	127
Real Estate Agents	133
Builders, Trades and Materials	136
Rosedale Architects	145
Rosedale Architects and the Homes They Designed	146
Heritage Toronto's Inventory of Heritage Homes	157
Rosedale Today	159
Notes and Sources	169
Photo Credits	171
Bibliography	172
Index	173

INTRODUCTION

For almost 150 years, Rosedale has been the home to Toronto's elite. It is the city's oldest surviving suburb; it is also its best-known and best-loved. The name itself evokes visions of winding tree-lined streets, stately old homes and well-manicured lawns. One can envision the Victorian Toronto of old; the horse-drawn carriages, coach houses, gas lamps and women in long bustled skirts. Rosedale, by any other name, would not carry the same mystique. Even the legend of how Toronto's charming suburb got its name is enveloped in romanticism. Mary Jarvis named her country estate "Rosedale" after the many roses growing wild on her property.

There is a mood to Rosedale that other neighbourhoods cannot replicate. The mystique goes beyond the wealth and fame of its residents, the grandeur of the houses and the beauty of its setting. Rosedale is the embodiment of Canadian culture and class, the home of old money and old families. It is steeped in history. The stories of the people who once lived here are interwoven into the eclectic spirit of the area and the uniqueness of the homes.

My interest in Rosedale dates back to the 1960s, when my husband and I began the search for our first home. We took the scenic route through Rosedale, goggling wide-eyed at the fine Victorian residences, which we certainly aspired to, but could hardly hope to afford.

Twenty years later, we bought a run-down rooming house on Crescent Road. From then on, my love-affair with Rosedale intensified. At the Metropolitan Toronto Reference Library, I found maps of Rosedale dated 1854, 1884, 1890 and 1905. They contained original street names, lot and plan numbers, and the names of owners. During renovations to our house, we discovered newspapers from June 1900 filled with articles and advertisements that revealed glimpses of Toronto life at the turn of the century. Our house itself was a historical gem, complete with its original butler's pantry, ice-closet, maid's staircase, marble shower, mother-of-pearl bells for calling the hired help, and a speaking horn from the kitchen to the third floor. Electric wiring for the many wall sconces had been run through the pipes formerly used for manufactured gas.

Carpenters' notes on the back of window frames in the sunroom referred to it as the "Palm Room." The garage even boasted a turn-table set into the floor to turn the car or coach around, ready for the next excursion.

Eleven years later, our family downsized to a smaller but older home on South Drive, vintage 1884. I have since discovered it was one of the first 42 homes built in Rosedale. By this time, my husband and I had taken early retirement, which left me time to renovate the house and research its history. The search for information became intoxicating and consuming.

Surprisingly, I found no books completely devoted to Rosedale, although many authors over the past 150 years have included descriptions of the area, its houses and estates, and histories of the interesting or famous people who lived in the suburb or were instrumental in planning and developing it. The Metropolitan Toronto Reference Library was a gold mine of information about historic Toronto. Personal diaries, letters and papers of the Jarvis and Cawthra families were found, along with the copious notes and writings of men like Henry Scadding and John Ross Robertson. Scadding was Rector of Holy Trinity Church and resident of York from the early to late 1800s, and Robertson was a newspaper reporter and founder of the Toronto *Evening Telegram*. Scadding filled his diary with detailed descriptions of the city and important local events. *Toronto of Old,* published in 1872, contains many of Scadding's reminiscences. John Ross Robertson gathered together an incredible number of articles and pictures about Toronto and released them in a six-volume work, *Landmarks of Toronto,* which was published between 1898 and 1914. These personal accounts bring the city's history alive with their representations of daily life in the 1800s.

I gathered details about property ownership and people living in Rosedale during the latter half of the 19th century from *Toronto Directories*, maps, newspapers, the Ontario Land Registry Office, and sources such as the *Macmillan Dictionary of Canadian Biography*. Visual impressions of the period were gleaned from paintings, sketches, illustrated newspapers and catalogues, as well as from the vast collection of photographs available in the Baldwin Room of the Metropolitan Toronto Reference Library.

As my pile of information grew, I decided to organize my research efforts into a book. In my mind, it seemed that Rosedale deserved more than a passing note in the history of Toronto. I wanted others to enjoy the interesting story behind this delightful suburb that is now in the heart of the city.

This book focuses primarily on the areas I had an interest in. The various chapters include a general history of the area between 1790 and 1910, accounts of real estate transactions, including subdivisions and land costs, the architecture of the houses and dates of construction, building methods, materials, finishes and amenities. There are also references to the people who commissioned homes and the families who lived in them. In some areas the information was endless; in fact, that was the reason I restricted research to the period from 1790 to 1910. In other cases, there were huge gaps in available information. Sometimes the accuracy of facts and figures was questionable. *Toronto Directories* were not always entirely correct, and names were often spelled differently from one year to the next. Where discrepancies arose, I had to judge which source was the most reliable. I hope any inadvertent errors will be met with understanding.

With the information contained in *Rosedale,* residents and weekend historians will be able to locate the lots on the historical maps, trace ownership back to the 1890s, and discover who the previous owners were and what they did. Pictures of 115 houses as they appear today and the architects that designed them are provided. Another 93 photographs of historic buildings, scenes, people, newspaper advertisements, and maps give the flavour of the times.

Many people have been gathering information about Rosedale throughout the years. Maybe their research projects will eventually be published as well. Undoubtedly, there is a tale for every old house, and it would take volumes to recount all of them. Hopefully *Rosedale* will not be the last word on Rosedale.

"Beyond its evident limitations, its mitigated stuffiness, its snobbery is neither better nor worse than I can find any day in any CBC office. Rosedale, and all other 'Rosedales' across the country, represent the difference between being merely housebroken, and being civilized. Canada both cherishes and loathes the 'Rosedale myth.' Yet, without it, without its quiet embodiment of decent manners and its sense of family and historical continuity, we might be merely Americans."

Scott Symons in Peter C. Newman's *The Canadian Establishment*

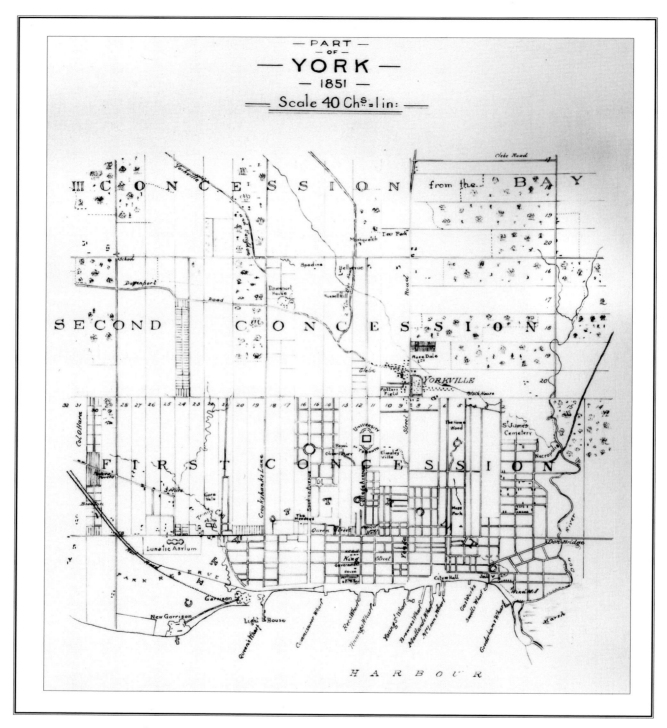

Copy of a portion of a map of Township of York by J. A. Browne, F.S.A., D.P., Surveyor.

Metropolitan Toronto Reference Library

THE STORY OF ROSEDALE

Rosedale, the charming, historic neighbourhood in the heart of Toronto, has been an enclave of Toronto's elite for almost 150 years. It is located only a few miles from the city's financial district at King and Bay; a short subway ride brings one to the station at Crescent Road and Yonge Street. Characterized by winding tree-lined streets, stately Victorian homes and well-manicured lawns, Rosedale is the home to old families and discreet wealth. Enveloping a geographic area of roughly 450 acres, its topography is traversed by two sizable ravines running on an angle roughly northwest to southeast that converge near Bloor Street East and Castle Frank. These ravines to a large extent dictate the layout of the streets and location of the homes. Over the past century and a half, more than 1,500 houses have been built here, most in the period from 1890 to 1910. About 2,500 families now reside in the area.

In the early 1820s, when the story of Rosedale began, the scene was much different. Toronto, then York, was only a small, insignificant town on the shores of Lake Ontario, with a population of fewer than 8,000 residents. The city limits extended only as far north as the Second Concession Line at Bloor Street, but most of the inhabitants were clustered near the lake. Well-to-do establishment families built their homes near the waterfront, close to the market, the wharfs and the Governor's residence on Front Street. The further north from the lake one travelled, the rougher the terrain, the more rural the complexion of the surroundings and the sparser the population.

In 1824 William Botsford Jarvis, a young gentleman of a well-known and respected local family, bought a 110-acre estate on the east side of the Yonge Street Highway, on the northern outskirts of Toronto. He was 25 years of age and worked as a clerk in the provincial secretary's office. For the purchase price of £1,150, the property included a simple farm house that had been erected by the previous owner, Mr. John Small.

"Rosedale,"
home of William
Botsford Jarvis
and family.
J. Ross Robertson,
Landmarks of Toronto, Vol. 1,
Toronto Reference Library

While the house was by all accounts quite basic, it was situated in a particularly beautiful and romantic spot, facing west towards Yonge Street with spectacular views to the ravines on the west, the south and the east.

A dense forest of cedars, maple, oak and aspen covered much of the property. The hillsides and natural clearings were blanketed with a wide variety of wild flowers, and a small stream meandered through the valley into a pond. On the hill to the north was a stand of pine trees, probably the present site of Pine Hill Road.

Imagine Mary Boyles Powell, the young bride of William Botsford Jarvis, leaving the refined home of her grandfather, Chief Justice William Dummer Powell, in 1827 to start her new life in the rustic far-reaches of the city. She was accustomed to living on Front Street in the heart of upper-crust society and the bustling activity of town near the wharfs, the market, and shops.

To reach their new home, Mary and William probably set out in a small buggy, or even a carriage or wagon, heading north up the Yonge Street Highway, which at the time was just a wide and straight dirt road. The couple traversed a countryside of forests and clearings, interrupted by large farms with fenced fields and the occasional house. As they neared the Bloor Street city limits, they might have pointed out to their left Potters Field, the burial ground for strangers and people without family, located north of Bloor and west of Yonge Street.

At this point, the couple would have left the Yonge Street Highway, and turned east along what is now Bloor Street. By this route they could detour the Yorkville toll-gate. The newlyweds might then have stopped for lunch at the Red Lion, a popular inn on the east side of Yonge Street, north of Bloor.

Setting off once more, they would have taken the first road running north (later known as Gwynne Street). This primitive track brought them down into a deep valley, over a small creek, and then up the steep sides of the ravine again. From this point on they were on their own property.

Their estate comprised the western portion of Township Lot 19 in the Second Concession from the Bay (for explanation see Early Beginnings). Today we know the site of their house as the northwest corner of Rosedale Road and Avondale Road.

Over the next few years, William and Mary Jarvis would make substantial improvements to their property. As children started to arrive on the scene, the original house was expanded. Local architect John Howard did most of the work, adding a large covered verandah, additional bedrooms, a sunroom and a conservatory. Outside, flower gardens were planted and fields enclosed with fences. The area to the south was allocated to orchards, while the area on the east, mid-way up what is now Avondale Road, became the vinery and gardens. Barns, a coach house, gazebo, gate house and peach house were constructed. By all accounts, the estate had by the late 1830s become quite a showplace.

For several years there were few other homes in the area. Judge Draper's rural cottage, "Hazeldean," was one of the closest, perched on the south side of the ravine overlooking the same valley and stream as "Rosedale."[1]

Little by little, other families moved into the burgeoning village of Yorkville, which spread north from Bloor Street on both sides of Yonge Street. William Botsford Jarvis was becoming an influential man. Following his appointment to the position of sheriff in 1827, he became more and more active in local affairs. He was also quite a speculator, investing in

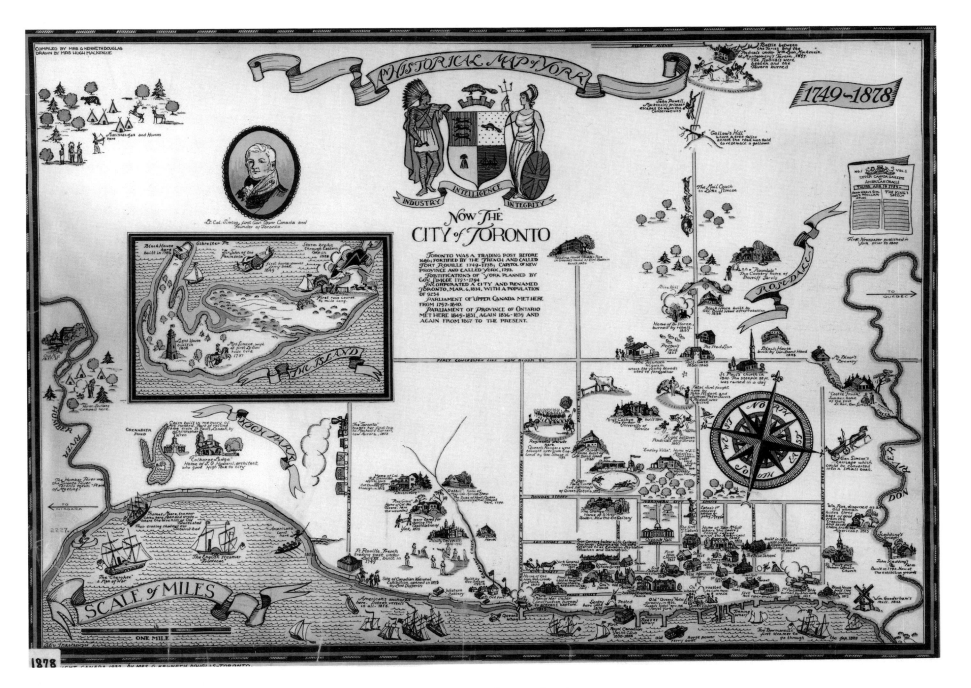

Historic Illustrated Map of York
Compiled by Mrs. G. Kenneth Douglas, drawn by Mrs. Hugh MacKenzie.
Toronto Reference Library

Severn Creek and Chief Justice Draper's house Hazeldean, circa 1860.

Watercolour over pencil.
Toronto Reference Library
T32210

various land deals, both in Toronto proper and in Yorkville, betting that population would eventually overflow the rapidly growing city into this outlying area. He, together with Joseph Bloor and Dr. Gwynne, physician to the Jarvis family, planned a land venture on the northeast corner of Yonge and Bloor Streets. The three men went as far as planning out streets and subdividing the property into housing lots.

Joseph Bloor had purchased a plot of land on the north side of what is now Bloor Street, which extended east as far as Sherbourne Street, west to Gwynne Street, then north into the Rosedale ravine. He situated a mill and brewery on the south bank of a pond located between the Sherbourne and Huntley Street bridges. Henry Scadding, a local Toronto diarist of the period, described the brewery as a squat, red brick structure, some 50 or 60 feet in breadth, by 100 feet in depth.[2]

Around the same time, the Severn Brothers also settled in Yorkville, locating a brewery and malting enterprise just north of Davenport Road, at the west end of the same ravine as Joseph Bloor. This brewery was much more commercial in size than Bloor's brewery, consisting of several buildings two or three storeys high, including residential quarters. Balconies adorned the upper floors, allowing the inhabitants a view of the idyllic countryside beyond.

Across the road, on the west side of the Yonge Street Highway, was the home of Dr. Horne, the brother-in-law of the first president of the Bank of Upper Canada and also its chief teller. During the uprising of 1837 and the fight for colonial self-government and autonomy from English rule, rebel leader William Lyon Mackenzie interrupted his march down Yonge Street to burn Robert Horne's house to the ground. Mackenzie was intent on inflicting a similar fate on "Rosedale," but rational minds intervened and the Jarvis homestead was saved.

After the rebellion, Governor Bond Head erected a two-storey block house on the east side of Yonge Street atop the Rosedale ravine (near Belmont Street) to protect the Yonge Highway. Another block house kept guard at the northeast corner of Sherbourne Street and the eastern terminus of Bloor Street.

By the mid-1830s Mary and William Jarvis had new neighbours to the immediate north. The family of Joseph Price had purchased a large farm and erected their home called "Thornwood." One of the sons, James Hervey Price, was an important personage of the period, Minister of Provincial Parliament and Commissioner of Crown Lands. Price was a known supporter of the Radicals and William Lyon Mackenzie in the Rebellion of 1837. James and his sister, Miss Sarah Price, sold off most of the family's property after their father's death in 1852. Sarah, however, remained in the house, later known as "Woodbine Cottage."

Mr. William Mathers, a local merchant, bought a large portion of the original Price family property in 1847 and built a home for himself, which he christened "Chestnut Grove." Mathers's land extended east as far as the Don Valley. Eight years later he sold his house and the land immediately surrounding it to Mr. David Lewis Macpherson, a newcomer from Montreal. Mathers kept his still sizable land holdings to the east.

Red Lion Hotel, circa 1885.
Toronto Reference Library
T11064

As the Yorkville area became more populated, brick and tile yards made their appearance in what is now Ramsden Park. The manufacturing concern was owned first by Messrs. James and William Townsley and later by Thomas Nightingale, who was connected to the Townsley family. Red and yellow bricks from these yards were used to build many of the homes in Rosedale. In fact, Thomas Nightingale used them to construct his own home in Rosedale at the corner of what is now Crescent Road and South Drive.

By 1854 when the first plan of subdivision for Rosedale was registered, the City of Toronto still extended only as far north as Bloor Street, but the Village of Yorkville had become a growing concern, extending north to Cottingham Street and the Canadian Pacific Railway lines, and east to Sherbourne Street.

The geographic area in current Rosedale includes most of what was defined in the mid-1800s as Township Lots 18, 19 and 20 in the Second Concession from the Bay. Township Lot 20 was the southernmost of these holdings, located north of Bloor Street East and stretching eastward to the Don Valley. It is the present site of South Rosedale. In 1796 this 200-acre

Joseph Bloor's Brewery, circa 1865.

Watercolour by R. Baigent. Royal Ontario Museum and Toronto Reference Library T10850

Block House, Yonge Street, 1863.

Watercolour by Henri Perre Toronto Reference Library, J. Ross Robertson Collection T11593

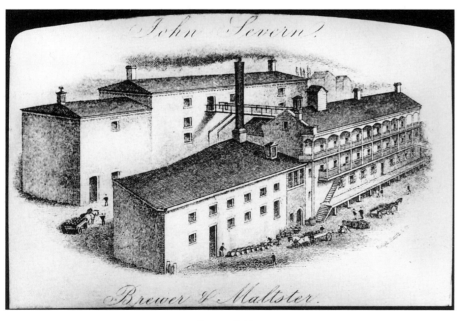

Severn's Brewery.
Engraving by Rolph, Smith & Co. Toronto Reference Library T10907

Brickyards, Yonge Street, circa 1880s.
Toronto Reference Library T10853

farm was granted to Captain George Playter. He put up a rustic log house on the summit of a hill, near the north end of Parliament Street. The eastern portion of this property, totalling 119 acres, was sold in 1834 to Francis Cayley and renamed "Drumsnab."[3]

It was around this time that Joseph Bloor had purchased his section of land in the western part of Township Lot 20. This property ran along the north side of the Second Concession Line (now Bloor Street), from about as far east as Sherbourne Street, to as far west as Gwynne Street, then north to the creek in the Rosedale ravine. Joseph Bloor bought this property as a land speculation venture with William Botsford Jarvis. The scheme was shortlived, and Bloor subsequently sold his land to Jarvis and moved to a cottage at 100 Bloor Street East. Mr. John Rose operated Bloor's brewery for a few more years, but it was eventually abandoned and some locals even though it was haunted.[4]

By 1843 much of the western part of Township Lot 20 had been acquired by Samuel Peters Jarvis, a cousin of William Botsford Jarvis. George Severn and his sons owned the plot of land in the northernmost sector of Lot 20 where their brewery stood, while the extreme eastern portion of Lot 20 still belonged to the Cayley family.

Township Lot 19, the area now known as West Rosedale, was from 1824 until 1854 William Botsford Jarvis's original Rosedale estate. This farm extended north from what is now Yonge and Aylmer Avenue/Rosedale Valley Road to Crescent Road. In 1854 Jarvis sold a large parcel of this farm to Frederick Carruthers and George Duggan, withholding only 41 acres of the original estate on which "Rosedale House" was located. It was George Duggan who registered Plan 104 of subdivision for the original Rose-Park, as the suburb was then called, in 1854.

As for the eastern portion of Township Lot 19, this was owned by the Helliwell family. Thomas Helliwell was a merchant from Todmorden, England who had immigrated to Canada in 1818. By 1821, he had purchased 10 acres of land on the Don River just north of the Town of York. He and his four sons built a brewery, distillery and malt house and called it Todmorden. Later, grist and paper mills were acquired and expanded. The family soon became well known in the community and was instrumental in the early commercial development of the Toronto waterfront. Thomas Jr., the oldest son, had offices at Market Square and owned property along Lake Ontario. Helliwell's Wharf was the site of considerable commercial activity.

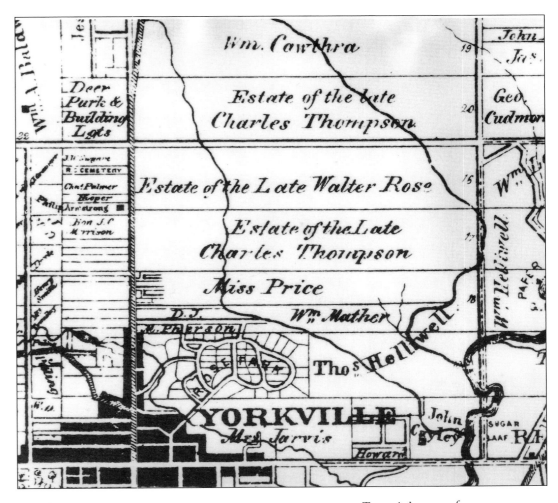

Tremain's map of the County of York Canada West, 1860.
Toronto Reference Library

Price's Mill
Watercolour by Joseph T. Rolph
Toronto Reference Library,
J. Ross Robertson Collection
T10893

Thomas Jr. bought grain for his father's mills and sold beer from the family brewery at the downtown location. After Thomas Sr.'s death in 1825, the brothers continued to operate the business. A fire destroyed the Todmorden mill and brewery in 1847. While Joseph, one of the brothers, rebuilt them shortly afterwards, the Helliwells sold to John, Thomas and George Taylor in 1855. The Taylors started three paper mills, and in 1880 George Taylor's sons took over and added the brickyards.

Further to the north was Township Lot 18, encompassing the area we know as Chestnut Park in the west and North Rosedale in the east. This property was purchased by Joseph Price in 1835. Price's Creek flowed through the ravine, roughly dissecting the farm. The family built a mill on the stream near the spot where the present Roxborough Drive crosses Mount Pleasant Road.

William Helliwell
J. Ross Robertson, *Landmarks of Toronto*, Vol. 2, Toronto Reference Library

Joseph Bloor
Toronto Reference Library T13662

The Price family sold the southern half of their farm to William Mathers in 1847. Mathers disposed of the western portion of this land in 1855 to David Lewis Macpherson, who took over the Chestnut Park estate, but he kept the large eastern part for himself. Eventually this was acquired from Mathers by Toronto lawyers James Edgar and Charles Ritchie and later still by the Scottish Ontario and Manitoba Land Company, who developed it into the residential neighbourhood of North Rosedale.

Today, the residential neighbourhood known as Rosedale encompasses an area of approximately 450 acres, and includes some 2,500 households.

Township lots in the second concession from the bay, circa 1855.
Adaptation of information obtained from the Ontario Registry Office and the Toronto Reference Library

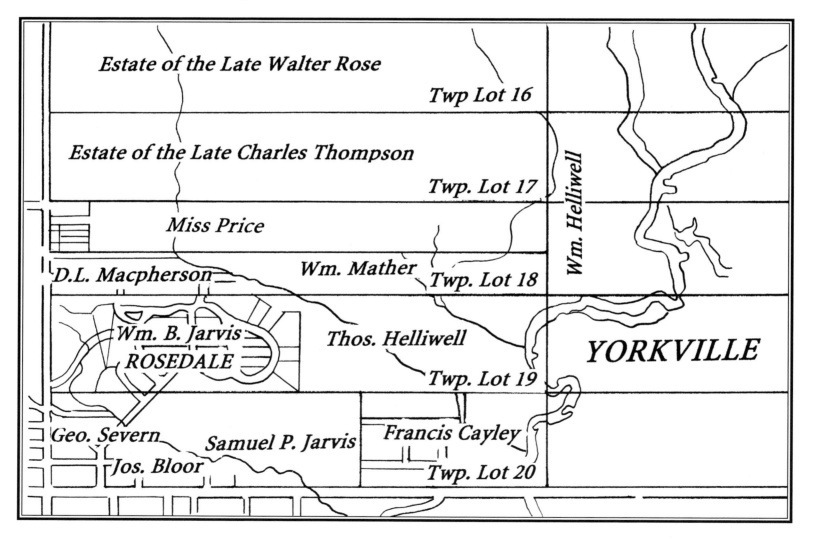

The physical character of the early suburb and the layout of the streets have not changed but are still determined to a large extent by the geographical positioning of the two ravines which meet at Castle Frank. The Rosedale ravine was the southern extension of what was known at the time as "Blue Hill," a steep gorge running north of Davenport Road, so called because of the bluish clay at the top of both its sides.

Rosedale today is contained by irregular boundaries that follow natural contours. Its border to the south is Rosedale Valley Road and the edge of the ravine that extends southeast to Bloor Street East at Castle Frank Road. The western perimeter follows Mount Pleasant Road north from Bloor Street as far as Rosedale Valley Road, and then cuts west to Yonge Street and north to Pricefield Road. The northern limit approximately follows the line of the Canadian Pacific Railway tracks, which run west to east along Pricefield Road, crosses over Mount Pleasant Road, and travels along Summerhill Avenue. It eventually meets the Glen Road extension and follows along Astley Avenue down to Chorley Park. The eastern boundary parallels Castle Frank Road and Bayview Avenue.

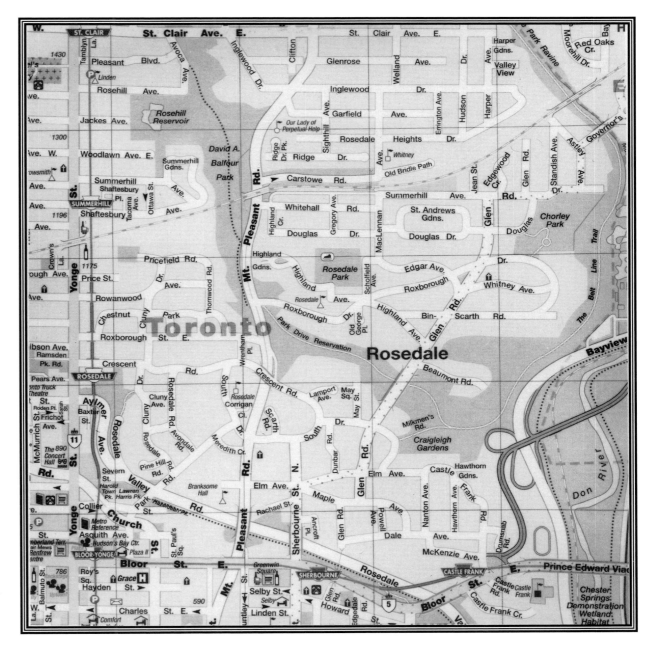

Present-day map of Rosedale.
Downtown Toronto Explorer, Map Art, Toronto Reference Library

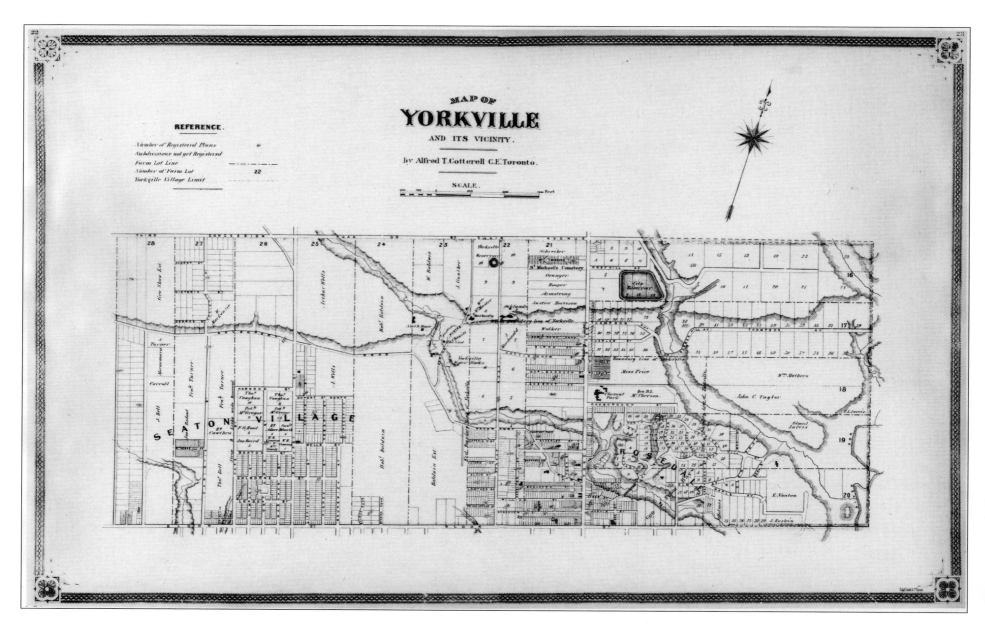

Map of Yorkville and its vicinity, circa 1875.
Alfred T. Cotterell, C. E., Toronto. Toronto Reference Library

EARLY BEGINNINGS

Township Lots in the Second Concession from the Bay

The course of development of the Rosedale suburb was haphazard at best, totally unlike fully planned residential communities such as Lawrence Park and the Kingsway. In these latter cases, visionaries Dinnick and Home Smith bought large parcels of land, subdivided them into lots, mapped out the streets, and hired architects and builders to design and construct homes of a similar architectural style. Both patterned their suburbs after the Garden City Movement, which was becoming popular in early 20th-century England. While Rosedale certainly has many of the same features as the Lawrence Park and Kingsway communities, namely the winding streets, tall trees, park-like setting and the interesting architectural style of the homes, there was no "grand scheme" envisioned by a single developer. Rosedale emerged in a very unorganized manner over an extended period. The fact that many individuals were involved in the process adds dramatically to its eclectic spirit.

We began our story with Mary and William Jarvis, but the history of Rosedale really starts in 1797, some 57 years prior to registration of the first plan of subdivision for Rose-Park. Originally all the land in the Township of York was owned by the Crown. In an organized effort to develop the region, the King's representative in Upper Canada, Governor Simcoe, divided the province of Ontario into counties. These counties were then sectioned off into townships, and each township was further divided into strips of land called concessions. These concessions were numbered in Roman numerals starting at Lake Ontario. They measured 100 chains across. Each concession was further divided into township lots. These lots usually contained about 200 acres, the area of an average farm. They were numbered in Arabic numerals and had a frontage of 20 chains (1/4 mile) and a depth of 100 chains (1 1/4 miles), the same as the concessions. Governor Simcoe granted these farm lots to important personages of the day.

Tracking ownership of the three large farms that comprised the original Township Lots 18, 19 and 20 in the Second Concession from the Bay reveals a wealth of information about events in 19th-century York. The detailed history of land sales in the area tells interesting family stories, charts an extensive record of land prices and paints a picture of the economic scene of the time. The record of transfers of ownership also gives us a glimpse of the legal system, the courts and the laws of the period. During periods of rapid growth, lots sold quickly and at ever-increasing values. Land speculation is documented by frequent subdivision of property that suggests rapid population growth and increasing personal wealth. Conversely, foreclosures and eroding property values signal recession and tough economic times.

While land sales and purchases in the original three Township Lots are quite easy to trace through the first half of the 19th century, the lineage of ownership becomes more complicated as frequent subdividing radically reduced lot sizes post-1860. The primary round of lot divisions is summarized in this chapter.

Township Lot 18

This portion of Rosedale, which includes the present Chestnut Park area and most of North Rosedale, was originally granted to Chief Justice Draper. The 200 acres of Township Lot 18 were purchased by Joseph Price in 1835, except for 10 acres in the southeast corner. Samuel Peters Jarvis put up the mortgage money of £480. Upon acquiring the property, Price immediately sold five acres in the southwest corner to his neighbour William Botsford Jarvis. In 1847 the Price family sold the southern half of Lot 18 to William Mathers for £550. Mathers, in turn, sold the western part of his southern half to David Lewis Macpherson in 1855 for £7,000. The property included the house "Chestnut Grove," recently built by Mathers. Mathers kept the eastern quarter of the property for himself.

In 1857 Sarah Price disposed of the southwest part of the northern half of Lot 18 for £2,375 to John Bugg, who almost immediately registered Plan 208 of subdivision. Sarah also sold the northwest part of the northern half of Lot 18 to Robert Robinson for £2,375.

The Price family made no new deals until 1873. At that time, Sarah sold more property to David Macpherson for $6,000. This must have been the remaining land on which the house "Woodbine Cottage" had stood. Also in 1873, Agnes Mathers granted William Mathers land on the extreme southern boundary of Lot 18 for $8,000.

By 1880 William Mathers had relinquished his southeastern sector of Lot 18 to the Scottish Ontario and Manitoba Land Company for $26,600. They in turn registered Plan 528. It is this subdivision that today forms most of the beautiful neighbourhood of North Rosedale.

Township Lot 19

Township Lot 19, the 192-acre farm lot on which the original Rose-Park suburb was located, was first granted to Abraham Lauraway in 1797. The property passed through a number of owners over the next two decades, including Isaiah Skinner in 1797, George Porter (for £600) in 1799, John Small in 1800 and finally William Botsford Jarvis, of York, gentleman, in 1824 for the price of £1,150.

The farmhouse originally built on the property by John Small was renovated and expanded by the Jarvises to accommodate their growing family. In 1851 William Botsford set up a trust with William Gwynne, Frederick W. Jarvis (William B.'s brother) and Philip Vankoughnet as joint tenants. Then, following the sudden death of his wife Mary in 1852, William Botsford moved out of "Rosedale House" to a residence on Front Street. While Jarvis did keep 41 acres including "Rosedale House" as an estate for his daughters, he ended up selling off the bulk of the property in the original farm lot to Frederick Carruthers and George Duggan in 1854 for £12,500. On December 20 of the same year, George Duggan registered Plan 104 of subdivision for Rose-Park.

Township Lot 20

As for the South Rosedale geographic area, Township Lot 20, its 200 acres were first granted in 1779 to Captain George Playter, who sold the western sector to Robert Horne in 1828 for £500. In 1831 the Playters sold another parcel of property, which fronted on Bloor Street and extended to the Rosedale ravine, to Joseph Bloor for £100. Bloor built a mill and brewery on the southeast banks of a pond in the valley fed by the Severn River. In addition to this enterprise, Bloor also had plans with William Botsford Jarvis to develop the small Village of Yorkville. The grand scheme, at least for Bloor, was shortlived. He sold his part of this property to Angus Fletcher and Peter McDougal. William Botsford Jarvis bought the Peter McDougal portion in 1835 for £1,000. Eventually, the plot was acquired by Samuel Peters Jarvis in 1843 for £4,300.

Playter sold 119 acres in the eastern portion of Lot 20 to Franklin Jackes in 1833 for £1,000; Jackes in turn sold to Francis Cayley the following year for £1,525.

Between 1835 and 1840, Cayley made land deals with Samuel Peters Jarvis for much of the western part of his original 119 acres. Samuel Peters would hold this property until his death. In 1872, his widow, Mary Boyles Jarvis (aunt of William Botsford Jarvis's wife, also named Mary Boyles Jarvis), sold the large parcel to a group of investors headed by Edgar John Jarvis.

While the Samuel Peters Jarvis property comprised the largest part of the original 119 acres in Township Lot 20, Francis Cayley did sell a 24-acre piece of land to Edward Nanton in 1866. Nanton acquired additional property from the Cayley trustees after Francis's death in 1872. The remaining 35 acres of Cayley land were sold to Maunsell Bowers Jackson in 1874 for $15,750.

Details of the numerous subdivisions occurring within the original three Township Lots are presented in the following chapters.

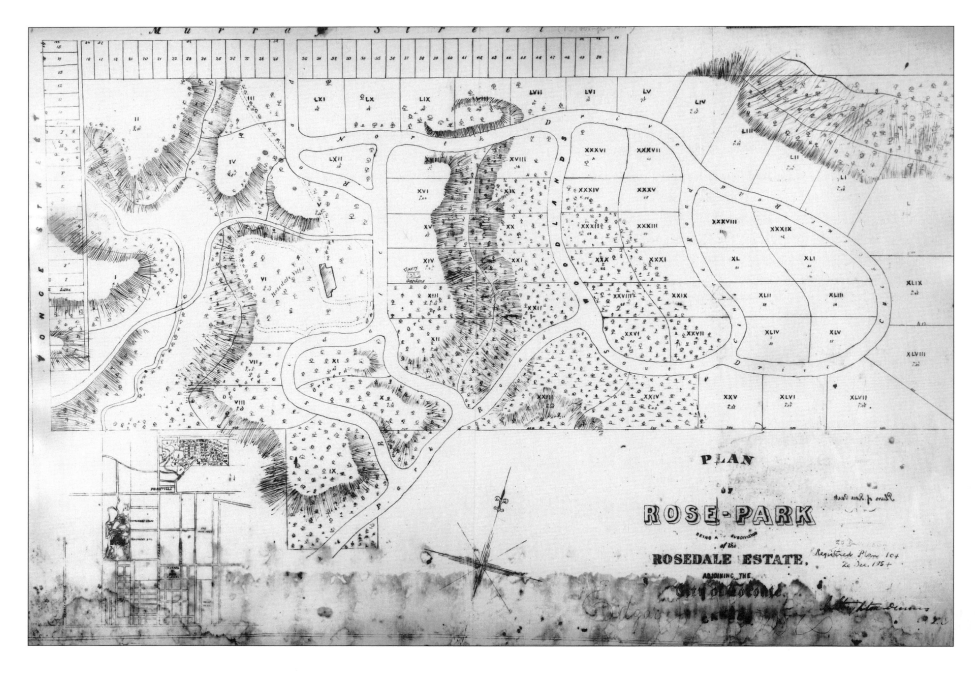

Plan of Rose-Park
Registered Plan 104, December 20, 1854, by George Duggan

THE ERA OF SUBDIVIDING

The first plan of subdivision for Rosedale, or Rose-Park as it was named at the time, was registered as Plan 104 by George Duggan on December 20, 1854, during an era of real estate speculation and considerable subdividing in the properties just outside the city of Toronto proper. The area now referred to as South Rosedale was not subdivided until 1872, almost 20 years after Rose-Park Plan 104. The plan for North Rosedale was submitted only in 1882, with actual development post-1907. The layout for the Chestnut Park area was registered first in 1890 and again in 1902, with construction commencing in the first decade of the 20th century.

In 1850–51 Toronto's population totalled only 30,775. While the general pace of expansion in Toronto was quite spectacular during the railway boom of the 1850s, development of the Rosedale area occurred only slowly. Many of the well-to-do considered the suburb too far from the city centre.

Rapid economic growth during the post-Confederation period from 1867 to 1875 saw population in the city almost double to 56,000, and by 1871 Toronto's affluent families were beginning to buy up lots in the new suburb. Nonetheless, by 1874 only 11 families were listed in the *Toronto Directory* as having a Rosedale address. More than a few of these were builders and land speculators who foresaw great things for this area, and purchased large properties with a view to subdividing them into smaller, affordable, city-sized plots.

The timing of the various subdivisions relates not only to economic climate and various cycles of boom and bust but also to population growth and accumulation of personal wealth. World depression and severe financial crises that spanned the years from 1873 to the mid-1890s were characterized by deflation and falling prices.

Despite the tough economic times, however, Toronto continued to experience phenomenal growth, with population in the city reaching 86,415 by 1880. The old estates in the city proper, especially those near Lake Ontario, were being gobbled up by commercial enterprises, thus putting upward pressure on residential land prices in other parts of the city. Speculation was rampant. New residential neighbourhoods were opened as fast as realtors could subdivide properties into smaller building lots.[1] By 1890 the city's population had more than doubled again to 181,220. Toronto had become the capital of Ontario and the undisputed centre for banking and finance. It had become the hub for numerous railway lines, and its harbour was one of the largest and busiest on the Great Lakes.[2] Consequently, lots in Rosedale were being rapidly bought up by the wealthy, who were building fabulous new homes.

Part of the allure of this new and picturesque residential area was the fact that it was by then considered relatively more accessible to the financial core of the city at King and Yonge. It was served by the newfangled street railway, inaugurated on September 10, 1861, by Alexander Easton. One of the first lines of the Toronto Street Railway Company travelled up Yonge Street to the northern city limits at Bloor Street, ending at the Town Hall in the small village of Yorkville. According to an

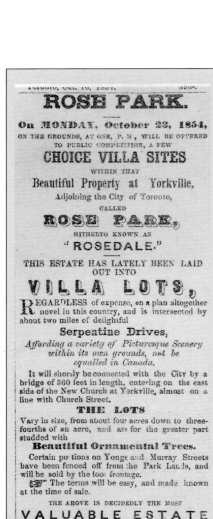

advertisement of 1875 the routes ran: from the St. Lawrence Hall to Yorkville; from the St. Lawrence Hall to the Asylum via Queen Street; from the Don River to Niagara Street via King; and from the St. Lawrence Hall to Winchester Street via Sherbourne, Carlton and Parliament Streets. Trips were made both ways every ten minutes. The large horse-drawn wagons operated only on weekdays for a fare of five cents.

The transit service was expanded to provide wealthy landowners on upper Jarvis Street, on Bloor Street East and in Rosedale easy transportation to their offices downtown.[3] It is hardly surprising that the first franchise-holder, William MacKenzie, resided in Yorkville, and that this small village and Rosedale probably enjoyed the best rail service of any area in the city. Lines to the less affluent areas were not constructed until later. Nonetheless, the company did not do well and ran into financial difficulties. By 1874 the Toronto Street Railway had been sold to new owners, and some moderate improvements in the city's transportation service finally occurred.

The street railway system's development reflected the rapid population growth in Toronto and its suburbs. Between 1891 and 1894 the lines were electrified. The first electric line travelled along Church Street. In 1889 the Belt Line Railway was chartered, and a track was laid through the Rosedale Valley, along what is now Mount Pleasant Road. The Scottish Ontario and Manitoba Land Company mentioned the Belt Line Railway on an advertisement for building lots in North Rosedale Park in 1908. The attractiveness of easy transportation to and from the business districts further south caused land prices to escalate in areas near the lines.

Despite economic hard times, the suburb continued to expand. The number of landowners in Rosedale jumped from 18 in 1879 to 42 by 1884, and to around 100 by 1890. The economic depression of 1893 did slow construction of many Toronto suburbs, but Rosedale was not affected to nearly the same degree.

The original 61 lots in the Rose-Park subdivision were auctioned off by the Wakefield and Coate Company in late October of 1854. They ranged in size from as small as three-quarters of an acre to four acres. Advertisements carried in *The Daily Leader* and *The Globe* described the properties in the flowery language common at the time. According to the articles, the Villa Lots were "intersected by two miles of delightful serpentine drives, affording a variety of picturesque scenery," and "studded with beautiful ornamental trees." The announcement goes on to say "the romantic grounds" are "unrivalled, for hill and dale, upland and valley, field and forest, woods and water." "Rosepark defies comparison, while the ever-varying diversity of its gently swelling banks, lovely vistas, mossy lawns, bold ravines and rocky glens, offers a home to all, such as the most fastidious could not fail to choose."[4] As a further enticement to would-be purchasers, the auctioneers boasted that the lots would soon be made much more accessible to the city by a new 360-foot bridge to be constructed north of Church Street.

In the second major subdivision, Plan 329 of South Rosedale, the lots were smaller, but still much larger than today's standards. Curving streets were adapted to the contours of the landscape — its ravines, valleys and tableland. In the case of Elm and Maple Avenues, Edgar Jarvis lined the quiet roadways with some 300 elm and maple trees.

The Daily Leader, October 20, 1854. Toronto Reference Library

Individuals planning to build large estates in a rural surrounding bought these over-sized lots in the two original plans of subdivision. Speculators on the future rise in Toronto property values also purchased them. As the area became increasingly popular and populated, their owners subdivided most of these original lots. Speculators like the Banks Brothers, James Henderson, David Macpherson, James Fraser, Henry Lamport and Benjamin Morton purchased several contiguous lots and later subdivided whole streets into smaller lots. The entire Rosedale area is made up of these mini-subdivisions.

The maps accompanying the next chapters outline the original lots in the various parts of Rosedale, the layout of the streets, the street names and the property owners, circa 1890. Not all the owners listed were the original ones since some of the properties had already changed hands. These detailed historical maps tell the story that thousands of words could not accurately recount.

Yonge Street at Price Street, circa 1908.
City of Toronto Archives
SC 244-7337

By 1884 some 42 people owned lots in Rosedale. They were men like William Davies, John Stark, John Hodgens, John Blaikie and Sir Edmund Osler. They were a virtual "who's who" of Toronto at the time — lawyers, senators, bankers, company presidents and business owners, as well as land agents, developers, architects and builders. Thomas Nightingale, for example, who purchased the lot on the southwest corner of what is now Crescent Road and South Drive, owned the brickyards on Yonge Street opposite Murray Street (now Roxborough Street East).

Many of these men were friends or at least acquaintances. They went to the same schools, worked together, served on the same boards of directors and were legal counsel for their friends' companies. Their sons and daughters married. For example, Dr. John Hoskin, Q.C., married the eldest daughter of Walter McKenzie of Castle Frank and built a home called "The Dale" nearby. And William Botsford Jarvis's second daughter, Louisa, married Augustus Nanton.

Surely not by coincidence, six of the original owners had lived on Jarvis Street, Yorkville (the present Asquith Avenue), and were neighbours of Frederick Jarvis, William Botsford's nephew and Edgar Jarvis's brother. The Jarvis family seemed to be working overtime selling property. Moreover, many of the land brokers and architects who bought, sold or designed homes in Rosedale had offices near Edgar Jarvis on Toronto Street.

ROSEDALE, PLANS OF SUBDIVISION, 1854 THROUGH 1910

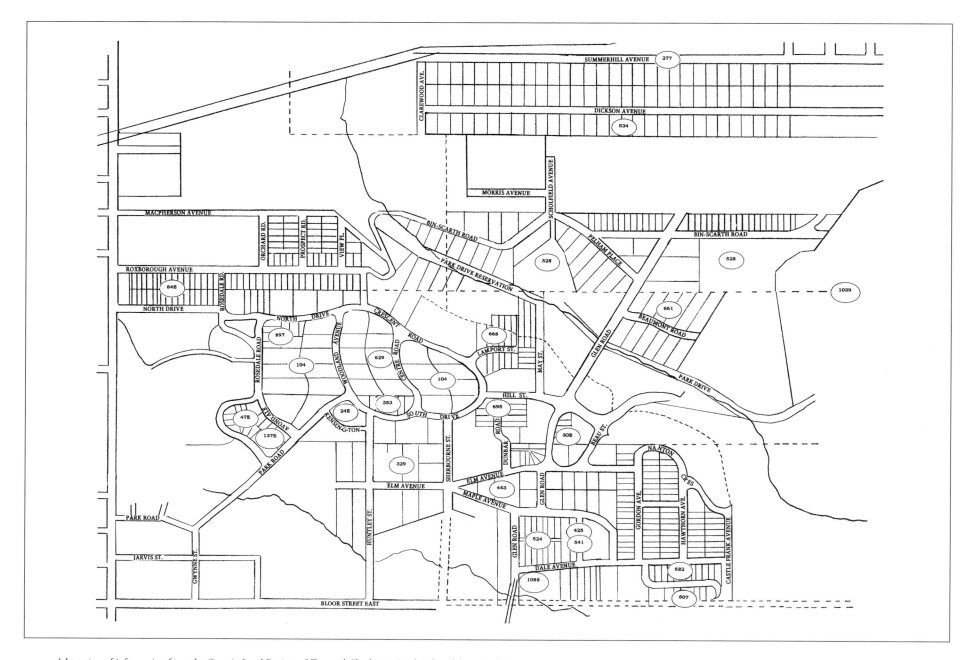

Adaptation of information from the Ontario Land Registry Office and Charles E. Goad, *Atlas of the City of Toronto*.

ROSEDALE PLANS OF SUBDIVISION
1854–1910

Plan 104 — Registered on December 23, 1854, by George Duggan
Consisting of the west half of Township Lot 19
Bounded on the west by Yonge Street, the north and east
by North Drive and Crescent Road,
and the south by the Rosedale ravine

Plan 241 — Registered on June 20, 1857, by Frederick Carruthers

Plan 277 — Registered on January 18, 1866, by John Griffith, executor
of the Francis Cayley Estate
Summerhill Avenue East

Plan 329 — Registered on October 26, 1872, by Mary Boyles Jarvis,
widow of Samuel Peters Jarvis
Consisting of the middle portion of Township Lot 20
Bounded on the south by Bloor Street East, on the west by
the west side of Huntley Street, on the north by the
northern boundary of Township Lot 20, and on the east by
the Edward Nanton and John Hoskin properties
Including the north side of Elm Avenue from west of
Bridge Street east almost to Glen Road, the south side of
Elm from west of Bridge Street to Sherbourne, the south
side of Rachael Street, the south side of Maple Avenue and
the west side of Glen Road

Plan 353 — Registered on June 15, 1874, by Benjamin Morton
Consisting of Villa Lots 9 and 10, Plan 104
Including the north side of South Drive between
Woodland Avenue and Centre Road

Plan 425 — Registered on April 3, 1877, by Samuel Jarvis Jr. and
Caroline Jarvis
A subdivision of Lots 27, 28, and 29 Plan 329
Including the block bounded by Powell, Maple and
Percy/Dale Avenues, including one lot on the south side of
Dale Avenue at the intersection of Maple Avenue

Plan 433 — Registered on November 16, 1877, by Edgar Jarvis
Including the north side of Maple Avenue, the south side
of Elm from Sherbourne to Edward Nanton's property, also
the east and west sides of Glen Road from Maple to the
North Iron Bridge, also the west side of May Street, the
northeast corner of Hill Street and Glen Road and the
northeast corner of Elm Avenue and Beau Street

Plan 137E — Registered on May 4, 1893, by Isaac Moody
Consisting of Villa Lots 10 and 11, Plan 104
Including the block bounded by Park Road, Rosedale Road
and Avondale Avenue

Plan 524 — Registered on August 22, 1882, by Elmer Henderson
Subdivision of Lots 25 & 26, Plan 329

Plan 528 — Registered on August 3, 1882, by the Scottish Ontario and
Manitoba Land Company
Including the southeast quadrant of Township Lot 18

Plan 534   Registered on November 25, 1882, by George and Isabella
            Dickson
            Consisting of Township Lot 17 east section and the
            northeast quadrant of Township Lot 18

Plan 541   Registered on January 15, 1883, by Edgar Jarvis, John
            Hoskin, and J. K. Fisker, an amendment to Plan 425
            Including Percy/Dale Avenue

Plan 607   Registered on October 20, 1886, to John Hoskin
            Including the south side of McKenzie Avenue

Plan 629   Registered on December 24, 1886, by Henry Lamport

Plan 661   Registered on May 7, 1886, by the Scottish Ontario and
            Manitoba Land Company
            Including the north and south sides of Beaumont Road

Plan 668   Registered on July 2, 1886, by Henry Lamport
            Consisting of Villa Lot 50, Plan 104
            Including the north and south sides of Lamport Street

Plan 682   Registered on October 20, 1886, by John Hoskin
            Including the north side of McKenzie Avenue

Plan 695   Registered on December 13, 1886, to John Paton
            Consisting of Lot 6, Plan 329
            Including Dunbar Road

Plan 897   Registered on July 8, 1887, by P. McDermid and W.E. Dixon
            Consisting of Villa Lots 16 and 17, Plan 104
            Including the southeast corner of Rosedale Road and
            North Drive

Plan 920   Registered on May 31, 1889, by Ann Hudson

Plan 24E   Registered on June 21, 1889, by William White
            Consisting of Villa Lot 23, Plan 104
            Including the north and south sides of Kensington Crescent

Plan 47E   Registered on December 12, 1889, by Jane Harvey
            An amendment to Plan 137E
            Consisting of Villa Lots 9 and 10, Plan 104
            Including Park Road, Rosedale Road and Avondale Avenue

Plan 1039   Registered on June 7, 1890, by the Toronto Belt Line Rail
            Company

Plan 79E   Registered on October 10, 1890
            Consisting of Lot 19, Plan 433 and part Lot 6, Plan 329
            Including the northwest corner of Glen Road and Elm Ave.

Plan 84E   Registered on November 18, 1890, by David L. Macpherson
            Consisting of Villa Lots 2 and 3, Plan 104
            Including the north side of North Drive between Yonge
            and Rosedale Road, also the south side of Roxborough
            Avenue from Yonge to the ravine and the north side of
            Roxborough east of Orchard Road, also the block east of
            Orchard Road south of Macpherson east as far as the ravine

Plan 1088   Registered on March 21, 1891, by Edmund Osler
            Including the north and south sides of Percy/Dale Avenue
            (west end), also the east side of Glen Road as far as Maple
            and the south side of Maple Avenue

Plan 204E   Registered on June 4, 1901, by the David L. Macpherson
            Estate

Plan 233E   Registered on December 20, 1902 by D.L. Macpherson
            Trustees

Plan 403E   Registered on April 29, 1910, by Maunsell Jackson

CHRONOLOGY OF DEVELOPMENT
1854–1890

Although Rosedale, or Rose-Park as the subdivision was originally named, did not officially exist until 1854, "Rosedale," referring to the William Botsford Jarvis country estate, appeared on maps as early as 1837. Rosedale, along with Bloorville and Cumberland were names suggested for the village of Yorkville, but Yorkville was the one eventually adopted.[1]

The surrounding area east of the Yonge Street Highway still consisted primarily of dense forest, ravines, streams and ponds. The suburb of Rosedale was originally much smaller than the current area. It included only the west-middle section of the suburb. Plan 104 mapped out the main residential streets, closely following the contours of the natural terrain that still exist.

Street names on the original plan of subdivision for Rose-Park included Park Road, Rosedale Road, Woodland Avenue, South Drive, Centre Road, North Drive and Crescent Road.

As early as 1855, the area north of Bloor Street East at the northern extremity of Jarvis and Sherbourne Streets was referred to as Rose-Park. The north side of Bloor Street East was quite a posh address at that time.

By 1877 maps were showing Roxborough Street East, in West Rosedale, Severn Street to the southwest and the "Chestnut Park" estate of Mr. Macpherson. The northern section of West Rosedale remained undeveloped. It was still the private domain of Mr. D.L. Macpherson and Miss Price. Plan 329 of subdivision for South Rosedale had been registered in 1872 with 29 lots designated. Streets had been mapped out but not named except for North Sherbourne Street. North Rosedale for the main part was still dense forest. Only the south side of Summerhill Avenue, or Thompson Avenue as it was then called, had been divided into lots.

Sometime between 1877 and 1884 further development occurred east of Crescent Road and South Drive. Hill Street (now the eastern extension of South Drive) was listed for the first time, as were May Street, Beau Street and Glen Road. In South Rosedale, Elm and Maple Avenues appeared. Maps noted large areas in South and North Rosedale owned by John Hoskin, Edward Nanton, John C. Taylor and William Mathers, but their holdings were not yet subdivided.

By 1885 West Rosedale had seen scant further growth. The large estates of Mr. Macpherson and Miss Price were still intact. A mini-subdivision, Plan 353, had been registered in the name of Benjamin Morton for the north side of South Drive between Woodland Avenue and Centre Road. In South Rosedale, Bridge Street and Percy Street/Dale Avenue were added to the roster of street names. Further subdivision of large lots also took place during this period. In North Rosedale major development occurred. Glen Road was extended north of Hill Street, and the North Iron Bridge was built, thus opening up

Advertisement for lots in the Pricefield Estate, circa 1908.
Toronto Reference Library

this area for much more rapid construction. Bin-Scarth Road, Pelham Place, Edgar Avenue, Dickson Avenue, Ritchie Crescent and Clarewood Avenue were roughed in on maps. Thompson Avenue had been renamed Summerhill Avenue and redivided into building lots. Plans 534 (99 lots) and 528 (65 lots) were registered to the Scottish Ontario and Manitoba Land Company for the holdings formerly owned by William Mathers and John C. Taylor.

By the late 1890s, development of all sections of Rosedale was proceeding at a considerably faster pace. In the western portion of the suburb, Avondale Avenue and Kensington Crescent were added. North Drive was extended west as far as Yonge Street, and the north and south sides of Roxborough Street East and the eastern extremity of the "Chestnut Park" estate were being divided into 108 lots as Plan 84E. Streets in the northeast sector of this area were named Orchard Road, Prospect Road and View Place. Also in the Macpherson Estate were plans 204E and 1233E. The block bounded by Rosedale Road, Park Road and Avondale Avenue was divided into Plans 47E and 137E by Jane Harvey and Isaac Moody. The north and south sides of Kensington Crescent (the old Davies estate) were divided into Plan 24E. Lamport Street was added under Plan 668 in 1886. In South Rosedale, Huntley Street, Dunbar Road, McKenzie Avenue, Castle Frank Avenue, Hawthorn Avenue and Nanton Crescent were named, and large original lots were divided into smaller ones. In North Rosedale, Beaumont Road now appeared on maps as well as Scholfield (formerly Clarewood) and Morris Avenue. Plans 661, 528 and 534 were registered.

Early in the 1890s Rosedale Lane was marked on maps. It ran east to Yonge Street, just south of the present day Crescent Road and the Rosedale subway station. The street was divided into building lots under Plan 241. Around this time, Pine Hill Road also appeared on maps and was ready for residential development under Plan M176.

By 1894, Lansdowne Place, Standish Avenue and Astley Avenue were named in North Rosedale.

Considerable growth occurred in the decade spanning 1895 to 1905, particularly in the region of West Rosedale, just north of the present day Crescent Road. North Drive was renamed Crescent Road, Scarth Road and Cluny Avenue were added, and the "Chestnut Park" estate of D.L. Macpherson was further developed. Plan 233E renamed Orchard Road, Prospect Road, Macpherson Avenue and View Place to Chestnut Park Road. Further south, Kensington Crescent became Meredith Crescent, Woodland was renamed Park Road, and Rosedale Ravine Drive opened. North Rosedale still remained largely undeveloped.

Another wave of development occurred between 1905 and 1910. In West Rosedale, Rowanwood Avenue and Thornwood Road (formerly Scarth Road) were added. The Woodland portion of Park Road was renamed South Drive. Centre Road was renamed Scarth Road with subdivisions 150E, 208E, 179E and 629. Rosedale Ravine Drive became Rosedale Valley Road, and Ancroft Place first appeared on maps. Hill Street was henceforth referred to as South Drive. In North Rosedale, Pelham Place was renamed Highland Avenue, the western portion of Bin-Scarth was renamed East Roxborough Street, and Lansdowne Place became an extension of Highland Avenue. The property now known as Chorley Park was owned by Toronto alderman John Hallam, who named the estate after Chorley, Lancashire where he was born. Within four years it would become the site of the lieutenant governor of Ontario's extravagant new home.[2]

The Jarvis Family

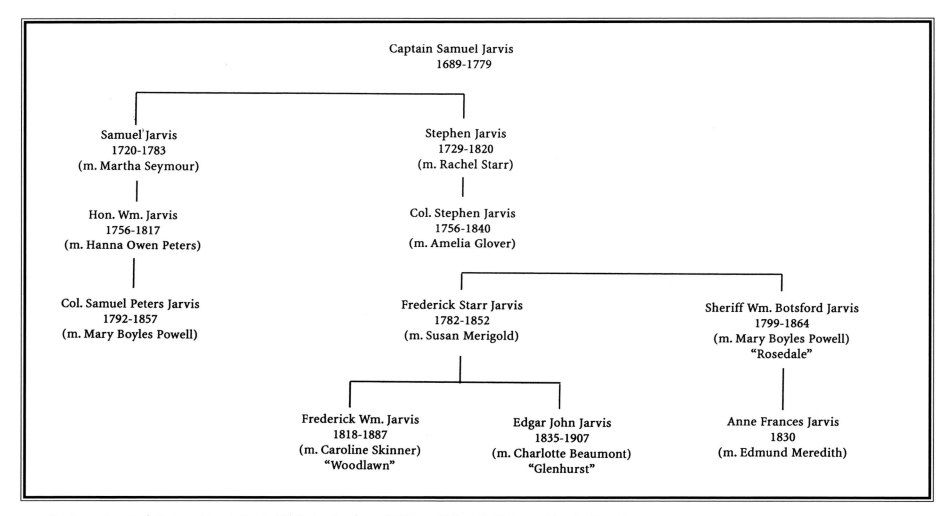

Captain Samuel Jarvis
1689-1779

Samuel Jarvis
1720-1783
(m. Martha Seymour)

Stephen Jarvis
1729-1820
(m. Rachel Starr)

Hon. Wm. Jarvis
1756-1817
(m. Hanna Owen Peters)

Col. Stephen Jarvis
1756-1840
(m. Amelia Glover)

Col. Samuel Peters Jarvis
1792-1857
(m. Mary Boyles Powell)

Frederick Starr Jarvis
1782-1852
(m. Susan Merigold)

Sheriff Wm. Botsford Jarvis
1799-1864
(m. Mary Boyles Powell)
"Rosedale"

Frederick Wm. Jarvis
1818-1887
(m. Caroline Skinner)
"Woodlawn"

Edgar John Jarvis
1835-1907
(m. Charlotte Beaumont)
"Glenhurst"

Anne Frances Jarvis
1830
(m. Edmund Meredith)

Data Source: Lucy Booth Martyn, *Aristocratic Toronto: 19th Century Grandeur,* and W. Stewart Wallace, *The Dictionary of Canadian Biography.*

Rosedale and the Jarvis Family
William Botsford Jarvis

William Botsford Jarvis
Alden G. Meredith,
*Mary's Rosedale
and Gossip of Little York*,
Toronto Reference Library

The history of Rosedale is as much a story of the Jarvis family as it is of land sales, subdivisions, development companies, architects and builders. Interwoven into the fabric of the suburb are the lives of William Botsford Jarvis, his cousin Samuel Peters Jarvis and his nephew Edgar John Jarvis. Their strong personal characters and incidents in their lives shaped the course of Rosedale's development as significantly as the economic, social and political events of the time.

The story of the Jarvis family's involvement with Rosedale starts with Colonel Stephen Jarvis, born on a farm in Connecticut. He craved a higher education, but his father had already sent his oldest son to study in England, and family finances were insufficient to pay for the education of another son. As a result, Stephen was forced to remain at home and work on the family farm. The father also refused permission for Stephen to marry his childhood sweetheart, Amelia Glover. So, when the Revolutionary War broke out in 1776, young Stephen ran away and joined the New York militia to escape the farm. Yet, being a Loyalist at heart, he did not remain with the American forces for long. Instead, when he arrived at Huntington, on the Atlantic coast, Stephen commandeered a canoe and paddled across the bay to a British sailing ship lying at anchor. He became a sergeant with the British Army and was invaluable to the English in locating and destroying a valuable cache of American supplies.

After the war, Stephen settled in Fredericton, New Brunswick, and finally married Amelia Glover. The couple had three children, the youngest of whom was William Botsford Jarvis.

In 1809, when William Botsford was ten years old, his family moved to the small town of York, where his father's cousin, William, was a local official. The relative had relocated to York from Newark (Niagara-on-the-Lake) after the Revolutionary War. Once in York, William Jarvis had become Provincial Secretary and Registrar of Records. He bought Park Lot 6 of 100 acres, which extended from Queen Street to what would later become Bloor Street. While he never actually built on this property, he did construct what was reputed to be the largest house in the town on a site near the present Sherbourne and King Streets. His cousin Stephen Jarvis's much less pretentious home was just a block away.

Mary Boyles Powell
Alden G. Meredith,
*Mary's Rosedale
and Gossip of Little York,*
Toronto Reference Library

William Botsford attended the local district school in York and was taught by John Strachan. On the completion of his education, he took up duties as a clerk in the provincial secretary's office, under his second cousin, Samuel Peters Jarvis. In May of 1827, William Botsford, at the age of 28, was appointed Sheriff of the Home District, a post he retained until he retired in 1856.

In 1824 William Botsford bought the Rosedale estate just north of the Town of York, and in July of 1827 married Mary Boyles Powell, granddaughter of Chief Justice Powell. The newlyweds moved into "Rosedale House" with William's father Stephen, by then 71 years old. The couple's first child (Frances or "Fanny" as she was called) was born in 1830, and as four more children appeared (Louisa, Colborne, William and Sarah), the Rosedale house was expanded to suit their needs. "A wing was added with a cheery morning room and additional bedroom space above. A large verandah made its appearance. A grape house, peach house and conservatory were built upon the sunny side."[1] Assorted vegetable gardens, orchards, winding pathways and flower gardens were added with a view out over the rolling hills and stream in the valley below. To the west one could see the Yonge Street Highway and the Hornes' house on the opposite side of the ravine.

In 1829, when William Botsford was 30, a vacancy in the representative House of Assembly of the Town of York became available. In the hotly contested election that followed, William Botsford opposed Robert Baldwin. Although Baldwin won the seat, the death of the King caused the Assembly to be dissolved. In the next election William B. took the day. Thereafter, he assumed a very active role on the civic and political scenes.

The Dictionary of Canadian Biography by Wallace Stewart describes William Botsford Jarvis as a man of above average height, slim of build, very athletic and active in both mind and body. He was a Conservative and avid Loyalist, with a keen sense of duty to his country and his family. He is said to have been gregarious and outgoing, with a good sense of humour. He was also a kind, gentle and loving husband and father. Judging from his letters to his children over the years, he had difficulty refusing any demands his daughters made of him.

Evidence of William Botsford Jarvis's character is offered by an incident that occurred during the outbreak of Asiatic cholera in 1832, when he was on the Board of Health. Greatly concerned for the debtors in York's jail, Jarvis freed them in order that they would not contract the deadly disease.

By the mid-1830s he was president of the Provincial Agricultural Association, a member of the Toronto Club and the Toronto Boat Club (later the Royal Canadian Yacht Club), and vice-president of the Toronto Turf Club. In 1834 he became chairman of the committee planning a railway link between Toronto and Lake Simcoe and was one of the first directors when the project finally got off the ground in 1844.

William Botsford Jarvis was also an entrepreneur and a land speculator. He and Joseph Bloor bought up land north and east of the present Yonge and Bloor Streets. Together they planned out lots for the new Village of Yorkville. He was one of the first to suggest a street railway on Yonge Street to facilitate access to his land holdings and make them more valuable. He was long associated with his second cousin Samuel Peters Jarvis in financial dealings and land speculation. William B. also avidly discussed with Francis Cayley his plans for the Cayley property, which lay to the east of Joseph Bloor's.

Despite appearances to the contrary, Jarvis was plagued by financial problems throughout his life. His letters clearly show that these problems centred around his difficulties in collecting his salary from the local officials.

Alden Griffin Meredith published many of William and Mary Jarvis's letters to various members of their family in the book *Mary's Rosedale and Gossip of Little York* (1928). Excerpts from these letters are presented in italics throughout this chapter.

William Dummer Powell
Chief Justice of Upper
Canada, 1816-1825.
Toronto Reference Library T13769

3rd April, 1833

...but the Government have withheld my salary £111 cy [currency] £20 cy for R.B. £80 lost by Suby's death and £40 pounds note endorsed for him has laid me on bare poles. I am really in great distress...[2]

14th June, 1833

I have received your letter about an increase of allowance and will bear it in mind when I forward you some dust which I shall do soon—but not just now, as I am below par, having made some purchases, etc., that have reduced my funds very low. To add this the disappointment in having not received my salary and allowances from the Government by which I am this half year their creditor to the amount of £200—which by the way, I fear I shall never get—and the losses I met with last year by the death of my jailer and other causes arising from the cholera. Notwithstanding this I am accumulating property—and if I am as fortunate in purchases and sales as I have been and meet with no very heavy losses, I hope in a few years to be pretty independent. I work hard, my expenses are large and my time so taken up that I most sincerely wish I was not in the House of Assembly.[3]

27th April, 1836

I have not yet recd. the money from Dr. C. in favour of Captain K.—he has been repeatedly promising to pay it, but is a very drunken miserable wretch having nothing but his half pay, which is I fancy ANTICIPATED for brandy long before it becomes due. I have not sued him lest he might refuse to pay & as he could evade it, not having property which could be seized and sold, the costs wd. fall upon the Plaintiff.[4]

William Botsford played an exciting role in the famous Rebellion of 1837. William Lyon Mackenzie, a radical Reformer, became so annoyed with the rule of Governor Sir Francis Bond Head and the inability of the colony to act independently of the King and British Parliament that he and his supporters began an uprising against the Crown and its Loyalist supporters.

On hearing that the rebels were amassing at Montgomery's Tavern (not the present site of the tavern but on Yonge Street north of Eglinton Avenue) on the evening of December 5, 1837, and fearing they would advance on the city, the Loyalists, including Colonel Fitzgibbon, Mr. Robinson, Bishop Strachan and William Botsford Jarvis, decided to act on their own. The governor had not taken Mackenzie's threats seriously and thus had not set up barricades on the roads leading into York or readied a volunteer militia.

The Loyalists sent Alderman John Powell, (Mary Boyles Jarvis's cousin) and Wharfinger MacDonald to ride up Yonge Street to see if they could find out what the rebels were up to. The two men had only reached Davenport Road when they encountered their friends Colonel Fitzgibbon, Brock and Bellingham, who had also been out reconnoitring the activities of the Radicals. Seeing nothing out of the ordinary, they had turned back towards town.

As Powell and MacDonald proceeded north on Yonge Street, they were apprehended by four horsemen. Thinking the riders were Fitzgibbon and his group who had decided to rejoin the search, the two Loyalists were caught off guard. The horsemen were the rebel leader Mackenzie himself, and Captain Anderson, the military leader of the insurgents, along with two others. Powell and MacDonald were captured. As they rode under guard, Powell learned that the rebel forces gathering at Montgomery's Tavern were in fact planning to advance on York that very night. Powell reasoned that unless he escaped and warned the sleeping undefended town, it would soon be set afire.

Powell pulled his pistol, shot Captain Anderson and galloped down Yonge Street toward York. Figuring that the tollgate at the northern city limits would slow him down, he abandoned his horse at Davenport Road and set off on foot across hill, dale, ploughed fields, fences and forests until he arrived at the governor's home on Front Street. Fitzgibbon, on horseback, arrived shortly after and together they briefed the governor, who, finally realizing the seriousness of the situation, began preparations for the defence of the town and its inhabitants.

William Botsford Jarvis would normally have joined Powell and MacDonald, but his wife and two of his children were quite ill. Given the long feud between him and Mackenzie, the lack of defences of the town, and the location of Rosedale right on the path the rebels were advancing along, Jarvis was a definite target. In anticipation of disaster, he readied horses and a carriage. If necessary, he could escape along a small road out the rear of his property, through the ravine, and on to Mary's grandparents' home on Front Street.

Early the next morning Jarvis set out for the city, first sending his coachman, Wilson, to get Dr. Gwynne to minister to his sick wife and children. By the time William B. reached city hall, a large crowd had gathered. They excitedly recounted the events of the previous night. Jarvis would have liked to meet with the Radicals but was advised by his friends not to do so, given the open animosity between Jarvis and Mackenzie. Moreover, Powell had just killed Captain Anderson, the Radicals' only military leader.

Jarvis happened to run into his neighbour James Hervey Price, a known rebel sympathizer. Jarvis suggested that Price meet with William Lyon Mackenzie and pass on the demands of the governor. While Price refused to do so himself, he suggested Dr.

William Botsford Jarvis with sons William and Colborne.
Toronto Reference Library
T13717

Rolph and John Baldwin for the task. Gathering these men, Jarvis went again to city hall where the messengers were given instructions. The envoys proceeded north to rebel headquarters at Montgomery's Tavern. Shortly after noon, the two men returned, reporting that Mackenzie had refused the governor's demands but, fearing the governor would charge the rebels with treason, asked for a written pardon for all involved if they dispersed.

In the meantime, reinforcements for the city arrived, and Governor Bond Head refused to give the pardon he had promised earlier. On hearing of the governor's change of heart, Mackenzie was enraged. Seeking some means of venting their anger, the unruly group set Dr. Horne's house on fire. Dr. Horne was a known Loyalist, chief cashier of the hated Bank of Upper Canada and a relative of its president. Mackenzie was by all accounts in an almost frenzied state, and suggested they burn the Jarvis house, "Rosedale," across the road. Mackenzie's men, however, did not support this destructive action and stated they would not continue to follow his orders. Colonel Samuel Lount and the others forcibly restrained Mackenzie and thus prevented the burning of "Rosedale." Lount, on learning of the capture of Jarvis's coachman earlier that day, had sent someone to give safe conduct to Dr. Gwynne to attend the Jarvis family at "Rosedale House."

The rebels retreated to Gallows Hill (St. Clair Avenue and Yonge Street) to regroup and organize another plan of action. By seven o'clock that evening they had headed south again for the city limits. Jarvis and his outpost guard saw them approach and ordered his men to fire. The volley, although inflicting little damage, caused great confusion among Mackenzie's forces. Those in the rear, thinking they had encountered a much larger government force, ran in complete disarray back to Gallows Hill. The uprising had ended. Jarvis and his men were heroes. They had saved the city.

In 1838 Jarvis was called upon to officiate at the execution of Samuel Lount for treason. It pained him deeply to put to death the man who had saved his home and possibly his family as well.

Later that same year, the William Botsford Jarvises held a grand masked ball for the establishment in York. It was a major social event. The "Society Notes" of the week in the *Patriot* newspaper describe the scene as follows: "We cannot estimate the numbers assembled at Rosedale at less than four hundred persons; the mansion was fitted up with equal taste and judgment for their reception, the hospitable owner seeming to have paid equal attention to pleasing the eyes and suitably accommodating the persons of his numerous guests. A large suite of apartments was thrown open, consisting of reception, dancing, and music rooms. A most extensive verandah was enclosed and fitted up as a picture gallery, lighted up with a profusion of coloured lamps, and affording a spacious and picturesque promenade. On entering the reception room, the guest was announced in his character, and presented to the fair hostess, who appeared on an elevated platform, in the admirably selected character of Mrs. Leo Hunter, the fascinating and all-accomplished lady patroness of the Pickwickian Revels. 'Mine Host,' in a striking garb of a Welsh noble, Baron Gwynn-wynn, was conspicuous in his endeavours to ensure the enjoyment of his visitors."[5]

One guest came dressed as a judge wearing an ass's head, and several others were costumed as Indians, including chiefs, warriors, and the beautiful Pocahontas and Squincanacousta.

Another account gives more descriptive details:
"The whole house, now enlarged to nearly twice its size since the Sheriff brought his bride there, was thrown open, heated by many stoves and lighted by innumerable lamps with coloured shades. Flowers spread their fragrance and beauty in every room, and even the tall old clock in the hallway was wreathed in vine leaves."[6]

Fanny, then a child of only seven, also recalled the event years later: "I remember the large verandah being closed in, with a stove at each end, and decorated with pictures. Some of the characters I have never forgotten. My Mother was costumed as Mrs. Leo Hunter, Sir John and Lady Colborne were present, but whether they were in costume or not, the deponent sayeth not."[7]

In 1841 William Botsford Jarvis was elected alderman. A year later, however, he resigned when the council did not elect him mayor. Among his other duties during this time, Jarvis was on the commission to supervise the construction of the Provincial Lunatic Asylum on Queen Street.

In the early summer of 1846, Mary made the decision to take her children to Europe in order to advance their education beyond what was possible in Canada. Moreover, their son William was ill and the doctors advised that he would benefit from a warmer climate. They planned to visit relatives in England, spend the winter in Avignon, and then further the children's schooling in Paris. William Botsford repeatedly made plans to join them but things always seemed to get in the way of his actually going.

Mary and the children were gone for two years. In the meantime, Jarvis moved out of "Rosedale" and rented the house until her return.

Toronto, 4th March, 1848

I have just returned from Rosedale, Dr. Clarke has given up the place, and compromised with me for the rent. It is I fear not likely to be tenanted this summer, in fact no one would take it for one year, and it will require new paper and painting before it will be fit for anyone to inhabit, so that all things considered I think we shall take possession upon your return, which must be this next Summer. I cannot be without you another Winter. It is becoming unbearable, and I have you not a moment from my thoughts.[8]

St. Paul's Anglican Church, Yorkville, 1848.
Watercolour by Wm. Arthur Johnson
Toronto Reference Library T10800

Not long after Mary's return with the children, a fire broke out on the Rosedale estate. The barn burned along with the peach house. Fortunately the main house was saved. She wrote:

January 1st, 1849

We are all very well after the fright we had at the burning of the barn on Saturday last. I do not know how it took fire, it was all consumed in ten minutes. The peach house is destroyed and the house was near going; now that it is over I am not sorry about the stabling, but at the time I was so frightened about the house and gave so many directions to the people in a screaming voice that it brought on an attack of asthma which though not important confined me to the house ever since.[9]

During this period, Fanny had been spending considerable time in Montreal as she was engaged to Edmund Allen Meredith, lawyer, principal of McGill University and provincial secretary. The couple was married at St. Paul's Church on Bloor Street near Sherbourne in 1851. In November that same year, the Jarvis family moved into town. William Botsford described the move to Fanny:

Toronto, 16th November, 1851

Your long and most acceptable letter should not have remained so long unanswered had I not been very much engaged in making arrangements for moving into town, and in moving, and as I saw long letters in progress from your Mother and sister, I thought I would put off until a later day and after we had got settled in town. We came on Monday the 13th, and Friday and yesterday were as disagreeable days as far as rain, nailing carpets and putting up curtains could very well make them. We are very comfortable. Your Mother and the girls like the house very much and we have only had one fire on this street since we came in.[10]

By May they were again moving back to "Rosedale House," as Mary Jarvis reported to Fanny:

Toronto, May 28th, 1852

I am afraid, my dearest Fanny, that you will be disappointed at not finding letters at Quebec on your arrival, for I have been so occupied in going up and down Yonge Street in daily visits to Rosedale where I have still an immense deal to arrange before we can move, that I have felt too much fatigued to write—your papa has also had a great deal of toil or he would have written.

I hope that we shall move out on Monday to Rosedale—Spring is looking lovely there and my strawberry hill is in the perfection of bloom. Next week we commence the planting of evergreens on the BLOCK HOUSE HILL. I have ordered red cedars, spruce, hemlock and fir in abundance, what think you of my promptitude? By July there will be quite a forest screen between us and Yonge Street.[11]

Mary Jarvis died suddenly in 1852 at only 49 years of age. As Meredith writes in his book *Mary's Rosedale and Gossip of Little York*, "The heart and hearth of Rosedale grew cold, silent and still."[12] William could not bring himself to continue living in Rosedale, home to so many warm family memories.

In 1853 he writes of "many heavy and pressing liabilities." He goes on to comment that he has much to do at Rosedale in the spring before he can lease the house. In another letter he mentions the property values on Front Street, speculates as to how much lots will increase in value and says that he has sold five lots for taxes in the West Division and made arrangements with the purchasers.

The *Globe*, October 5, 1854, Toronto Reference Library

Toronto, 22nd January, 1853

I have been so much engaged in Court during the week since I received your letter that I have not had time to answer it and scarcely to think of the proposition with that attention that it deserves. I telegraphed you that I fully approved of your plan and that I would endeavor to be of your party and it would be a great gratification if I could so arrange it to accompany you, but when I think of it seriously I almost fear that at this period of the year when you would be going it would almost be impossible for me to get away. There would be a good deal to have done at Rosedale in the Spring preparatory to letting the house and the idea of leaving the girls even for three months I cannot scarcely make up my mind to. Still I will not say no, but will keep the idea in view and if possible will accompany you.

I am sure that it would benefit you and if I do not go I will at least assist you in going and I think I may promise you £100 towards your travelling expenses. My office this year has been exceedingly profitable and has enabled me to pay off many heavy and pressing liabilities, and should the next year be as good as the last I will, if I have health, be rendered much more at my ease in financing matters. I am, I may say, quite well so that I will have no excuse on the plea of ill health, still I do not think that there would be any difficulty in obtaining leave of absence. I fully intend visiting England if I live but the time when I shall be able to accomplish the object is uncertain.[13]

The weather is as mild as March, great-coats, uncomfortable. Fur caps not to be worn. The ice on the bay is as smooth as glass, and the iceboats and people are gliding about in great numbers.

I shall send down your deed for the lot which Miss Powell has given for the land in Front Street in lieu of your relinquishment to Sarah and Louisa of your interest in the other lots, so that you each will have one. Henry Bolton offered yesterday £12.10s, per foot for the whole plot in front of the old rookery but he also agreed with me that it would in a year or less bring £20 per foot. So that your twenty-six feet, would be worth at least £500. The railroad terminus of the Guelph line will be at the foot of York Street and the Esplanade which is to be built and the northern terminus in front of Mrs. Justice Jones' house so that the whole of the front along Front Street will become most valuable. Give my love to Coly and say I will write him a long letter in a few days, at present I have not time. I sold five 55-ft. lots of land for taxes in the W. Div. and I am kept busy arranging with the purchasers.

God bless you, my child, may you be returned to health is the prayer of your affectionate Father.[14]

William Botsford Jarvis and his daughters.
Alden G. Meredith,
*Mary's Rosedale
and Gossip of Little York,*
Toronto Reference Library

Before April 1851, William Botsford and Mary Jarvis had drawn up a Grant of Trust Deed for the southwest corner of Lot 18 and half of Lot 19, consisting of 119 acres. William Gwynne, Frederick William Jarvis and Philip Vankoughnet were to be joint tenants of the property. Then, in 1854, William Botsford, along with the three aforementioned trustees, Edmund Meredith and his wife Fanny, Louisa Jarvis and Sarah Jarvis sold much of the Rosedale property (except Villa Lot 6 on which "Rosedale House" was situated, a total of 41 acres of the original estate) to Frederick Carruthers and George Duggan for £12,500.

Jarvis had also decided to divide Rosedale into two houses to be leased to tenants. He wrote to Fanny about his plans to make numerous repairs to the property, and to erect a stable and coach house.

Toronto, 9th April, 1854

My darling child,

I received this morning a letter from Mr. Meredith in which amongst other things he mentions your delight in the arrangement which I have made respecting the retention of a portion of Rosedale—that is the house lawn and the portion of ground encircled by the road leading to what was the stables, and so round to the…fence and to a certain distance below the brow of the hill. This embraces 41

acres and has been reserved from the sale to Mr. Carruthers, and for the remainder he is to pay £12,500 in place of £15,000 for the whole, but in order to affect this I engaged to pay Mr. Carruthers £1000 out of my own means so that neither you nor the girls will be deprived of your full share of the property. I did this to gratify the desire which you have for the retention of a portion of the property, and it gives me great happiness to be able to gratify you in this as it always has been in every other wish that you or they ever desired. I intend to put the house in thorough repair, and erect a stable and coach house on the northeast corner of the portion retained and put a substantial fence around it so that it will be protected from injury, and if a good tenant offers let it for two years. It is also my intention to enclose the Caer Howell property and if you all agree to the sub-division which I shall propose to you, to build on that portion which I intend for Coly and occupy it so long as I live, or at least, should I live so long until he arrives at the age of twenty-one years, when I shall surrender it up to him.[15]

Edmund A. Meredith House, Rosedale Road, circa 1900.
Photograph by Galbraith Photo Co. Toronto Reference Library T11418

In a letter of October 13, 1854, to her father Fanny suggested that Jarvis himself be one of the tenants of Rosedale. Jarvis responded that he had placed an advertisement to lease Rosedale but that the house was still under repair. Sarah, his youngest daughter, was to marry Lewis Ord, a government official, that winter, and William B. felt that since she was so young, the couple should live for a time with him and Louisa. These plans were thrown awry when Louisa announced her own engagement to marry Augustus Nanton, barrister, in the spring of 1855. Nanton had been a law student at Osgoode Hall in 1846 and was called to the bar in 1852.

Lewis Ord house,
162 Crescent Road.
Photograph by
Mario Angastiniotis

October 13th, 1854

My darling child,

Louisa does not leave till Monday, in consequence of the arrival of Mrs. William Robinson who thereby prevents her husband from departing till that day. I have just received your letter of the ninth, and have only retained that portion of it which contains your suggestion as to the occupancy of Rosedale and the proposal that I should be one of the tenants. I had placed an advertisement offering it to be let but as it is not yet in a state fit for occupation, being under repairs, I have not placed it beyond my control. I quite agree with you that it is better for all new married parties to be by themselves and I would only in consequence of Sarah's extreme youth have consented to her marrying this early with the understanding that she was to remain for a time with Louisa and me. Thinking it possible that I might be absent this winter. This plan will be carried out as far as I am concerned, but what changes Louisa's engagement may make remain to be yet discovered and ascertained.

Louisa and Sarah would neither of them desire to live at Rosedale should the present prospects be carried out. Indeed persons having anything to do, and I trust that will be the case, should always be near their business.

I think, too, that they should commence on a small scale and study economy. It has not been taught to them, they do not know how to attempt it while with me, and I cannot and will not while I have a dollar, refuse to gratify every wish that they may express. In new establishments and with new servants and new ideas it will be easier.

All these matters require forethought and when I begin to study them out I GET RATHER BEWILDERED.

MARY CARNWAMM is here staying with Stephen, and the girls have got up a little party for her to-night.

God bless you, my child, with best love to Coly, I remain yours, affectionately.[16]

Large gathering at "Rosedale House," October 23, 1861.
Toronto Reference Library T11364

In a following letter, we read that Fanny and her husband Edmund Meredith had also decided to live in the Rosedale house. Therefore Jarvis removed the advertisement from the local paper. The newlyweds, Louisa and Augustus Nanton, planned to move into the Rosedale house as well.

Toronto, 29th October, 1854

My dear Fanny,

Most assuredly you shall have Rosedale as a residence if you desire it. I imagined that so large a house and one so far from town would be an objection to your inhabitation but as my desire the remainder of my life is to devote myself to the comfort of you all surely whatever is in my power will not be refused. I had taken the notice from the paper the moment you expressed a desire respecting it.

I expect to leave on this Friday or Saturday and will probably be with you on Monday or Wednesday if all goes right. I should most likely have left on Monday but Mary Stephen wishes me to remain to her party, and Mrs. Widder will not consent to my declining with her on that day. She gives a party to Sarah who lunched with Frank Cayley and dined at Gzowski's yesterday. Goes to a dinner at Schriebers on Monday, dines at Mr. Nashes on Wednesday, and Widders on Monday. So much for one week. Is Louisa aware that her old friend Fred — is married. Mrs. Broadfoot gave a soiree on the occasion.[17]

Toronto, 6th February, 1855

I have had a good deal of repairs done at the house at Rosedale at a cost of nearly £150. And there are other expenses to be incurred in the Spring. The house is too large for one family unless a very large one, and cannot, as I think, be so arranged so as to accommodate two—you and Mr. Meredith have this house at your disposal to do as you think best.

Consult together, and whatever you may think best I will on my part, endeavor to carry out.

God Bless you, and may we meet in May if not before.

Your affectionate Father.[18]

The last large public gathering held by the Jarvis family at "Rosedale House" took place in 1861. The occasion was the distribution of prizes won at the rifle match held at Garrison Common. Veterans of the War of 1812, including William Botsford Jarvis, attended.

Sheriff William Botsford Jarvis died at "Rosedale House" on July 26, 1864.

In 1856 the *Toronto Directory* had already listed Edmund A. Meredith, Fanny's husband, as resident of a property on the west side of Rosedale Road, just north of Pine Hill Road. By 1859 Charles Jarvis was living at "Rosedale House," according to the *Toronto Directory* of that year.

In 1861 Lewis Ord, Sarah's husband, purchased a picturesque property on the north side of Crescent Road overlooking the ravine, just east of the present Mount Pleasant Road. Lewis and Sarah built a yellow brick Victorian house in 1882 well set back from the road. Today, 162 Crescent Road is covered with ivy and all but hidden by a tall and dense privacy hedge.

All three daughters lived at "Rosedale House" at various times from around 1855 until after William Botsford's death. What happened to the Jarvis homestead after that date has been pieced together from the *Toronto Directories*, Ontario Land Registry Office documents and various newspapers of the period.

The Jarvis daughters and their husbands took an active part in Rosedale property sales throughout the 1860s, 1870s and 1880s. An advertisement in *The Leader* of May 16, 1870, shows "Rosedale House" for rent. By that time, only six acres of the original property remained with the house. Another advertisement found in *The Globe* of May 1874 gave particulars regarding another attempt to rent the home.

"Rosedale House" was finally bought by David Lewis Macpherson in 1878. According to historian Lucy Booth Martyn, Macpherson's daughter Christina and her husband, Percival Ridout, resided there from 1889 until 1905, when the historic house was demolished.

TO RENT.

THE HOUSE AND GROUNDS KNOWN AS

ROSEDALE,

ADJOINING THE

VILLAGE OF YORKVILLE.

The house has been thoroughly repaired, and is now ready for occupation. Arrangements have been made to divide the place into TWO PARTS—should it be required.

There are about Six acres of ground attached; also a Garden stocked with some choice fruit trees

The property is beautifully situated; and with in a few minutes walk of the Street Railway Terminus. It is free from City Taxes.

Possession given at once.

Apply to

J. W. G. WHITNEY,

Corner Church & Court Sts.,

Toronto.

May 4, '70.

VALUABLE BUILDING LOT FOR SALE IN ROSEDALE.

Pursuant to a power of sale contained in a mortgage from Hector Cameron and R. Selby Cameron to F. F. Carruthers, bearing date the tenth day of December, 1855, there will be sold by PUBLIC AUCTION, at the Rooms of F. W. COATE & CO., on

SATURDAY, THE 30TH DAY OF MAY, INSTANT,

Villa Lot number IX. in Rosedale, containing about three and a half acres.

This Lot, beautifully situated, comprises the pine and oak-covered knoll immediately on the left when crossing Rosedale Bridge, and commanding fine views up and down the Ravine and over Rosedale Estate, and is undoubtedly one of the most desirable building sites for a gentleman's residence in the neighbourhood of Toronto.

The property will be offered at an upset price of $4,000.

TERMS—One-fourth down; balance in three yearly instalments, with interest at six per cent. on unpaid purchase money.

For further particulars and condition of Sale, which will be made known at the time of sale, apply to

J. & R. C. HENDERSON,

Vendors' Solicitors, Toronto.

Toronto, 7th May, 1874.

Above:
The *Mail*, May 22, 1874,
Toronto Reference Library

At left:
The *Leader*, May 16, 1870,
Toronto Reference Library

William Jarvis, Registrar, with son Samuel (died 1792).
Rotunda, Spring 1982, Toronto Reference Library

Hanna Peters Jarvis with daughters Maria and Augusta.
Rotunda, Spring 1982, Toronto Reference Library

ROSEDALE AND THE JARVIS FAMILY
SAMUEL PETERS JARVIS

Samuel Peters Jarvis
Toronto Reference Library T30358

S amuel Peters Jarvis, a cousin of William Botsford Jarvis, was one of the more colourful characters of this period in Toronto history. He is described as an impulsive man with a passionate nature, committed to upholding his own personal reputation as well as that of his family. These attributes landed him in more than a few controversial incidents and scandals throughout his lifetime.[1]

While his cousin William Botsford Jarvis was the key figure in the shaping of southwest Rosedale (the area south and east of the Rosedale subway station), Samuel Peters Jarvis features strongly in the early development of South Rosedale. The two men, however, could not have possessed more different personalities.

Samuel's father, William Jarvis, was born in 1756 on the same farm in Connecticut as Stephen Jarvis (father of William Botsford). William, being the eldest son, received the English education so dearly coveted by his younger brother Stephen. While in England, William married Hannah Peters, a woman of high spirit and determination. On receiving an appointment as provincial secretary and Registrar of Upper Canada by Governor John Graves Simcoe in 1792, he and his wife set out for Upper Canada with their three children. They first settled in Newark (now Niagara-on-the-Lake), where Samuel Peters Jarvis was born shortly after their arrival. By 1798 the William Jarvises had moved to York.

Governor Simcoe granted them Park Lot 6 of 100 acres for the modest sum of £100. The property extended from Lot Street (now Queen) northward to Bloor Street, between John and Mutual Streets.

The William Jarvises, while not from a particularly wealthy family, were ostentatious and extravagant, living well above their means. They built one of the largest homes in town and reputedly owned one of the first carriages. To compound the problem, William lost most of his income as registrar in 1795, when fees on land patents (grants) were redistributed among colonial officials.[2] All efforts at frugality failed and the family continued to mount up debts they could never hope to repay.

Undaunted by mounting financial concerns, the family sent Samuel Peters to Cornwall, Ontario for a formal education at the grammar school of the renowned Dr. John Strachan. He studied law, articling under Attorney General William Firth, until the War of 1812 interrupted his studies. Samuel saw active duty at the battles of Queenston Heights, Lundy's Lane and Stoney Creek. Following the war, in 1815, Samuel was called to the bar and appointed assistant secretary and registrar to his father. In 1817 he was made clerk of the Crown in Chancery in the Legislative Assembly, a post he held for 20 years.

The most notorious incident of Samuel Peters Jarvis's life was the duel he fought with his friend John Ridout in 1817. The Ridouts and Jarvises had been embroiled in a family feud spanning the better part of a decade. Both families had lived in Newark during the early 1790s, moving to York later in the decade. Tom Ridout Jr. became deputy to his father, who was registrar of deeds for York County. The younger son, John Ridout, was appointed clerk to brother Tom in 1814. The Ridouts were one of the oldest families in York and were Reformers. The Jarvises, on the other hand, were United Empire Loyalists and staunch supporters of the Tories and the Family Compact.

The incident started on July 11, 1817, possibly with an insult that led to fisticuffs between young John Ridout and Samuel Peters Jarvis in the streets of York. It ended the next day in a deadly duel. Samuel was 25 years old, John only 18. Their seconds, Henry Boulton and James Edward Small, respectively, joined the two young men at a spot near the present College and Yonge Streets, where John Ridout was killed in the ensuing shootout. Sam Peters spent several months in jail, but was eventually cleared of the murder charge and set free.

This was a particularly bad time for the Jarvis family. While Samuel was in prison awaiting trial, his father died, leaving his son a mountain of debts to repay. Samuel did get title to the land in Park Lot 6, but with a reputation now stained by the scandalous duel, it seemed prudent for the young man to leave town for a short while.

Sam married Mary Boyles Powell, daughter of Chief Justice William Dummer Powell, and the couple moved first to Queenston, then later to Niagara, where Samuel practised law until 1824.

On returning to Toronto, Samuel cleared 50 acres of pine forest on Park Lot 6 and had John Ewart build a two-storey brick house with a verandah in the vicinity of the present Jarvis and Shuter Streets. The handsome "Hazel Burn" was accompanied by brick outbuildings including stables, smoke house, hen house, carriage house and shed. Ten acres of garden and orchards were planted. To help pay for the grand new house, Samuel used £1,000 he had received as compensation for his father's lost fees as registrar.

After William Jarvis's death in 1817, Samuel's mother, Hannah, had moved to Queenston to be with her daughter, Hannah Owen Hamilton. The young woman's husband had died leaving her penniless. With only a small pension to support them and several young children, the two women worked in drudgery, taking in laundry and sewing to help supplement their meagre allowance. Hannah Peters Jarvis died destitute. It seems that Samuel did little to alleviate their poverty.

By 1827, despite his earlier transgressions, Samuel obtained the post of deputy provincial secretary and registrar. He held this office until 1839, but never attained the position of head secretary and registrar that he sought. It seemed that his reputation as a hothead would continually thwart his lofty career ambitions.

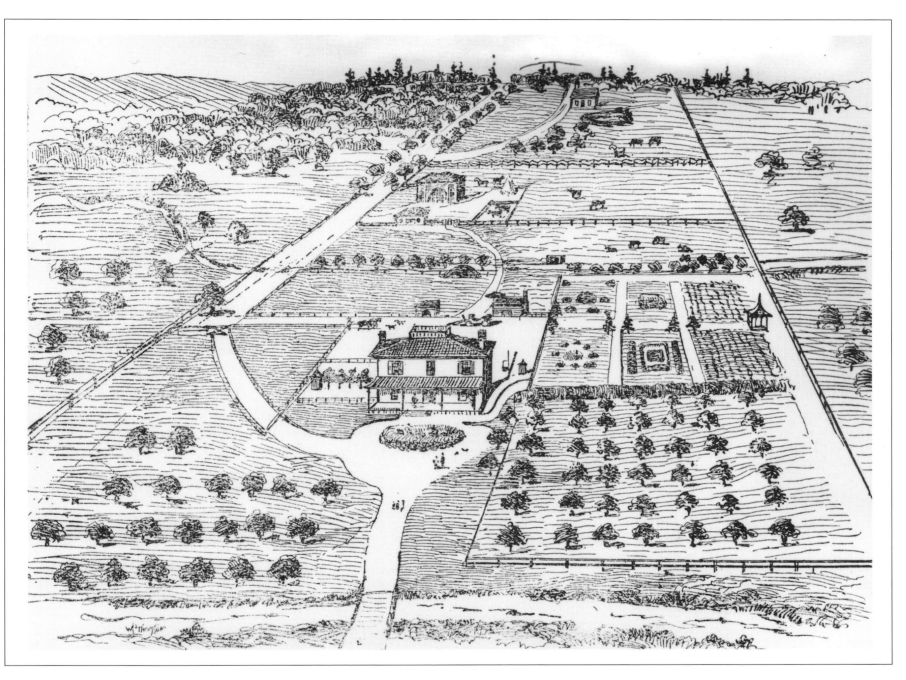

Residence of Samuel Peters Jarvis, Park Lot 6.

J. Ross Robertson, *Landmarks of Toronto*, Vol. 2, Toronto Reference Library

Another notorious incident in Samuel Peters's life took place four years after his return to York. The press labelled it "the type riot" of 1828. Seeking to silence the increasingly rebellious and often personal attacks printed by William Lyon Mackenzie, a group of young Tories under the leadership of Samuel Peters Jarvis raided William Lyon Mackenzie's printing shop, damaged the premises and dumped the print type into the Toronto harbour. The court awarded Mackenzie £625 to compensate for damages, a figure well in excess of their actual worth. Not only was Samuel Peters responsible for paying part of the settlement costs but the incident also ended up helping Mackenzie, who had been facing bankruptcy at the time. Instead of stopping the reformer from printing his views against the Family Compact, the raid ultimately assisted him.

In 1837, with the Family Compact still in force, albeit tenuously, and Tory supporters still receiving preferred government positions, Lieutenant Governor Bond Head assigned Samuel Peters the lofty post of Chief Superintendent of Indian Affairs for Upper Canada, a position he would retain until 1845, when he left amidst another scandal.

Indian Affairs was a highly visible portfolio and under the constant scrutiny of both government and public. Inquiries into the affairs of the department in April 1839 and again the next year found Samuel Peters to be hardworking and diligent in his duties. A third review by a three-man Royal Commission in January 1844, however, came to a markedly different conclusion, one that would taint Jarvis's reputation for the rest of his life. James Macaulay, a close personal friend of Jarvis, had headed the initial examinations. The final, more impartial investigation judged that the management of the Indian Department was disorganized and that its administrator was inept and even of questionable honesty. An accounting of department books found as much as £9,000 missing, a total subsequently amended to a lower amount. Attempts by Samuel to clear his name only spurred further evidence to support the embezzlement. The commission found him uncooperative and evasive, and stripped him of his post in 1845.[3]

Was Sam Peters truly guilty of misappropriating these funds or was he merely a poor bookkeeper? Apparently Jarvis kept his personal funds in the same Bank of Upper Canada as his business accounts for the Department of Indian Affairs, shifting money back and forth in a casual, offhand style of someone not accustomed to formal business dealings. Perhaps he was just unlucky to be the first Toronto administrator to have his financial records examined so closely. It has even been hinted that his clerk George Vardon, who was actually responsible for carrying out the day to day financial transactions of the department, may have had an axe to grind and wanted to see Jarvis's reputation tarnished. Whichever story was true, neither version was ultimately proved.[4]

Needless to say, Jarvis left in disgrace and although he tried repeatedly to clear his name throughout his lifetime, it was to no avail. The fact that the government never asked him to repay the supposedly missing funds suggests the matter was far from clear-cut.

Despite no obvious means of support, Samuel Peters still managed to live the life of the landed gentry, fishing in the Gaspé, hunting on the Bruce Peninsula and touring England and Europe. Even so, he always seemed to be sorting out either his own or his family's financial difficulties. His cousin, William Botsford Jarvis, had disagreements with him on more than one occasion over the equitable division of Jarvis family debts and a family trust fund.

Financial worries did not stop Samuel from pursuing any of the many land speculation deals he embarked on. In 1840 Frank Cayley sold him 44 acres in the south middle portion of Township Lot 20 for £900, and in 1843 sold him additional land for £4,300. This was property on the north side of Bloor Street near Sherbourne that would later be developed into the area now known as South Rosedale. He was also involved in a deal with his cousin William Botsford Jarvis involving the development of property in the neighbourhood of Yonge and Bloor Streets.

But all these deals undoubtedly had their toll on his finances. Around 1845 he commissioned John Howard to subdivide the property in Park Lot 6, his father's original grant from the Crown. His house was torn down to allow for the extension of Jarvis Street northward as far as the city limits at Bloor Street. In order to help pay off his debts, Samuel eventually sold 40 acres of this property for £7,307 to John Howard, who in turn would market the one-acre lots on both sides of Jarvis Street for £500 each. Samuel Peters and his family moved to the north side of Bloor Street.

In 1856 Samuel Peters Jarvis managed to pay off his mortgage of £4,300 to the Bank of Upper Canada on the South Rosedale property. He died a year later in 1857 at the age of 65. There would be no new land deals by his family until 1865.

From that point onward, the name of his widow, Mary Boyles Jarvis, is listed frequently in land transfer office documents. Perhaps to pay off an ever-rising mountain of debts, Mary Boyles Jarvis sold some of her property to Samuel Hume Blake in 1865 for the sum of £590. The next year she remortgaged the remainder of her large landholdings in South Rosedale for £1,000. By 1866 Elisha Gilbert and others had brought legal actions against her. In 1870 Samuel Blake sought action from the Court of Chancery for repayment of a bad debt. Records in the Ontario Land Transfer Office show that Samuel Peters Jarvis Jr. went to court to settle family financial matters, first to call into question his mother's title to the South Rosedale property, and second to release himself from any claims. In essence, he wanted to facilitate the sale of his mother's property. By October of 1872, Mary had registered Plan 329 of subdivision for her 44 acres in South Rosedale. Before the end of that year, the court had ordered Mary Boyles to relinquish numerous lots in the new suburb to a long list of people including Elisha Gilbert and Samuel Blake, William Stanley, James Metcalfe, John Strathy, William Hope, John Hallam, Thomas Henry Ince, and Edgar John Jarvis as payment for bad debts.

William Botsford Jarvis and his cousin Samuel Peters Jarvis were well-known men in York between 1800 and 1860, and were especially instrumental in the development and growth of the newly emerging Town of Yorkville. The two were not only large property owners and land speculators but they were also local government officials and led active public lives. They were at the centre of the upper crust social scene. In later life, as their influence waned, a new generation of Jarvises was advancing from the rear to take their place. The Jarvis family would continue to figure strongly in Toronto history for many years to come.

Between 1872 and 1878, Edgar Jarvis, William Botsford and Samuel Peters's young relative, would by one means or another acquire most of the land in South Rosedale, a story continued in the next chapter.

The Edgar Jarvis family
Lucy Booth Martyn, *Toronto: 100 Years of Grandeur*, Toronto Reference Library

Rosedale and the Jarvis family
Edgar John Jarvis

E dgar John Jarvis was born on January 28, 1835, to Frederick Starr Jarvis, the older brother of William Botsford Jarvis. His grandparents, the Stephen Jarvises, originally from Connecticut and later New Brunswick, arrived in the town of York in 1809, when Frederick Starr was 27. Fred married Susan Merigold and bought land four miles east of Oakville, remaining there until his death in 1852. Their son Edgar, by then 19 years old, moved to Toronto where his older brother, Frederick William, was living. The two men were apparently quite close to their uncle, William Botsford. Fred William was the first of the succeeding generation to appear on the Rosedale scene. As early as April 1851, he was one of four men named in a Grant of Trust Deed for 110 acres of William Botsford's Rosedale farm. When the Rosedale property was sold to Frederick Carruthers and George Duggan in 1854, Frederick William Jarvis, Philip Vankoughnet and William Gwynne held the mortgage for £10,000.

On William Botsford Jarvis's retirement, Frederick William Jarvis became sheriff of the Home Office. By 1859, his brother Edgar, 17 years his junior, was appointed sheriff's clerk. The lad remained in this capacity only a short time, however. He was destined for a much different career. Two years later the *Toronto Directory* listed him as a land agent and broker, with offices in the Whittemore Building on Toronto Street. Edgar Jarvis would be remembered as the man most influential in the development of Rosedale.

Edgar had established himself in the land business by 1862. This career change may well have been related to the death of Samuel Peters Jarvis in 1857, as well as to the Jarvis family's still extensive land holdings in Yorkville. Edgar did not inherit either Samuel's land in South Rosedale or William Botsford's property from the original "Rosedale." Nor did he buy the property in several neat, large packages. Edgar acquired the property over a lengthy period of time with considerable deliberation and planning. He had conceived a grand dream for the Rosedale suburb; one that would incorporate not only the original Rose-Park in the west, but also the South Rosedale land of Samuel Peters and the undeveloped property to the north that would become North Rosedale. Jarvis envisioned an exclusive enclave to accommodate the rich and famous of Toronto society, complete with spacious mansions surrounded by extensive grounds.

The first step in putting this dream into reality was the construction of a landmark residence for himself, one that would not only set the standard for but also advertise the select suburb. Around 1863, after his marriage to Charlotte Beaumont, Edgar bought several acres on the east side of Park Road near "Rosedale House." The purchase encompassed the area north and east of the present intersection of Park Road and Rosedale Valley Road, extending almost as far north as the present Meredith Crescent, running east to Mount Pleasant Road and south into the Rosedale ravine. At that time, although this part

*Edgar John Jarvis
house, "Glen Hurst,"
circa 1920.*
Toronto Reference Library
976-47-10

of Rosedale had already been subdivided into 61 lots, it was still largely a rural area. The only residences nearby were "Rosedale House," the home of William Botsford Jarvis, "Chestnut Park," the home of David Macpherson, "Woodbine Cottage" of Sarah Price, James Boyd Davis's new house on the west side of Park Road (later known as "Caverhill"), and "Idlewold," Walter Brown's home on Rosedale Road (later known as "Rose Cottage"). The surrounding countryside remained dense forest, with occasional clearings around the few homes for orchards and gardens.

Edgar and Charlotte's large house sat on a hill facing west towards Yonge Street, commanding a grand panorama of the valley and stream below. During the construction period from 1863 until 1866, the newlyweds resided at "Rosedale House." The estate was named "Glen Hurst," a combination of the Welsh word "glen," meaning a small, narrow, secluded valley, and the Old English word "hurst," meaning a wooded hill or high spot.[1] More apt names for the picturesque situation could hardly be imagined. Access to the property, however, was another matter, as William Botsford had already discovered. The dirt road running north from Bloor Street, began as Gwynne Street, then turned into Park Road, progressed through the Rosedale ravine where it traversed a somewhat precarious bridge over the Severn River, then went further north up a steep hill. Conditions were almost impassable during the autumn and spring rains, when mud made the road a quagmire of ruts from wagon wheels. At least William Botsford could reach his estate from the north via Murray Street (now Roxborough Street East), then by going south on Rosedale Road.

"Glen Hurst," designed by the architectural firm Gundry & Langley, was an impressive two-storey yellow brick structure, large enough to accommodate the Edgar Jarvises' 13 children (ten boys and three girls), the first of which appeared on the scene in 1864, the last around 1881. Set amidst a broad expanse of lawn, the house sported a large Romanesque-style wrap-around verandah, a standard feature at the time.

Edgar's land deals began in earnest in the early 1870s with the forced sale of the late Samuel Peters's South Rosedale property. He was to continue acquiring land throughout most of the 1870s. Some of the lots that Mary Boyles Jarvis, Samuel's widow, had subdivided in 1872 as Plan 329 were used to repay Edgar, among others, for outstanding debts. At this moment in Toronto history, those who could scrape together a minimal downpayment bought up as much property as they could conceivably manage the mortgage and tax payments for. But, as always, the reality was not always the same as the forecast. Periodic recessions ushered in eras of falling prices. Individuals and banks were forced to foreclose on mortgages.

Newspapers constantly advertised auctions of property seized by mortgagees for non-payment of debt. Such sales were carried out by the sheriff's office.

Edgar Jarvis acquired many lots in South Rosedale because of foreclosures. Others he would purchase outright from men who had been given lots in payment for outstanding debts. Edgar either gave them hard cash in exchange or allowed the original owner to hold a mortgage. Over a period of 15 years he assumed title to much of the land in South Rosedale and registered Plans 433 and 541 of subdivision in this part of Rosedale.

Edgar's brother, Frederick William, was also active in the land business from 1851 until 1866. Registry Office documents list him in land dealings concerning several lots in the original Rosedale estate, by then subdivided as Rose-Park. He traded lots on Roxborough Street East, as well as Villa Lots 1, 2, 11, 12, 26, 27 and D through I. After that date Frederick seems to have retired from the land business. Perhaps by coincidence, his brother Edgar's activity was just beginning to gather momentum. Through the 1870s, Edgar acquired Villa Lots 9, 19, 20, 23 and 24 in Plan 104.

Spurred on by the new estates of Messrs. Blaikie, Alexander and Ellis at the western end of Elm Avenue, Edgar embarked on a building program of his own, constructing another select grouping of sizable country manors to lure the wealthy into Rosedale. None of these houses remains standing today.

The first of these mansions of high Victorian style was on the east side of Beau Street set on 13 acres of land overlooking the Don River Valley. The residence was built in 1876 and purchased by Sir Edmund Osler, who christened it "Craigleigh." Records at the Ontario Land Registry Office show many financial transactions between Osler and Edgar Jarvis. Osler put up the mortgage money for several of Edgar's land purchases and house building ventures. Osler, a financial baron in his own right, got into the speculative spirit as well, subdividing the land south of his home in 1890 as Plan 1088. The Osler house was demolished in 1932 and part of the property was turned into a beautiful park.

Edgar constructed "Sylvan Towers" for himself during the period from 1877 to 1880. It was located on the northeast corner of Glen Road and what is now Milk-men's Road on Lot 33, Plan 433, a subdivision Edgar had registered in November 1877. Within a month he had taken out a mortgage for $4,000 from Edmund Duggan. A year later, he received additional financing of $10,000 from the Canada Life Assurance Company to finish building the house.

John Ellis house, 8 Elm Avenue.
Photograph by
Mario Angastiniotis

"Norcastle,"
Hill Street and
Glen Road.
Toronto Reference Library
T14018v

"Sylvan Towers" may have been Edgar Jarvis's own personal version of the Sleeping Beauty castle, complete with turret to view the ravines to the north. He sold "Glen Hurst" in 1881 to Bernard B. Hughes, an important railway contractor, and moved his family into "Sylvan Towers." The Jarvises lived here until 1889. After that, the property was first rented, then sold in 1908 to James Plummer. It was eventually torn down in 1933.

Across the street, on the northwest corner of Glen Road and Hill Street (now South Drive), Edgar built the grandiose "Norcastle" estate. The financing was obtained in two lumps, the first for $4,000 in 1878, and an additional $18,000 in 1880. The turreted castle was quite a spectacle, the huge home sitting on expansive wooded grounds, soaring above the Glen Road ravine. Encircled by a fence and gates, it was a testament to Toronto's rich and famous of the late 1800s. The grand home was bought in July 1882 by Henry W. Darling, owner of a well-known woollens wholesaling company, for $29,166. The Darlings renamed the house "Hillcrest." Almost 20 years later, on February 1903, Sir Albert Gooderham purchased the mansion and renamed it "Deancroft" in memory of his mother Harriet Dean.[2] This home also suffered the fate of "Sylvan Towers." It was torn down in 1933 to make room for a mini-subdivision.

89 Glen Road

Evenholm, 157 South Drive

Edgar's career was a roller coaster ride of successes and failures, his fortunes rising and falling with the economy and the real estate market. Others would reap the benefits, financial and otherwise, of his grandiose plan.

After the financial success of "Craigleigh," "Norcastle" and "Sylvan Towers," Edgar fell on hard times. By 1896 his resources were vastly reduced and the family moved into 46 Elm Avenue, a semi-detached house built in 1875. According to author Lucy Booth Martyn, Charlotte gave music lessons to supplement her husband's income.[3] By 1901 they had moved yet again, this time to 89 Glen Road, another semi-detached house. Edgar built his final residence at 157 South Drive in 1905–06. Designed by his oldest son, Edgar Beaumont, the Jacobethan gem, with its characteristic parapeted gables, was called "Evenholm." Edgar died there a year later in 1907 at the age of 72.

Rosedale was just coming into its own, experiencing the rapid growth, prestige and attention he had craved 40 years earlier. Edgar was before his time. His wife, Charlotte, remarked that upper-crust Toronto women considered Rosedale "too far from town; too difficult to find domestics who would go there; too lonely."[4]

The era from 1900 to 1910, Laurier's Golden Age, witnessed a real estate boom of massive proportions, initiated by increased population growth, expansion of personal wealth and the emergence of the middle class. The new Chestnut Park development, designed by Hamilton Townsend along the lines of the increasingly popular Garden City Movement, certainly gave Rosedale the publicity long sought by Edgar Jarvis. Elsewhere in the suburb, a spate of new homes was being erected on the many remaining homes on Rose-Park and South Rosedale.

1872

In the vicinity of Trinity College

A Stroll in old Moss Park Shuter St. in 1876.

1885

Fashion in 1885 said "No surrender" where formality was concerned, and the summer costume relaxed not a whit from boned bodices, draperies and bustles. The little kiddy looks neither easy in mind or body—a less willing martyr to style than her elders.

Toronto fashions in the 1860s, 1870s and 1880s.
T. Eaton Company, Golden Jubilee 1869-1919,
Toronto Reference Library

SETTING THE SCENE

Everyday life in Toronto during the middle of the 19th century was by today's standards primitive. While the upper class did enjoy a few basic comforts, the great majority lived in shocking conditions. Streets were glorified dirt tracks, covered with manure. Sidewalks were made of wood planks. The mode of transportation for most was walking. Only the upper classes owned horses, and travelled by horse and buggy, or in carriages and stagecoaches when venturing further distances. Most homes lacked running water, and central heating was not yet invented. There were outhouses and open sewers. Candles, oil lamps and, later, wall sconces fuelled by manufactured gas were the primary source of lighting. Bathtubs were exclusively for the rich.

Only the very wealthy owned a private residence. For the seemingly modest sum of between $2,000 and $2,500, an eight-room house, with stone foundation, brick facade, furnace, white enamel bathtub, sinks, hardwood floors and oak trim could be purchased. A three-acre lot in Rosedale went for $3,000 in 1867. But even workers lucky enough to earn $245 a year in the 1870s, had to spend some $180 for renting a room with board; for them, owning their own home was unthinkable. Tenement houses were freezing cold in winter and unbearably hot in summer, and families often had to share only one or two rooms.

Most manufactured goods came from Europe. The major dry goods companies placed advertisements in the local newspapers advising customers when the latest shipments had arrived from England. The ports of Toronto and Montreal were closed during the winter, and although New York was open year round, shipment of goods overland during the winter months was uncertain until railways were built near the end of the 1850s. As a result, people often waited months to purchase an item not produced locally.

Barter was common at most stores until the late 1860s, when Timothy Eaton introduced the radical idea of marking prices on individual merchandise and accepting only hard cash for the purchase. The Pound Sterling was the currency until Confederation in 1867, and demand notes were frequently used.

Conditions did improve dramatically, however, during the years from 1850 to 1900, due to the Industrial Revolution and full-scale growth in Toronto manufacturing. In addition, many new inventions, including the telephone, electricity, the electric light bulb, central heating, and iron stoves for cooking and heating, along with revolutionary advances in building construction, did increase daily comforts, at least for the well-to-do.

MILESTONES 1840-1900

1840s

1842   Gas lines laid in Toronto

1843   Water lines laid in Toronto

1846   First telegraph line out of Toronto

1848   Consumers Gas Company of Toronto formed

1850s

1851   St. Lawrence Hall completed

1852   Canadian Yacht Club founded

1852   Toronto Post Office at King and Adelaide Streets completed

1853   St. James Cathedral opened

1854   Birks, Ellis, Ryrie opened for business

1856   Grand Trunk Railway, first train left Toronto for Montreal

1858   Union Station built

1859   Toronto Turf Club petitioned Queen Victoria to give an annual prize for the Queen's Plate horse race

1859   University College completed

1860s

1860   Osgoode Hall completed

1860   St. Paul's Anglican Church completed

1861   Toronto Street Railway started

1864   John A. Macdonald and George Brown formed a coalition government

1864   Charlottetown Conference; first ideas for Confederation formed

1866   Fenian Raiders captured Fort Erie

1867   British North America Act and Confederation

1867   Sir John A. Macdonald (Conservative) elected Prime Minister

1869   Timothy Eaton started business at Queen and Yonge Streets

1870s

1870   Granite Club opened

1870   Metropolitan Church completed

1872   Robert Simpson opened his store

1873   Alexander Mackenzie (Liberal) elected Prime Minister

1873   Toronto Post Office opened at Adelaide and Toronto Streets

1870s *continued*

1873   Union Station (second) opened, west of York Street south of Front Street

1876   First telephone line strung

1878   John A. Macdonald elected Prime Minister under "National Policy" platform

1878   Toronto Stock Exchange incorporated

1878   Coal first used to generate steam

1878   Toronto Telephone Dispatch Company Limited formed (it became The Bell Telephone Company in 1881)

1879   Toronto Industrial Exhibition (CNE) opened

1879   Vice-Regal Reception for The Marquis of Lorne and Princess Louise (Queen Victoria's daughter)

1879   Invention of the light bulb

1880s

1880   Royal Canadian Yacht Club acquired Toronto Island property

1883   Woodbine Race Track opened

1884   Toronto Corn Exchange amalgamated with the Board of Trade

1884   Electric arc lights invented; street lighting by electricity installed at Yonge and King Streets

1885   Yonge Street shopping arcade opened

1885   Canadian Pacific Railway completed

1885   Louis Riel Rebellion

1886   National Trades and Labour Congress of Canada formed

1890s

1891   Sir John A. Macdonald died

1894   Toronto Street Railway electrified

1894   Massey Hall opened

1896   Sir Wilfred Laurier (Liberal) elected, the "Golden Age of Laurier" began (he was in office for 15 years)

1896   New Union Station completed on Front Street

1897   Queen Victoria's Diamond Jubilee

1899   Toronto City Hall at Queen and Bay Streets completed

ROSEDALE, Plan 104
Residents, 1890

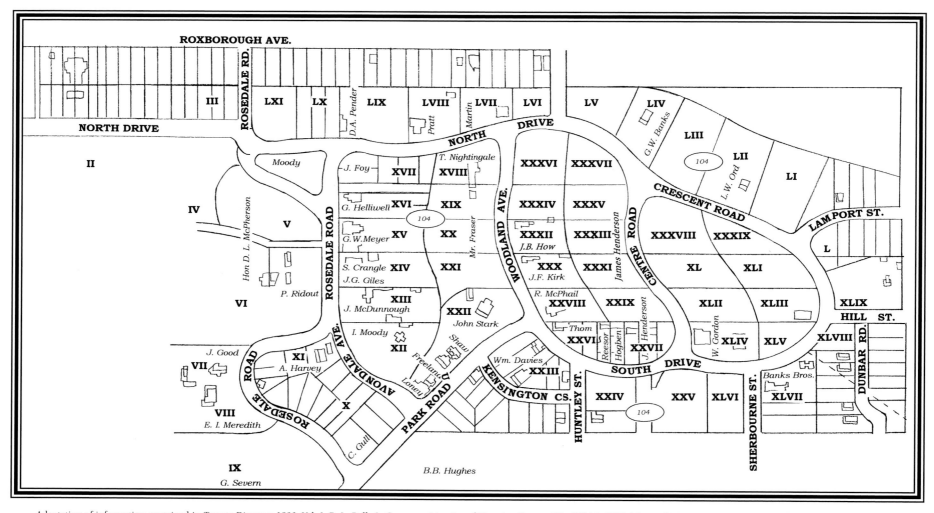

Adaptation of information contained in *Toronto Directory 1890, Vol. 1*, R. L. Polk & Company, *Mapping of Victorian Toronto (The 1884 & 1890 Atlases of Toronto in Comparative Rendition)*, Charles Edward Goad, Plate 31 and Plate 34.

A BIRD'S-EYE VIEW
OF ROSEDALE BY STREET, 1890

By 1890 approximately 100 families lived in Rosedale. The houses were located mainly in West Rosedale (Plan 104) and in South Rosedale (Plan 329). Much of the area had been subdivided into building lots, but many of them had not been built on. Often, there were only a few homes on a street. The following excerpts taken from the *Toronto Directory 1890* give the reader a good idea of what the suburb was like before full-scale development began in the early 1900s.

Current residents or neighbourhood aficionados can use the maps in this chapter to locate a lot, determine who its owner was in 1890, and then use the "Who's Who" chapter to find out that person's occupation and place of business.

Information for this chapter was obtained from *Toronto Directories,* 1850 through 1890. These directories were an early version of today's telephone books. Of course there were no telephone numbers in the 1800s. The volumes were published primarily by R.L. Polk & Company, of 14 King Street West. From about 1860 onwards, these books were put out annually and contained an alphabetical listing of businesses, private citizens and public institutions. A cross-referencing of citizens by street was also provided. They are an invaluable source of information about Toronto from 1833 onwards, since they also included statistics about population, government, public office holders, the courts, laws, regulations, taxes and a wealth of other facts and figures. Publishing costs were covered by the companies advertising and by the sale of the books to the public. The cost in 1890 was $5.

Cluny Avenue and Crescent Road.
Toronto Reference Library
T34891

CLUNY AVENUE & CRESCENT ROAD, ROSEDALE, TORONTO.

ROSEDALE, Plans 329, 524 541, 425, 433
Landowners, 1890

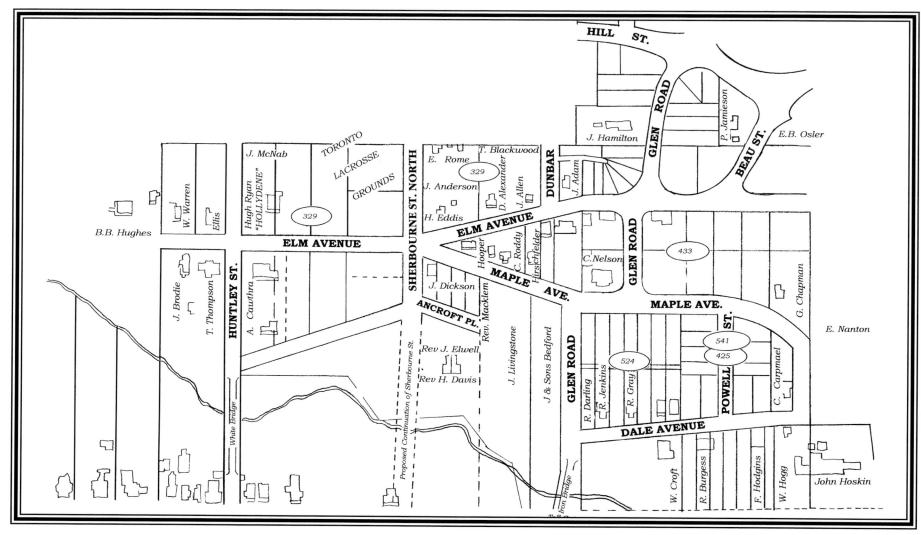

Adaptation of information contained in *Toronto Directory 1890, Vol. 1*, R. L. Polk & Company, *Mapping of Victorian Toronto (The 1884 & 1890 Atlases of Toronto in Comparative Rendition)*, Charles Edward Goad, Plate 31 and Plate 34.

ANCROFT PLACE, not listed in the 1890 *Toronto Directory*

ASTLEY AVENUE, not listed

AVONDALE ROAD, not listed

BEAU STREET, runs north from Elm Avenue, first east of Glen Road
East side
  private grounds
  Edmund Osler
West side
  12 Philip Jamieson

BEAUMONT ROAD, not listed

BIN-SCARTH ROAD, runs east from foot of Macpherson Avenue East
North side
  private grounds
  vacant lots
  Ritchie Crescent commences
  vacant lots
  vacant house
  vacant lots
  Pelham Place intersects
  vacant lots
  Glen Road intersects
  vacant lots
  Francis A. Despard
  vacant lots
  unfinished house
  private grounds
  Julian Sale
  vacant lots
South side
  vacant lots
  Pelham Place intersects
  vacant lots
  Glen Road intersects

Crescent Road, west of Cluny Avenue.
Toronto Reference Library T34889

  private grounds
  Ebenezer Stovel
  vacant lots

CASTLE FRANK AVENUE, not listed

CHESTNUT PARK ROAD, not listed

CENTRE ROAD, runs north from South Drive opposite the Toronto Athletic Grounds to North Drive and Crescent Road
East side
  1 James Haverson
  vacant lots
West side
  Not built on

CLUNY AVENUE, not listed

CLUNY CRESCENT, not listed

CRESCENT ROAD, runs north from South Drive to North Drive
East side
  house
  vacant lots
  Hill Street commences
  vacant lots
  Lamport Avenue commences
  vacant lots
  private grounds
  30 Lewis W. Ord
  vacant lots

West side
  Not built on

DALE AVENUE, runs east from Glen Road to city limits, first north of Howard
North side
  house
  private grounds
  4 Robert Jenkins
  private grounds
  8 Robert M. Gray
  10 unfinished houses
  vacant lots
  a lane
  vacant lots
  private grounds
  36 Charles M. A. Carpmael
  Maple Avenue ends
  vacant lots
  Gordon Avenue commences
  vacant lots
  Hawthorn Avenue commences
South side
  private grounds
  1 Wm. Croft
  stables
  5 Ralph K. Burgess
  private grounds
  9 Francis E. Hodgens
  stable
  15 Wm. Hogg
  private grounds
  21 John Hoskin
  private grounds
  McKenzie Avenue ends
  vacant lots

DRIVE, not listed

DRUMSNAB ROAD, not listed

DUNBAR ROAD, runs north from Elm Avenue to Hill Street, first west of Sherbourne Street
East side
  Not built on
West side
  vacant lots
  Thomas F. Blackwood
  private grounds
  Robert J. Montgomery
  vacant lots
  unfinished house
  Frederick E. Phillips

EDGAR AVENUE, runs east from Ritchie Crescent to city limits, first north of Bin-Scarth Road
  Not built on

EDGEWOOD CRESCENT, not listed

ELM AVENUE, runs east from west of Huntley to Gordon Avenue
North side
  2 Wm. A. Warren
  private grounds
  8 Eliza Ellis (widow John)
  Huntley Street intersects
  private grounds
  10 Hugh Ryan
  private grounds
  Toronto Athletic Grounds
  Sherbourne Street intersects
  house
  private grounds
  44 vacant
  46 David W. Alexander
  private grounds
  52 John Allen
  Dunbar Road commences
  54 James Adam

vacant lots
Glen Road intersects
vacant lots
Beau Street commences
vacant lot
South side
  1 Johanna Brodie (widow, R. S.)
  private grounds
  3 Thomas Thompson
  private grounds
  Huntley Street intersects
  5 Joseph Cawthra
  private grounds
  vacant lots
  junction of Sherbourne & Maple Avenue
  private grounds
  house
  private grounds
  rear entrance to Maple Avenue
  vacant lots
  51 Reverend T.C. Street Macklem
  private grounds
  53 John Livingstone
  55 J. & Sons Bedford, builders
  vacant lots
  Glen Road intersects
  vacant lots

GLEN ROAD, runs north from opposite 27 Howard to Maple Avenue, first east of Sherbourne Street
East side
  vacant lots
  toll-gate
  bridge
  Dale Avenue commences
  Robert Darling
  private grounds
  vacant lots
  Maple Avenue intersects

vacant lots
Elm Avenue intersects
vacant lots
Hill Street intersects
private grounds
stable
bridge
Park Drive intersects
vacant lots
private grounds
Charles Davidson
a lane
private grounds
Samuel Beatty
private grounds
Bin-Scarth Road intersects
Rosedale Park
West side
private grounds
vacant lots
Maple Avenue intersects
60 Charles H. Nelson
private grounds
vacant lots
Elm Avenue intersects
vacant lots
private grounds
James C. Hamilton
vacant lots
Hill Street intersects
private grounds
Henry W. Darling
private grounds
bridge
Park Drive intersects
vacant lots
Roxborough Avenue ends
    (Pelham Place)
vacant lots
Bin-Scarth Road intersects

ROSEDALE, Plans 425, 682, 607, 626, M16, 266E
Landowners, 1890

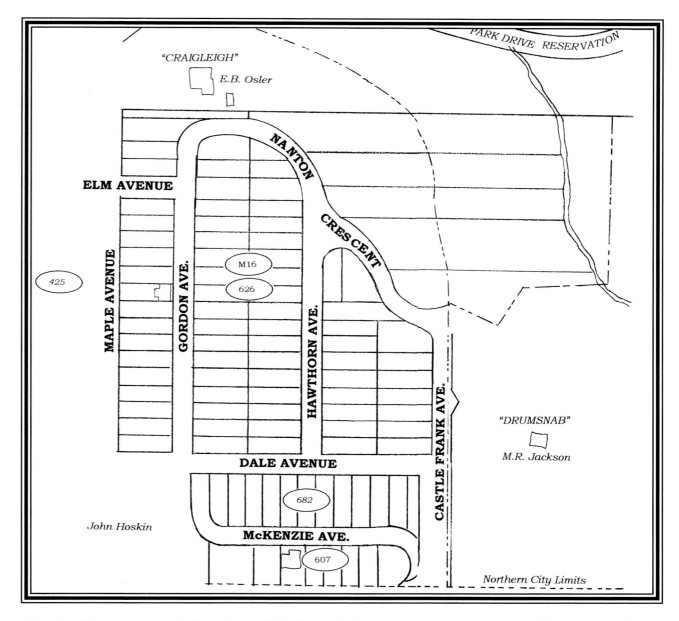

Adaptation of information contained in *Toronto Directory 1890, Vol. 1*, R. L. Polk & Company, *Mapping of Victorian Toronto (The 1884 & 1890 Atlases of Toronto in Comparative Rendition)*, Charles Edward Goad, Plate 31 and Plate 34.

ROSEDALE, Plan 84E
Landowners, 1890

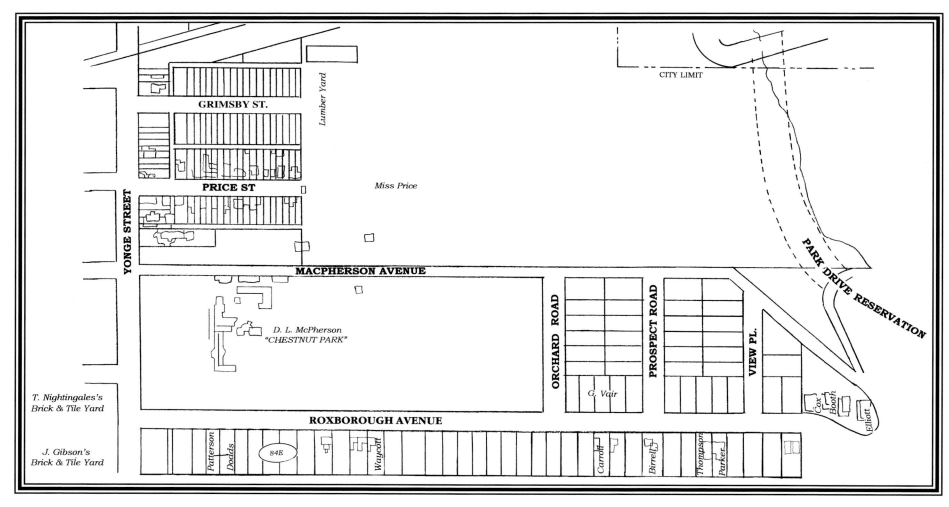

Adaptation of information contained in *Toronto Directory 1890, Vol. 1*, R. L. Polk & Company, *Mapping of Victorian Toronto (The 1884 & 1890 Atlases of Toronto in Comparative Rendition)*, Charles Edward Goad, Plate 31 and Plate 34.

GREGORY AVENUE, not listed

HAWTHORN AVENUE
  Not built on

HIGHLAND CRESCENT, not listed

HIGHLAND GARDENS, not listed

HILL STREET, runs east from junction of South Drive and Crescent Road
North side
  10 Walter Jackson
  12 Frederick Buckler
  14 Helen McDonald (widow Archibald)
  vacant lots
  May Street commences
  private grounds
  Glen Road intersects
  private grounds
South side
  Not built on

HUNTLEY STREET, runs north from the head of Earl to South Drive, first east of Jarvis Street
East side
  Bloor Street
  bridge
  private grounds
  Elm Avenue intersects
  private grounds
  125 James McNab
  vacant lots
  South Drive
West side
  bridge
  private grounds
  house
  Elm Avenue intersects
  house

  private grounds
  Kensington Crescent commences
  unfinished house
  private grounds
  South Drive

KENSINGTON CRESCENT, runs east from Park Road to Huntley Street, first south of South Drive
North side
  private grounds
  Lawrence Coffee
  vacant lots
South side
  Not built on

LAMPORT AVENUE, runs east from Crescent Road, first north of Hill Street
North side
  2 Alexander Y. Scott, M.D.
  vacant lots
South side
  Not built on

MACLENNAN AVENUE, not listed

MACPHERSON AVENUE EAST, runs east from 1085 Yonge Street to private lane, first north of Roxborough
North side
  private grounds
  2 Caroline Ridout (widow Joseph)
  stables
  private grounds
  Walter Daniels
  private grounds
South side
  "Chestnut Park," D.L. Macpherson
  George Wright
  private grounds

MAPLE AVENUE, runs southeast from Sherbourne Street and Elm Avenue to Dale Avenue
North side
  private grounds
  2 vacant
  private grounds
  4 Captain Henry Hooper
  private grounds
  6 Charles Roddy
  vacant lots
  10 Jacob M. Hirschfelder
  private grounds
  vacant lots
  private grounds
  house
  Glen Road intersects
  vacant lots
  46 George A. Chapman
South side
  private grounds
  house
  private grounds
  Glen Road intersects
  vacant lots
  Powell Street ends
  vacant lots
  house

MAY STREET, runs north from Hill Street, between Glen and Crescent Roads
East side
  private grounds
  stables
  private grounds
West side
  vacant lots
  8 John Massey
  10 James F. Smith, Q.C.

ROSEDALE, Plan 528
Landowners, 1890

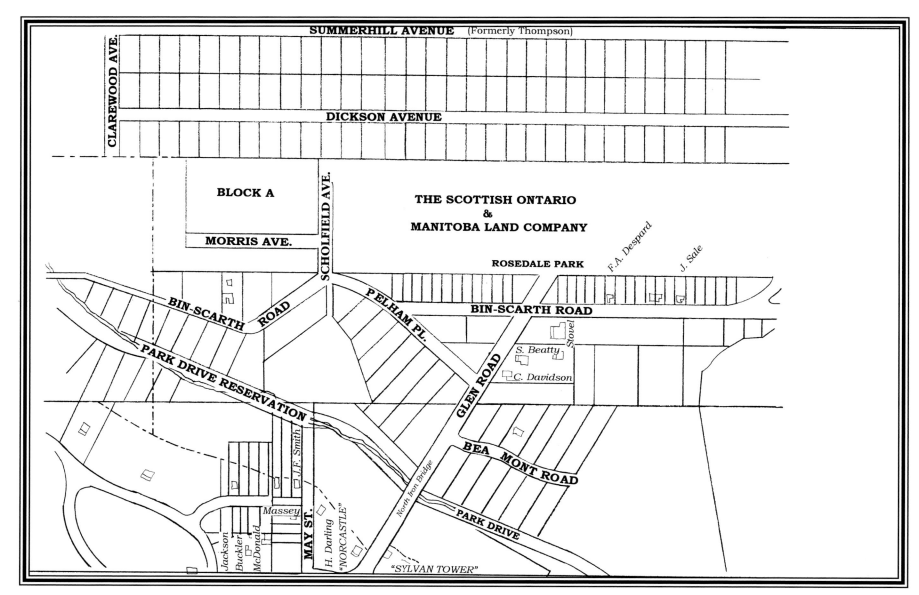

Adaptation of information contained in *Toronto Directory 1890, Vol. 1*, R. L. Polk & Company, *Mapping of Victorian Toronto (The 1884 & 1890 Atlases of Toronto in Comparative Rendition)*, Charles Edward Goad, Plate 31 and Plate 34.

MCKENZIE AVENUE, not listed

MEREDITH CRESCENT, not listed

MILKMEN'S ROAD, not listed

NANTON CRESCENT, not listed

NORTH DRIVE, runs south and east from Roxborough to Crescent Road, first east of Yonge Street
East side
  vacant lots
  private grounds
  88 David A. Pender
  private grounds
  98 Alfred J. Pratt
  private grounds
  110 Thomas M. Martin
  vacant lots
  142 Greenhow Banks
  Crescent Road commences
  private grounds
West side
  vacant lots
  a lane
  vacant lots
  Rosedale Road ends
  private grounds
  unfinished house
  Woodland Avenue ends
  vacant lots
  Centre Road ends

OLD GEORGE PLACE, not listed

PARK ROAD, runs east from 807 Yonge Street to South Drive
North side
  Rosedale Road commences

private grounds
Moody lane commences
private grounds
170 James E. Loney
private grounds
172 Edward B. Freeland
vacant lots
176 William Dick
private grounds
178 Frederick W.L. Shaw
private grounds
190 John Stark
private grounds
Woodland Avenue commences
vacant lot
South side
  Not built on

PELHAM PLACE, runs southeast from Bin-Scarth Road, first west of Glen Road
  Not built on

PINE HILL ROAD, not listed

POWELL AVENUE, not listed

PRICEFIELD ROAD, not listed

RACHAEL STREET, runs east from Sherbourne Street, first south of Maple Avenue
North side
  private grounds
  stables
South side
  1 Reverend Joseph Elwell
  3 Reverend Henry W. Davies

RITCHIE CRESCENT, runs north from Bin-Scarth Road, second west of Glen Road
  Not built on

ROSEDALE ROAD, runs north from Park Road, first east of Gwynne Street
East side
  private grounds
  5 Charles Gull
  private grounds
  21 Arthur Harvey
  Moody lane ends
  25 Isaac Moody
  27 James McDunnough
  private grounds
  31 James G. Giles
  private grounds
  35 Samuel Crangle
  private grounds
  vacant lots
  39 George W. Meyer
  private grounds
  41 Grant Helliwell
  vacant lots
  North Drive commences
West side
  vacant lots
  private grounds
  6 Edmund A. Meredith
  a lane
  8 James Good
  private grounds
  12 Percival Ridout
  private grounds
  a lane
  private grounds
  a lane
  vacant lots

ROWANWOOD AVENUE, not listed

ROXBOROUGH STREET EAST, runs east from 1083 Yonge Street to private grounds, first south of MacPherson Avenue East

Henry Osler house, Rosedale Road near Park Road, circa 1935.

Photograph by Pringle and Booth, Toronto Reference Library 976-47-21

North side
    "Chestnut Park," Sir D.L. Macpherson
    74 George Vair
    private grounds
    vacant lots
    170 Arthur Cox
    172 George Booth
    unfinished house
    176 George A. Elliott
South side
    vacant lots
    9 Robert L. Patterson
    15 Edward K. Dodds
    private grounds
    53 Charles Waycott
    North Drive commences
    vacant lots
    113 John Carroll
    private grounds
    123 Charles Birrell
    private grounds
    133 Allen Thompson
    private grounds
    139 Thomas Parker
    4 unfinished houses

ROXBOROUGH DRIVE, not listed

ST. ANDREWS GARDENS, not listed

SCARTH ROAD, not listed

SCHOLFIELD AVENUE, not listed

SHERBOURNE STREET, runs north from the Esplanade to Bloor, third east of Jarvis
East side, north of Bloor Street
    Rachael Street commences
    Reverend Henry W. Davies
    Reverend Joseph Elwell

    stables
    James Dickson
    junction of Maple and Elm Avenue
    private grounds
    Henry W. Eddis
    private grounds
    James Anderson
    private grounds
    David Rome
    private grounds
West side
    Bloor Street East
    ravine
    vacant lots
    Elm Avenue intersects
    Toronto Athletic Grounds

SOUTH DRIVE, runs east from the junction of Park Road and Woodland Avenue to Hill Street
North side
    2 John H. Thom
    private grounds
    8 Hon. David Reesor
    10 Henry Hogben
    private grounds
    a lane
    private grounds
    16 Charles Smith
    vacant lots
    Centre Road commences
    private grounds
    22 James D. Henderson
    private grounds
    26 William Gordon Sr.
    Crescent Road commences
South side
    private grounds
    Huntley Street ends
    vacant lots
    Toronto Athletic Grounds

    Sherbourne Street ends
    house
    private grounds
    Hill Street commences
    City limits

STANDISH AVENUE, not listed

SUMMERHILL AVENUE EAST, not listed

THORNWOOD ROAD, not listed

WHITEHALL ROAD, not listed

WOODLAND AVENUE, runs north from junction of South Drive and Park Road
East side
    private grounds
    1 James B. How
    private grounds
    vacant lots
    private grounds
    19 James F. Kirk
    private grounds
    25 Robert McPhail
    vacant lots

West side
    vacant lots
    36 Thomas Nightingale
    private grounds

WHITNEY AVENUE, not listed

WRENTHAM PLACE, not listed

Greenhow Banks
Adam, *Toronto Old & New*,
Toronto Reference Library

John L. Blaikie
Toronto Illustrated

Francis Cayley
Adam, *Toronto Old & New*,
Toronto Reference Library

Dr. John Hoskin, Q.C.
Adam, *Toronto Old & New*,
Toronto Reference Library

A WHO'S WHO
OF ROSEDALE'S FIRST CENTURY

The original lot owners in Rosedale were a virtual "who's who" of Toronto in the late 1800s. Lawyers, bankers, corporate presidents, company owners and senators, as well as land agents, architects, developers, builders or, like Thomas Nightingale and Isaac Moody, owners of brickyards.

In 1884 only about 40 people owned lots in Rosedale and by 1890 the total was still as few as 100. It is hardly surprising that many of these families knew each other. They were personal friends, they went to school together, worked together, were on the same boards of directors, and their sons and daughters married.

The *Toronto Directories*, published by R.L. Polk & Company, indicate that at least six of the original purchasers of Rosedale lots were neighbours on Jarvis Street, Yorkville (the present Asquith Avenue) prior to moving to the new elite suburb. During this period various members of the Jarvis family also lived on Jarvis Street. They were presumably marketing the Jarvis family's properties to their neighbours. Moreover, many of the land developers, real estate agents and architects who eventually bought lots in Rosedale had offices near Edgar Jarvis on Toronto Street.

As Henry Scadding aptly put it in his *Toronto of Old* , "This ruling elite clearly rested on personal wealth." But it was not wealth alone. There were other criteria: one had to give the right parties, "not too lavishly ostentatious...for the right guests, belonging to the right community organizations and churches (preferably Anglican or Presbyterian, though more urbane Methodism increasingly would do), display the right furnishings and 'tasteful' art objects, and, especially, engaging in philanthropy." It was also necessary to have the most upwardly mobile profession. "Shopkeepers and manufacturers, however large their operations, were not deemed as socially admirable as big wholesalers and financiers, unless, like the distillery based Gooderhams, they had been present long enough and had acceptably diversified their business concerns."[1]

OSLER & HAMMOND,
18 King street west, Toronto,
STOCK BROKERS,
DEALERS IN
Railway and Municipal Debentures.
E. B. OSLER,   H. C. HAMMOND,
Members Toronto Stock Exchange.

Toronto Mail, December 5, 1883, Toronto Reference Library

BLAIKIE & ALEXANDER,
WILLIAM ALEXANDER.   JOHN STARK.
(Members of the Stock Exchange,)
Stock Brokers and Estate Agents.
Stocks, Bonds, Debentures, Houses, Lands, &c., bought and sold.
Money loaned on mortgage.   Mortgages negotiated, and investments made.
Orders by letter or telegraph will receive prompt attention.
10 KING STREET EAST, TORONTO.   d

The Mail, May 23, 1874, Toronto Reference Library

The Leader, February 19, 1870, Toronto Reference Library

Toronto Mail, December 5, 1883, Toronto Reference Library

ADAM, John
Manager Smith & Keighly,
residence 54 Elm Avenue

ALEXANDER, David
Wholesale leather goods, 65 Front Street,
residence 46 Elm Avenue

ALEXANDER, William
1864–65 Blaikie & Alexander, accountants, brokers
& estate agents, President National Investment Co.,
residence "Denbrae," Rosedale

ALLEN, Alfred
Contractor, builder, residence 10 South Drive

ALLEN, John
Traveller, residence 52 Elm Avenue

ANDERSON, James
Hees, Anderson & Co.,
residence Sherbourne Street

BANKS, Arthur
1864–65 clerk, 1978 of Kay & Banks

BANKS, George
1874 bookkeeper, 1879 estate agent

BANKS, Greenhow W.
Banks Brothers, Accountants, Real Estate
General Agents
1864–65 clerk, 1878 assistant manager Isolated
Risk Fire Insurance Co., residence "Heyroyd,"
Rosedale

BANKS, William
clerk 1864–65

BANKS, Robert
bookkeeper and accountant

BEATTY, Samuel
George D. Beatty & Stovel Real Estate
64 Victoria Street, 6 York Chambers,
9 Toronto Street, residence Glen Road

BEATTY, W.H.
Vice President Bank of Toronto 1884

BEDFORD, Jeremiah
Builder, J. & Sons Bedford,
residence 55 Elm Avenue
Sons Frederick, John & Henry

BIRRELL, Charles
Milk dealer, business 123 Roxborough,
residence same

BLACKWOOD, Thomas F.
Residence 6 Dunbar Road

BLACKWOOD, Arthur E.
Clerk H.S. Howland & Sons & Co., rooms,
6 Dunbar Road

BLACKWOOD, Charles K.
Clerk A. R. Williams, rooms, 6 Dunbar Road

BLACKWOOD, Thomas F.
apprentice, rooms, 6 Dunbar Road

BLAIKIE, J.L.
1864–65 Blaikie & Alexander, accountants, brokers
and estate agents, 1864-65 residence 352 Jarvis
Street, 1880 president Canada Landed Credit Co.,
residence Rosedale

BOOTH, George
George Booth & Son, wallpaper, house, sign and fresco painters, 21 Adelaide Street, residence 172 Roxborough

BOOTH, Arthur
Clerk Booth & Son, rooms 172 Roxborough

BRODIE, Johanna
Widow Richard S., residence 1 Elm Avenue

BUCKLER, Frederick
Peddler, residence Hill Street

BURGESS, Ralph K.
Clerk Imperial Bank, residence 65 Dale

CARPMAEL, Charles M. A.
FRAS, Director Meteorological Office, Queen's Park, residence Dale Avenue

CARROLL, John
Milk dealer, business 123 Roxborough, residence same

CAWTHRA, Joseph
Retired, formerly successful retailer and general store owner in Newmarket

CAYLEY, Francis
Bank of Toronto, Land agent
Residence "Drumsnab"

CAYLEY, John
Rector of St. George's, Church of England
Residence "Drumsnab"

CHAPMAN, George A.
G.A. Chapman & Co., 1883 produce commission

merchant of 91 Front Street, residence Maple Avenue, Rosedale

COFFEE, Lawrence
Coffee & Co. & Thomas F. Flynn Grain Commission Merchants, residence Kensington Crescent

COFFEE, John L.
Cashier, Coffee & Co.

COX, Arthur
Treasurer GNW Telegraph Co., residence Roxborough

CRANGLE, Samuel
Mariner, residence Rosedale Road

CROFT, William
William Croft & Sons, fishing tackle and needles, of 37 Colborne Street, residence Dale Avenue

DARLING, Henry W.
Wyld, Brock & Darling, wholesale dry goods, of Bay & Wellington Streets, President Canadian Bank of Commerce, residence "Norcastle," Glen Road, Rosedale

DARLING, Robert
Robert Darling & Co. wholesale woollens, 234 Wellington Street, residence "Ravensmount," Rosedale

DAVIDSON, Charles
C. Davidson & Co., saddlery and carriage hardware, of 118 King Street East, residence Glen Road

DAVIES, William
Provision dealer, provision merchant, residence 1859–60 Jarvis Street, 18 Kensington Crescent

DAVIS, Dr. James B.
1880 Principal Normal School, Rosedale east of the White Bridge, Sherbourne Street

DESPARD, Francis A.
Secretary-treasurer The Ammonia Company of Toronto, residence Bin-Scarth Road

DICK, William
Assistant accountant Bank of Montreal, residence 176 Park Road

DICKSON, James
James Dickson & Co., provision dealer, residence Sherbourne Street

DODDS, Edward K.
Excise officer Internal Revenue Department, rooms, 15 Roxborough

DODDS, E. King
Manager Canadian Sportsman & Livestock Journal, residence 15 Roxborough

EDDIS, H.W.
1874 Public accountant, also accountant for Coffee & Co., residence "Aldbury Lodge," Rosedale

EDDIS, E. H.
1880 of Boswell, Robertson & Eddis, barristers, of 20 Adelaide Street East, residence "Aldbury Lodge," Rosedale

ELLIOTT, George A.
Builder, carpenter, residence 176 Roxborough

ELLIS, Eliza
Widow John, residence Elm Avenue

ELLIS, John
Residence 10 Park Road

ELLIS, Henry H.
1883 barrister, rooms, corner Bridge & Elm Avenue

ELWELL, Reverend J.
Pastor Apostolic Church, residence Sherbourne St.

FOY, J.J.
Foy, Tupper & Macdonell, barristers of 20 Adelaide Street East, later of Patrick Foy & Sons (James & John), residence 18 Rosedale Road

FRASER, James
1870 secretary & treasurer Metropolitan Permanent Building Society, agent Liverpool & London & Globe Insurance Co. and Briton Medical & General Life Association

FREELAND, Edward B.
Accountant John Stark & Co., residence 176 Park Road

GILES, James G.
J.G. Giles & Son, grocer 37 Yonge Street, 1879 residence Rosepark, Rosedale Road

GOOD, James
James Good & Co., groceries, wines & liquors, Agent Labatt's Ale & Porter 220 Yonge Street, also owner of foundry near Victoria & Yonge Streets, residence Rosedale Road

GORDON, William Jr.
Junior clerk Imperial Bank, rooms 26 South Drive

GRAY, Robert M.
R. H. Gray and Co., residence Dale Avenue and Huntley Street

GULL, Charles
Traveller, residence 5 Rosedale Road

HAMILTON, J. Cleland
1867-68 Patterson, Beaty & Hamilton, residence 107 Bay, 1880 of Beaty, Hamilton & Cassels, residence Glen Road Rosedale

HARVEY, Arthur
Haverson & St. John, barristers 28 Wellington Street Toronto, 1874 secretary manager Provincial Insurance Co. of Canada, 1878 receiver Provincial Insurance Co., manager Toronto Life Assurance Co. & Tontine, President Land & Loan Co., residence Rosedale Road

HAVERSON, James
Barrister, Haverson & St. John, residence 9 North Drive

HELLIWELL, Grant
Gordon & Helliwell architects, 23 Scott, residence Rosedale Road

HENDERSON, James
1856 Broker, land agent,
1861 Home District Savings Bank 1864-65 President Savings Bank, Royal Insurance Building, residence Bloor Street, Yorkville
1870 clerk R.A. Hoskins & Co., President Savings Bank, James D. Henderson Co., real estate, insurance, rents collected, estates managed, financial broker, arbitrator and valuator, office 8 King Street, residence 22 South Drive

HIRSCHFELDER, Jacob M.
Professor, residence Maple Avenue

HIRSCHFELDER, Charles A.
U.S. Vice Consul, residence 10 Maple Avenue

HODGENS, Francis E.
Coatsworth, Hodgens & Company, residence 9 Dale Avenue

HOGBEN, Henry
Saloon 4 Court, residence South Drive

HOGG, William
Coachman J. Hoskin, residence 15 Dale Avenue

HOOPER, Captain Henry
Residence "Fermoy Lodge," Sherbourne Street

HOSKIN, John
Q.C. McCarthy, Osler, Hoskin & Creelman, President National Investment Company of Canada residence 21 Dale Avenue

HOW, James B.
Dentist 17 King Street, residence Woodland Avenue

HUGHES, B.B.
1880 of Hughes Brothers, residence Elm Avenue

JACKSON, Maunsell B.
Clerk, registrar of Common Pleas Division, residence "Drumsnab," Castle Frank Avenue

JACKSON, Walter
Gardener, residence 10 Hill Street

JAMES GOOD & CO.

One of the leading among the established wholesale and retail dealers in general groceries, wines and liquors in this city is the firm of James Good & Co., located at 220 Yonge street, corner Albert. The business was established 26 years ago, and is under the control of Mr. James Good, the sole proprietor, who occupies a position in the front rank of the trade and numbers among his patrons the best families in the city. The premises comprise three flats, each 20 x 110 feet in area, and the stock consists of everything in the line of staple and fancy groceries, including hermetically sealed fruits, vegetables, etc., in tin and glass, table luxuries and delicacies of every kind, and the choicest imported French and other imported wines, fine old whiskies, malt liquors etc. In the bottling department Mr. Good is doing an extensive trade. He is sole agent for Labatt's renowned ale and stout and for the Pabst Brewing Co,, and also agent for St. Leon mineral water, and in this branch of the business employ about fifteen hands. Mr. Good, who was born in Ireland, and has resided in Toronto twenty-seven years, has always sustained a high reputation. He deals in goods only of a superior quality.

Toronto Illustrated.

R. HIGGINS AND SON.

The Rosedale Grocery, located at 804 Yonge street, conducted by R. Higgins and Son, is among the most complete and best stocked concerns on the street. Mr. R. Higgins was born in England and his son, Mr. F. higgins, was born in Brooklyn, U.S., but has been a resident in this city since boyhood, and they have had many years experience in the family grocery line. this establishment was founded ten years since and under its able management has always enjoyed a good patronage. the store is 20 x 75 fet indimensions and is well supplied with a choic line of goods. as a partiial enumeration may be named teras, coffees, spices, pure baking poowders, best flour for family use, a gret variety of fresh canned goods, corn meal, fruits, vegetables, and all and singularthe article consumed in families, hotls and restaurants. this house enjoys a fine reputation, both on account of the qualityof the goods handles and sold, and also for its fair dealing. Both gentlemen composing the firm are thorough business men and enjoy the confidenc eof the public in a high degree.

Toronto Illustrated.

JOHN STARK & CO.

With the rapid growth of Toronto and the ever increasing demand for residences and manufacturing and commercial buildings, the real estate and financial interests of the city have received a wide expansion and naturally come to form one of the chief investments for capital. Among the most enterprising and popular firms of stock and exchange brokers and real estate agents and valuators is that of Messrs. John Stark & Company, of No. 26 Toronto street, whose business had its inception thirty-five years ago. They are members of the Toronto Stock Exchange, and promptly fill orders for the purchase or sale of bonds, stocks, or miscellaneous securities, giving the utmost care and attention to the interests of their customers. The firm possess the best facilities for the receipt of the earliest information regarding stock interests, and the advantageous placing of orders. They also transact a general real estate business, manage estates, collect rents, and negotiate loans on mortgage. The telephone call is 880. The firm enjoy the confidence and esteem of leading financial circles, and are in every way worthy representatives of the stock and real estate markets of the city.

Toronto Illustrated.

JAMIESON, Philip
Merchant, tailor and clothier 180 Yonge Street, residence Beau Street

JARVIS, Charles
1859–60 Rose Park, Yorkville

JARVIS, Edgar John
1859 Sheriff's clerk, 1861 Land agent and broker, Whittemore Building, Toronto St.
1878 land agent, "Glenhurst," Rosedale

JARVIS, Frederick William
1856 Deputy Sheriff, 1859–60 residence Jarvis Street

JARVIS, Samuel P.
1856 of Bloor Street, Yorkville

JARVIS, William Botsford
1856 Sheriff, residence Front Street, formerly of Rosedale Road

JENKINS, Robert
R & T Jenkins Estate Agents, Assignees in Trust, Accountants and Auditors, 15 Toronto Street, residence Dale Avenue

KIRK, Ferrier
Residence Woodland Avenue

KIRK, James F.
1884 accountant London & Canada Loan & Assurance Co., Manager London & Canadian Loan Agency, residence Woodland Avenue

LIVINGSTONE, John
Agent and trustee, 31 York Chambers, residence Maple Avenue

LIVINGSTONE, F.W.
1864–65 barrister, agent and trustee 31 York Chambers, residence 53 Elm Avenue

LONEY, James E.
Real estate 828 Yonge Street, residence 170 Park Rd.

MACKLEM, Reverend T.C. Street
Rector St. Simon's Anglican Church, residence 51 Elm Avenue

MARTIN, James
Artist, residence North Drive

MASSEY, John
Assistant manager Western Canadian Loan &
Savings Co., residence 10 May Street

MATTHEWS, Wilmot D.
W.D. Matthews & Co., president Toronto
Incandescent Electric Light Co.,
residence 56 Elm Avenue

MCDONALD, Helen
Widow Archibald, residence Hill Street

MCDUNNOUGH, James
Manager carpet department R. Walker & Sons,
residence 27 Rosedale Road

MCNAB, James
Residence Huntley Street

MCPHAIL, Robert
Wilson & McPhail Co., residence 25 Woodland

MACPHERSON, Sir David Lewis
1856 Contractor Toronto Rolling Mill,
Speaker and Senator of the Dominion of Canada,
residence "Chestnut Park," Yonge Street

MEREDITH, Edmund A.
Vice Pres. Toronto General Trusts,
residence Rosedale Road

MEYER, George W.
1878 law student, 1881 barrister,
residence Rosedale Road

MONTGOMERY, Robert J.
Manager Canadian Bank of Commerce
791 Yonge Street, residence Dunbar Road

MOODY, Isaac
1880 brick manufacturer, residence Rosedale Road

MURRAY, George
Barrister 60 Church Street, 1884,
residence 40 Huntley Street

NANTON, Edward
Broker Imperial Bank Building, residence York Twp.

NELSON, Charles H.
H.A. Nelson & Son, residence Glen Road

NIGHTINGALE, Thomas
1862–63 manufacturer of red and white brick,
sewer and drain tile, Yonge Street, 1880 residence
"White House," Woodland Avenue

ORD, Lewis W.
1880 assistant auditor Parliament Buildings,
Director Dominion Bank of Canada,
residence 30 Hazelton, 1881 statistical clerk
Treasury Department, residence Crescent Road

OSLER, Sir E.B.
1867–68 of Pellatt & Osler, residence 25 Grenville,
1880 of Pellatt & Osler, residence "Craigleigh,"
Beau Street

PARKER, Thomas
Principal Winchester Street School,
residence 139 Roxborough

PATTERSON, Robert L.
Manager Miller & Richard,
residence 9 Roxborough

PENDER, David A.
T. G. Foster & Co., residence North Drive

PHILBRICK, Dr.
1870 Doctor and coroner, Bloor Street, Yorkville

PHILLIPS, Frederick E.
House and sign painter 115 Church Street,
residence Dunbar Road

PRATT, Alfred J.
Cabowner, residence North Drive

PRICE, Miss Sarah
Residence "Woodbine Cottage," Yonge Street

REESOR, Hon. David
Senator, residence 8 South Drive

RIDOUT, Percival
Residence Rosedale Road

RODDY, Charles
Porter & Son (Robert E. Porter),
residence Maple Avenue

ROME, David
Secretary, The Williams, Greene & Rome
Company, residence Sherbourne Street

RYAN, Hugh
Contractor 20 Manning Avenue,
residence 10 Elm Avenue

SALE, Julian
Julian Sale & Co. Manufacturers of pocket books,
Sample Room 24 Front Street, residence Bin-Scarth
Road

SCOTT, Alexander Y.
M.D., residence Lamport Street

SEVERN, George
1859-60 Yorkville Toll Gate

SEVERN, Henry
Severn Brothers Brewery, brewers and maltsters, Yonge Street, Yorkville

SEVERN, William
Severn Brothers Brewery, Yonge Street, Yorkville

SHAW, Frederick W.L.
S.R. Warren & Sons, residence 178 Park Road

SMITH, Charles
Coachman Joseph Cawthra, residence 16 South Drive

SMITH, James F.
Q.C. Smith, Smith & Greer, residence 10 May Street

STARK, John
1867–68 bookkeeper, Blaikie & Alexander, John Stark & Co. Stock brokers & financial agents, 28–30 Toronto Street residence 34 Gloucester, partner Wm. Alexander & Lawrence Buchan, 1874 residence Park Road

STOVEL, Ebenezer
Stovel & Co., merchant tailors, 73 King Street West, residence Bin-Scarth Road

TAYLOR, John
1880 constable county court, residence "Rosedale Lodge," Rosedale

THOM, J.H.
1880 Barrister, taxing officer, Accountant's Office, Osgoode Hall, residence Woodland Avenue, Rosedale

THOMPSON, Allen
Labourer, residence Roxborough

THOMPSON, Thomas
Thomas Thompson & Son, Mammoth House dry goods store, residence 3 Elm Avenue

WARREN, William A.
Warren Brothers (Charles D. & William A.) & Henry Boomer, wholesale grocers 35–37 Front Street, residence Elm Avenue

WAYCOTT, Charles
Coachman to Sir D.L. Macpherson, residence 53 Roxborough

WHITE, Mrs. Louisa
Widow George, builder, Bloor Street, residence Rosedale Road

STREET NAMES:
Their Origin and Evolution

A variety of sources yielded information about the origin of street names in Rosedale. Aside form the purely descriptive names like Crescent Road, Park Road, South Drive, Dale Avenue, Bridge Street and Woodland Avenue, most of the others are named after people, either because of their personality and prominence, position and wealth, or because of their ownership of land in Rosedale. Authors Henry Scadding and John Ross Robertson offered up derivations for some of the oldest streets, but for the most part, clues about the source of the street names came more or less by accident while searching through land transfer documents, registrations for subdivisions, or on forays for other Rosedale-related topics at the Toronto Reference Library. *Toronto Directories* also proved to be a fertile cache of intelligence. Some of the spellings of names have altered slightly from the originals, as in MacPherson (not Macpherson) and Sherbourne (not Sherborne) and in the case of Bin-Scarth, we see both hyphenated and non-hyphenated versions used.

Northeast corner of Maple and Dale Avenues, 1913.
City of Toronto Archives
RG 8-10-101

ANCROFT PLACE was named for Anthony Croft, owner of a property on nearby Maple Avenue.

BEAU STREET was probably a truncated form of Beaumont, for Edgar Jarvis's wife, Charlotte Beaumont; also after Beau, Edgar Jarvis's son.

BEAUMONT ROAD was named for Edgar Jarvis's wife, Charlotte Beaumont.

BIN-SCARTH ROAD was named after William Bain Scarth, land commissioner, born in Scotland in 1837. His father, James Scarth was descended from the Scarths of Binscarth, Orkney Islands.

BRIDGE STREET was referred to this way because of the white bridge over the Rosedale ravine just north of Bloor Street.

CASTLE FRANK AVENUE commemorates "Castle Frank," the summer home of John Graves Simcoe.

CHESTNUT PARK commemorates the residence of Sir D.L. Macpherson of the same name. Originally horse chestnut trees lined Yonge Street and MacPherson Avenue, where the estate was located.

CRESCENT ROAD was so called because of its shape.

DALE AVENUE is a fanciful designation.

DICKSON AVENUE was named after George Pennie Dickson, large landowner in North Rosedale in the 1880s. It was later renamed Whitehall Road.

DRUMSNAB was named after Francis Cayley's "Drumsnab Farm."

EDGAR AVENUE was named after James Edgar, Toronto lawyer and later MP. In 1880 he and Charles Ritchie owned much of the land in North Rosedale.

ELM AVENUE was given this name because of the trees Edgar Jarvis and his gardener planted there.

HIGHLAND AVENUE was possibly named after John Herbert Hyland, speculator in North rosedale property in 1887. Otherwise a purely fanciful name.

HOWARD STREET was named after Allen MacLean Howard, clerk of the Division Court.

HUNTLEY STREET was named after Huntley, Aberdeenshire, Scotland, birthplace of Col. William Allan, second postmaster and customs collector of York.

LAMPORT AVENUE was named after Henry lamport, merchant in Norfolk county, purchaser of Villa Lots 35 and 50 in Rose-Park. Lamport registered Plans 629 and 668 subdividing these lots in 1886.

Eli Whaley house, 74 Roxborough Street East, circa 1906.
Toronto Reference Library T31237

MACPHERSON AVENUE was named after Sir David Lewis Macpherson of "Chestnut Park" Estate, Speaker and Senator of the Dominion of Canada.

MAPLE AVENUE was given this name because of the trees of that name planted by Edgar Jarvis.

MAY STREET was named after Edgar Jarvis's twin daughter May.

MCKENZIE AVENUE was named after Walter McKenzie of "Castle."

MEREDITH CRESCENT was named after Edmund A. Meredith, author and principal of McGill College. He was the husband of Anne Frances "Fanny" Jarvis, favourite daughter of William Botsford Jarvis.

MORRIS AVENUE was named after Laura Morris, owner of property in North Rosedale in the 1880s.

MURRAY STREET was named after the wife of Chief Justice William Powell, whose maiden name was Murray. Her granddaughter married William Botsford Jarvis. It was later renamed Roxborough Street East.

NANTON AVENUE was named after Edward Nanton. Louisa Jarvis, second daughter of William B. Jarvis, married Augustus Nanton in 1855.

NORTH DRIVE, so named to distinguish it from South Drive.

PARK ROAD was purely a picturesque, descriptive name.

Roxborough St. E., near Mt. Pleasant Rd., 1927.
Dept. of Public Works, Toronto Reference Library 976-47-6

PELHAM PLACE derived its name from George Pelham (1766–1827), bishop of Bristol, Exeter and Lincoln or John Thomas Pelham (1811–1894), bishop of Norwich.

PERCY STREET was named after one of Edgar and Charlotte Jarvis's twins.

POWELL STREET was named after William Dummer Powell, Chief Justice of Ontario. Samuel Peters Jarvis married his daughter Mary Boyles Powell in 1818. William Botsford Jarvis married his granddaughter Mary Boyles Powell.

PRICEFIELD ROAD derives its name from the large plot of land on the east side of Yonge Street, just south of the railway tracks as far as Rowanwood owned by Miss Sarah Price. What is now Price Street was also part of the estate. Her home was called "Thornwood," later "Woodbine Cottage."

RACHAEL STREET was named after Rachel Starr, wife of Stephen Jarvis, or after Rachel Patrick, who from 1874 until the mid-1880s lived nearby on the south side of Maple Avenue, Lot 22.

RITCHIE CRESCENT was named after Charles Henry Ritchie, prominent Toronto lawyer. He and James Edgar owned most of North Rosedale in 1880. Later renamed Scholfield Avenue.

ROWANWOOD AVENUE was the name of James Grant Macdonald's home located just north of D.L. Macpherson's "Chestnut Park."

ST. ANDREWS GARDENS, named after St. Andrews College. The boys' school was originally located at the "Chestnut Park" estate from 1899 until 1905, then moved to North Rosedale.

SCARTH ROAD was named after W.B. Scarth, land commissioner and manager of the Scottish Ontario and Manitoba Land Company.

SCHOLFIELD AVENUE, named after Alexandra L. Scholfield, who bought land in North Rosedale from Miss Sarah Price circa 1880.

SHERBOURNE STREET was named after the small town of Sherborne in Dorset, the original home of Toronto's Tom Ridout, cashier of the Bank of Upper Canada 1822–1861.

SOUTH DRIVE was named so as to distinguish it from its complement North Drive.

SUMMERHILL AVENUE commemorates the house of the same name built by Charles Thompson on a hill east of Yonge Street with a view to the valley below.

THORNWOOD ROAD originates from Thornwood, Essex, England, birthplace of Joseph Price, owner of the large farm on Township Lot 18, now Chestnut Park and North Rosedale.

WHITNEY AVENUE was either named after Sir James Pliny Whitney, prime minister of Ontario 1905–08 or after J.W.G. Whitney, land and estate agent of 25 Toronto Street.

WOODLAND AVENUE was merely a fanciful name.

CHANGES IN STREET NAMES

ANCROFT PLACE

1910   First appeared on maps.

ASTLEY AVENUE

1890   First appeared on maps.

BEAU STREET

1877   First appeared on maps. It ran north from Elm Avenue to Hill Street (South Drive.)

BEAUMONT ROAD

1890   First appeared on maps.

BIN-SCARTH ROAD

1884   First appeared on maps.

1908   Western portion from the Mount Pleasant ravine to Scholfield Avenue was renamed East Roxborough Street.

BRIDGE STREET (MOUNT PLEASANT ROAD)

1877   First appeared on maps. It ran north from Bloor Street East to South Drive.

1890   Renamed Huntley Street.

CASTLE FRANK AVENUE

1890   First appeared on maps.

CENTRE ROAD (SCARTH ROAD)

1854   First appeared on maps.

1905   Renamed Scarth Road. The portion north of Crescent Road was added.

1910   The northern portion was renamed Thornwood Road.

CLAREWOOD AVENUE (HIGHLAND CRESCENT)

1884   First appeared on maps. It was a northern extension of Ritchie Crescent.

CLUNY AVENUE

1905   First appeared on maps.

CRESCENT ROAD

1854   First appeared on maps. It ran east from the intersection of Centre Road (Mount Pleasant Road) to Sherbourne Street.

DICKSON AVENUE

1884   First appeared on maps. It was located near the present Whitehall Road.

DUNBAR ROAD

1890   First appeared on maps.

EAST ROXBOROUGH STREET

1908   First appeared on maps.

EDGAR AVENUE

1884   First appeared on maps.

ELM AVENUE

1877   First appeared on maps.

GLEN ROAD

1877   First appeared on maps. It ran north from Maple Avenue to the North Rosedale Ravine.

1884   Extended north into North Rosedale after the North Iron Bridge had been built. Extended south to Bloor Street East after the Iron Bridge over the South Rosedale ravine   had been built.

GORDON AVENUE (NANTON AVENUE)

1890   First appeared on maps.

1905   Renamed Nanton Crescent.

HAWTHORN AVENUE

1890   First appeared on maps.

HILL STREET

1877   First appeared on maps. It ran east from Crescent Road to Beau Street.

1905   Renamed South Drive.

KENSINGTON CRESCENT (MEREDITH CRESCENT)

1890   First appeared on maps. It ran east from Park Road to Bridge Street (Mount Pleasant Road).

1905   Renamed Meredith Crescent.

LAMPORT STREET

1890   First appeared on maps. It ran east from Crescent Road, first street north of Hill Street (South Drive).

MACLENNAN AVENUE

1908   First appeared on maps.

"Heyroyd," home of the Banks brothers,
Sherbourne Street and Crescent Road.
Photograph by Mario Angastiniotis

MACPHERSON AVENUE

1884	First appeared on maps.
1905	Renamed MacPherson Avenue East.
1910	Renamed Rowanwood Avenue.

MAPLE AVENUE

| 1877 | First appeared on maps. |

MAY STREET

| 1877 | First appeared on maps. |

MCKENZIE AVENUE

| 1890 | First appeared on maps. |

MORRIS AVENUE

| 1890 | First appeared on maps. It ran roughly along the western path of Douglas Drive. |

MURRAY STREET (ROXBOROUGH STREET)

1954	First appeared on maps.
1877	Renamed Roxborough Street.
1890	Renamed Roxborough Avenue.
1905	Renamed Roxborough Street East.

NANTON CRESCENT
(CASTLE FRANK AVENUE)

| 1890 | First appeared on maps. |
| 1905 | Northern portion renamed Castle Frank Avenue. |

NORTH DRIVE (CRESCENT ROAD)

1854	First appeared on maps. It ran east from the present Cluny Avenue to Centre Road (Mount Pleasant Road).
1890	Extended west to Yonge Street.
1905	Renamed Crescent Road.

PARK ROAD

| 1854 | First appeared on maps. |

PELHAM PLACE
(HIGHLAND AVENUE)

1884	First appeared on maps.
1905	Western portion also called Lansdowne Place.
1908	Renamed Highland Avenue.

PERCY STREET

| 1884 | First appeared on maps. |
| 1890 | Renamed Dale Avenue. |

PINE HILL ROAD

| 1905 | First appeared on maps. |

POWELL AVENUE

1884   First appeared on maps.

PROSPECT ROAD
(CHESTNUT PARK ROAD)

1890   First appeared on maps.

1905   Renamed Chestnut Park Road.

RITCHIE CRESCENT

1884   First appeared on maps. It ran roughly along the path of the present Highland Gardens.

ROSEDALE RAVINE DRIVE

1905   First appeared on maps.

1910   Renamed Rosedale Valley Road.

ROSEDALE ROAD

1854   First appeared on maps. It ran north from Park Road to Murray Street (Roxborough Street East).

1890   Southern portion renamed Avondale Avenue.

1905   Northwestern portion renamed Cluny Avenue.

SCHOLFIELD AVENUE

1890   First appeared on maps.

1910   Renamed Scholfield Street.

SHERBOURNE STREET

1877   First appeared on maps. It started one block north of Bloor Street East.

1905   Renamed North Sherbourne Street. The road was extended south to Bloor Street East after the bridge over the ravine had been built.

SOUTH DRIVE

1854   First appeared on maps. It ran east from the intersection of Park Road and Woodlands Avenue.

STANDISH AVENUE

1890   First appeared on maps.

THOMPSON AVENUE
(SUMMERHILL AVENUE)

1877   First appeared on maps.

1884   Renamed Summerhill Avenue.

VIEW PLACE
(CHESTNUT PARK ROAD)

1890   First appeared on maps.

1905   Renamed Chestnut Park Road.

WHITNEY AVENUE

1908   First appeared on maps.

WOODLANDS AVENUE
(SOUTH DRIVE)

1854   First appeared on maps. It ran south from North Drive (Crescent Road) to the intersection of South Drive and Park Road.

1877   Renamed Woodland Avenue.

1905   Renamed Park Road.

1910   Renamed South Drive.

The *Leader*, May 16, 1870, Toronto Reference Library

THE FIRST LANDOWNERS

Prior to 1854, there were seven estates in the neighbourhood we now know as Rosedale. Even after the registration of the Rose-Park Plan of subdivision by George Duggan in 1854, development of the new suburb proceeded only slowly. While Toronto enjoyed a period of rapid expansion during the railway boom of the 1850s only six lots had been sold in Rosedale by 1864. Part of the problem in the early years was its distance from the city centre and the fashionable residences of establishment families near the lake. Another problem was the lack of public transportation to the area. This was alleviated to some extent in the 1860s by the inauguration of the Toronto Street Railway in 1861. One of the lines ran along Yonge Street from King Street in the south to the Yorkville Town Hall just north of Bloor Street.

Another period of economic prosperity spanned the years from 1867 to the mid-1870s, but still the total number of properties sold in Rosedale stood at a meagre ten by 1874. By this time the old estates in the vicinity of Front and Sherbourne Streets had been replaced by railway lines. The land on the east was being taken over by factories and the area on the west, along Yonge Street, witnessed commercial development with retail stores such as those of Timothy Eaton and Robert Simpson springing up. On King Street, both east and west of Yonge Street, an important financial centre was being established. High society families were building homes at the northern end of Jarvis and Sherbourne Streets and on Bloor Street.

The economy suffered an acute and prolonged slowdown from the mid-1870s until well into the 1890s, which was marked by falling prices and declining incomes. In spite of this, Toronto continued to grow in leaps and bounds. Population skyrocketed from 56,000 in 1871 to 86,415 in 1881 and to 181,220 in 1890. But by 1884 the number of lots sold in Rosedale still totalled a mere 42. It wasn't until 1890, that activity really started to take off and the count jumped to about 100. During this era public transportation in Toronto improved dramatically. The number of miles of track increased from 19 in 1880 to 68.5 in 1891.[1] Moreover a new middle class was emerging in the city, composed of entrepreneurs who owned businesses and had the financial means to build grand houses in the suburbs and to pay for transportation into the city core.

THE ORIGINAL ROSEDALE ESTATES

1824	"Rosedale House"	William Botsford Jarvis, Rosedale Road
1830		Joseph Bloor, mill, brewery and residence, east end Rosedale ravine
	"Hazeldean"	Chief Justice Draper, north banks of Rosedale ravine, east of Park Road
1834	"Drumsnab"	Francis Cayley
1835	"Thornwood"	Joseph Price, block bounded by Price Street, Yonge Street and MacPherson Ave.
		George Severn, brewery and residence, Yonge Street and Park Road
1850	"Chestnut Park"	Sir D.L. Macpherson, block bounded by Yonge Street, Roxborough and MacPherson Avenue
1855	"Caverhill"	James Davis, Park Road (west side)
1856	"Idlewold"	Walter Brown, Avondale Avenue and Rosedale Road
1861		Lewis W. Ord, Crescent Road (house not built until 1881)
		Thomas Hodgins, Dale Avenue

1862	"The Dale"	John Hoskin, Dale Avenue (south side) near Maple Avenue
1863	"Glen Hurst"	Edgar Jarvis, Park Road (east side) north of Severn Creek
1870		George White, Rosedale Road
1874		Arthur Harvey, purchased "Idlewold," Rosedale Road and Avondale Avenue
	"Heyroyd"	Robert G. Banks, Sherbourne Street
	"Aldbury Lodge"	H.W. Eddis, Sherbourne Street and Elm Avenue
1876	"Denbrae"	William Alexander, Elm Avenue and Bridge Street (southwest corner)
	"Lorne Hall"	William Davies, Meredith Crescent (north side), formerly Kensington Crescent
	"Craigleigh"	Edmund B. Osler, Beau Street north of Elm Avenue
1877	"Sylvan Towers"	Edgar Jarvis, Glen Road and South Drive (northeast corner)
1878		Greenhow Banks, southeast corner North Drive and Woodland Avenue

1878 "Glenpatrick"
continued

Reverend J. Elwell, Sherbourne Street

Reverend Davis, Sherbourne Street

"Norcastle"

Henry W. Darling, Glen Road and South Drive (northwest corner) later known as "Hillcrest," "Deancroft" and "Ravensmount"

1879 "Hollydene"

John Lang Blaikie, 10 Elm Avenue and Bridge Street (northeast corner)

J.G. Giles, Rosedale Road

1880

Isaac Moody, North Drive and Cluny Avenue, also Avondale Road (southeast corner) and Park Road and Woodland Avenue (west corner)

John Taylor, Glen Road

B.B. Hughes, purchased "Glen Hurst," Park Road north of Severn Creek

1881 "The Thom House"

John H. Thom, South Drive, Woodland Avenue and Park Road (north side)

Lewis Ord, Crescent Road (north side)

1882 "White House"

Thomas Nightingale, Woodland Avenue and North Drive (southwest corner)

G.W. Meyer, Rosedale Road

1882 "Fermoy Lodge"
continued

Henry Hooper, Sherbourne Street (southeast corner)

1883

G.A. Chapman, Maple Avenue

1884 "Guiseley House"

Joseph Cawthra, Huntley Street and Elm Avenue (southeast corner)

Ferrier Kirk, Woodland Avenue

James How, Woodland Avenue

Robert McPhail, Woodland Avenue

James Comfort, Woodland Avenue

J.J. Foy, North Drive and Rosedale Road (southeast corner)

H.L. Ellis, Elm Avenue and Bridge Street (northwest corner)

W. Warren, Elm Avenue

G. Murray, Huntley Street and Glen Road

James Henderson, Centre Road

F.W. Livingstone, Powell Avenue and Dale Avenue (northeast corner)

ARCHITECTURE OF ROSEDALE HOMES

From its beginnings, Rosedale has had a distinctive character. Even the very first homes, "Rosedale House" (1824), "Drumsnab" (1834), and "Chestnut Park" (1850–55) were as varied in style as their owners and the originality of their individual tastes. While large, ostentatious estates can certainly be found in Rosedale, in large measure the residences were built for middle to upper middle class families. "Rosedale House" of Sheriff William Botsford Jarvis started out as a simple four-square farmhouse, and was added to over the years. "Drumsnab," Francis Cayley's dwelling, was a simple Regency villa that made the most of the incredible view over the Don River Valley, while the sprawling "Chestnut Park" estate of David Macpherson exhibited a whimsical nature not evidenced in the other two.

Rosedale's uniqueness as a suburb can be attributed largely to its variety of architectural styles. Since development extended over a long period, numerous architectural styles went in and out of vogue. Many architects were involved in the design of the homes. Advances in industry brought innovations in construction methods, heating systems, and building materials. During the course of development in the suburb, the number of companies in Toronto producing building products increased dramatically, allowing a much greater variety to the finishes, fixtures and trims found in the homes. General economic conditions and personal wealth were additional factors influencing the appearance and size of homes. As a result, a stroll through Rosedale today abounds with surprises on every block.

With even a modicum of architectural knowledge, the date of construction of a particular home can be estimated. The first clue, in addition to the style of the home itself, is that more often than not the oldest homes are the ones placed well back on their lot.

The railway boom of the the early 1850s was a period of rapid growth and prosperity. Many Toronto men made it rich as contractors, owners of steel foundries and manufacturers of railway tracks and locomotives. It was amidst this era of unparalleled expansion that the original subdivision of Rose-Park was registered in 1854. But the new suburb did not open up as quickly as envisioned. Economic boom was soon followed by bust, the subsequent recession spanning the years from 1855 until

Glen Road looking north.
Toronto Reference Library
T34890

1865. Only three homes were constructed in Rose-Park during these 10 years. In 1855, James Davis, a lawyer, built 124 Park Road (later known as "Caverhill"). In 1857–58 financier Walter Brown built the Italianate "Idlewold" at 23 Rosedale Road (later known as "Rose Cottage"). Between 1863 and 1866, Edgar Jarvis constructed "Glen Hurst" at 2 Elm Avenue, a home that sported a grand Italianate verandah, hipped roof and central front-facing gable.

During this period the basic shape of homes changed noticeably due to technological advances in heating and construction methods. Until the 1830s large fireplaces for burning coal or wood were the primary methods of heating houses. The first cast iron stoves were introduced around 1830. They were vented with metal stovepipes or small masonry flues, both much easier to install than massive fireplaces and chimneys. Both stove and fireplace were used together until the late 1800s. In many of the Rosedale homes built before 1900, the old hole for the stovepipe can still be recognized in the kitchen despite being plastered over.

It wasn't until after 1880 that central furnaces burning wood or coal were in common use. This invention allowed even greater flexibility to the architect and builder, and home layouts consequently became more irregular.

Most of the earliest Rosedale houses were of four-square plan (basically a four-cornered box). As post and beam construction was very difficult, costly and time-consuming, builders usually kept designs as simple as possible. Consequently, all but the rich built simple four-square homes. The Rosedale residences constructed before 1860 were originally of relatively uncomplicated design. In most cases, various wings, additional stories and other embellishments were added at later dates.

Balloon framing, a revolutionary advance in wood housing construction introduced in the 1830s, made construction faster, easier and less costly. A few two-inch studs, joists and rafters along with wire nails were all that was needed. At first only expensive architect-designed homes in major North American cities used the new technology. But balloon framing soon became the standard, allowing the architect much greater leeway in design ideas, and facilitating irregular plans with wings and extensions. Toronto in the 1830s was still pretty much a rural backwater. It was not until the 1860s that balloon framing came into common usage, and homes in Rosedale became more elaborate.

The years from the mid-1860s to the mid-1870s were economically prosperous, engendering a mood of optimism amongst most people and an expectation of unlimited growth. The homeowner had not only the ability but also the inclination to be extravagant. During this period, several more homes graced the new suburb. Ornate Italianate and Second Empire styles were the most popular from the late 1860s into the 1870s and even the early 1880s. The William Davies house at the current 3 Meredith Crescent is an excellent example of the latter style, and the Thom house at 54 South Drive a particularly fine example of the former. The late 1870s and early 1880s ushered in the gradual appearance of High Victorian homes. Queen Anne and Richardsonian Romanesque styles became popular, their lavish embellishments increasing as the century neared its end. The enclave at the west end of Elm Avenue, including the estates of John Blaikie, William Alexander and Joseph Cawthra, were the large but rather plain forerunners of what was to come only a few years later. Edgar Jarvis's three mansions at Glen Road, Hill and Beau Streets also were of the 1876 to 1882 vintage, but had significantly more pretentious and decorative features.

During the period from 1892 until 1900 Toronto experienced another economic downturn, during which only a few houses were erected in Rosedale. It was not until the first decade of the 20th century that the main thrust of house building began. Laurier's "Golden Age" saw spectacular development. Chestnut Park and North Rosedale were both opened up, and the previously undeveloped parts of the original Rose-Park and South Rosedale were filled in.

The early Edwardian period (the early 1900s) started with a hodgepodge of new designs all trying to gain recognition. Styles were generally simpler. Architects discarded many of the intricate details of the earlier Victorian era. Neo-Tudor, English Cottage Style (in brick), Neo-Georgian, Prairie School, Beaux Arts and Classical Revival were introduced in the early 1900s. Often houses combined several styles, taking the most desirable features of each. As the decade progressed this confusion died down, and the Neo-Tudor and Neo-Georgian styles became the most popular.

Italianate
1850-1880

The Italianate style was dominant in Rosedale from 1850 to 1880. It was patterned after the timeless Italian country homes with their trademark square towers.[1] These are recognizable by their low-pitched roofs and widely overhanging eaves adorned by decorative brackets beneath. They are usually two or three stories in height, many with a square cupola or tower. The windows are tall and narrow, usually curved or arched above, often with elaborate crowns of inverted U shape. A fine example is found at 54 South Drive, originally the residence of Mr. Thom, built in 1881.

By 1880 the western world was suffering a long and severe economic depression. To be sure, families building mansions in Rosedale may not have been too concerned with the mundane costs of constructing a new home. Nonetheless, there was a certain restraint evident in the late 1870s and extending through the 1880s, which dissipated only gradually in the early 1890s. As the end of the century approached, and the Victorian era approached its end, architectural styles became increasingly elaborate and fanciful.

Second Empire
1860-1880

Second Empire was a prevalent style of architecture between 1860 and 1880 in northeast North America. It was modelled after a construction style very popular in France during Napoleon III's regime in the period from 1852 to 1870. North American architects were familiarized with the design at the Paris Exhibitions of 1855 and 1867.[2] It was used extensively for a few years but went out of fashion after the economic decline that started in the mid-1870s. Its main identifying feature is the mansard roof with inset dormer windows. Deep cornices normally frame the top and lower edges of the roof. As in the Italianate style, the widely overhanging eaves are accentuated with decorative brackets. Square towers or cupolas are also a feature of many of these homes. Elaborations include decorative window surrounds and dormers, and cresting on the roof line.

A wonderful example of this style, perhaps the only one in Rosedale, is "Lorne Hall," at 3 Meredith Crescent, built by Mr. Davies in 1867.

Queen Anne
1880-1900

The Queen Anne style was the most popular architectural form between 1880 and 1900 when large numbers of Rosedale homes were designed. Architect Richard Norman Shaw and his colleagues christened the style and brought it to prominence.[3] Actually the style copies the late Medieval Elizabethan and Jacobean eras more than the Queen Anne period. Its fanciful spindlework is mainly a North American addition.

While styles of earlier periods may have been characterized by their relative uniformity and symmetry, Queen Anne was quite the opposite. These homes are identified by the irregularity of their roof shapes and the detailing on exterior walls and facade. Some of the recognizable features include steep roofs, primary front-facing gable, projecting bay windows, patterned shingles and patterned brickwork.[4] The facade is asymmetrical with a partial or full-width porch that is usually one storey high, often encircling more than one side. Most of the Queen Annes in Rosedale can be recognized by their patterned brickwork. They are fairly austere examples of the Queen Anne style, as they lack the incredibly fanciful gingerbread trim and spindlework found on their frame cousins in the American south. In southern examples, it is quite unusual to see Queen Anne homes such as those in Rosedale with masonry walls, patterned brickwork and relatively little wooden detailing. Most were designed by architects who were given wide scope for personal expression.

Richardsonian Romanesque
1880-1890

Many of the public buildings built in Toronto during the late 19th century are of the Richardsonian Romanesque style. The Old City Hall at Bay and Queen Streets and the Ontario Legislature buildings at Queen's Park Circle are easily recognizable examples.

It is a prerequisite that Richardsonian Romanesque houses be built of masonry and almost always include some squared, rough-hewn stone insets to lesser or greater degrees.[5] A particularly common identifying feature is the rounded arch (often of stone) above windows, front doors, and porticos.[6] Most have towers that are normally round with conical roofs. The facade is usually asymmetrical.

It is more common to see this style in Toronto's Annex neighbourhood than in Rosedale. In most Rosedale adaptaions of this style, designers merely added Romanesque detailing to the typical hipped-roof-with-cross-gables shape of the then-dominant Queen Anne style.

Colonial Revival
1880-1955

The Queen Anne style became increasingly inventive in the late 1890s, with architects veering away from the primary features of the true design. It was hardly surprising that they pretty much abandoned the style entirely after the turn of the century. Colonial Revival, along with other competing designs, fully displaced Queen Anne after about 1910. Many of the homes in North Rosedale, especially those built after 1910, are Colonial Revival. Such styles are much more common in the Moore Park area, which was developed at a slightly later date.

Colonial Revival became very popular between 1900 and 1950. The Georgian and Adams styles provide the main source of inspiration for the Colonial Revival. Architects borrowed details from the above styles and often combined them with others so that exact reproductions of colonial houses are almost never found. More often than not these homes are eclectic mixtures of designs.

Some of the predominant features of Colonial Revival are symmetry of design with the front door the main focal point in the centre. These are usually adorned with a pediment and pillars, sidelights on either side of the front door, and transom or fanlight above. Windows are almost always regularly spaced across the front and are multiple-pane in double-hung sashes.[7]

Tudor
1890-1940

As the 20th century approached, architects began to experiment with a variety of different styles. Tudor became an important influence in Rosedale.

Stucco, half-timbering and leaded windows are the most readily recognized features of the Tudor style. Classic brick and stone examples are seen in North Rosedale. These were built circa 1910 and after. However, there are examples of Tudor inspiration in South and West Rosedale from as early as the mid-1890s. These are called Jacobethan and are identified by front-facing Flemish gables. In these ostentatious, architect-designed homes, the parapet extends above the roof. Easily identifiable versions line Crescent Road and Chestnut Park.

As time went on, the style became more informal. Typically, these homes have casement windows grouped in twos, threes or fours with stone or tabbed stone mullions, often complete with transoms. Roofs are generally steeply pitched with a side gable and one or more dominant cross gables on the front. It was typical to inset front porches under an upper room.

"Rosedale House,"
home of William Botsford Jarvis, circa 1832.
Watercolour by James W. Hamilton
Alden G. Meredith, *Mary's Rosedale and Gossip of Little York,*
Toronto Reference Library

ROSEDALE HOUSE

William Botsford Jarvis of York, gentleman and later sheriff, purchased a 110-acre farm on the east side of the Yonge Street Highway in 1824 for £1,150. The property encompassed the northwestern part of Township Lot 19 in the Second Concession from the Bay, owned by John Small since 1800. It included a simple one-storey farmhouse built three years earlier. The residence perched on a hill approximately where Rosedale Road meets Cluny Avenue today, facing west towards Yonge Street and overlooking the deep ravine where the subway now runs south from the Rosedale station.

"Rosedale House" was certainly not the grand mansion that one might imagine of the estate that gave its name to this wealthy suburb. It was more a rustic farmhouse or villa. The land around the house was cleared, with orchards, vinery and gardens neatly laid out. Various barns and outbuildings dotted the property. Rough-hewn fences meandered their way along the rolling hills nearby. In the rear, thick forest remained.

At first, William Botsford lived here with his father Stephen Jarvis, Registrar of Ontario, and later with his wife, Mary Boyles Powell, after their marriage in 1827. Extensive renovations to the house were undertaken in 1835 to accommodate William and Mary's growing family. John Howard, later of Colborne Lodge in High Park, remodeled the simple four-square house into a more substantial residence, adding a front verandah, a wing with a sun room, and a conservatory. A peach house and grape house were also constructed.[1] A sweeping drive winding around a circular garden led to the front door.

The Jarvises' closest neighbours were the Severn Brothers, who lived at their large brewery south on Yonge Street, the Joseph Price family at "Thornwood" further north on Yonge, and the Hornes on the west side of Yonge between Davenport Road and Belmont Street. But rebels loyal to William Lyon Mackenzie burned this home in 1837. "Rosedale House" only escaped a similar fate due to the intervention of Colonel Samuel Lount (see pages 42–43).

Although the home was torn down in 1905, paintings by artists of the time give us some idea of its appearance. The earlier versions, dating after 1837 when the second storey was added, show a rather simple house, of symmetrical design with low-pitched hipped roof, two chimneys (one at each end) and shuttered windows. A large low verandah extending the full width of the front had a lattice trim beneath the porch and simple criss-cross railings. A later watercolour by James Hamilton shows a much grander entrance and various wings, one on either side of the main house. An advertisement in *The Globe* of October 1854 to rent the house, described it as including: "breakfast, dining and two drawing rooms, two large bedrooms with dressing rooms attached, six smaller bedrooms, bath room, store room, butler's pantry, two kitchens, larder, wine and vegetable cellars, and servants' rooms, an excellent well, and other conveniences."[2]

When Mary Jarvis died suddenly in 1852, William Botsford could no longer bring himself to reside in the Rosedale house. He divided it into two sections, judging it too large to be occupied by one family. In 1854 repairs were made to the residence, a stable and coach house were constructed on the northeast corner of the lot, and a fence was erected around the property. His daughter Fanny, along with her sister Louisa and her husband, Augustus Nanton, lived in one half. Professor and Mrs. Kingston leased the other half. All of William Botsford's daughters lived here with their husbands and families at various times throughout the 1850s and 1860s. Even their cousin Edgar John Jarvis set up housekeeping at "Rosedale House" during the period between 1863 and 1866 while his own residence was being constructed on nearby Park Road.

In 1854 much of the original estate was sold off to Frederick Carruthers and George Duggan, William keeping only 41 acres, including Villa Lot 6 on which "Rosedale House" was situated. Duggan registered Plan 104 of subdivision for Rose-Park on December 23, the same year. The three Jarvis daughters and their husbands would all buy and sell Rosedale properties throughout the latter half of the 19th century; so would their cousins Frederick William and Edgar John Jarvis. By 1870 only six acres remained around the original Rosedale house.

David Lewis Macpherson bought "Rosedale House" in 1875 for his daughter Christina and her husband, Percival Ridout. The couple lived there until 1905, when the building was demolished. The Macpherson estate subdivided the property in Villa Lot 6 in 1901. Plan 204E sectioned off lots on Cluny Drive.

DRUMSNAB 1834

Francis Cayley bought the 118-acre "Drumsnab" estate in 1834. The property stretched from the northeast corner of Parliament and Bloor Street East, as far as the Don River. It was part of a 200-acre farm lot originally granted by the Crown to Captain George Playter.

The western part of this farm, consisting of 81 acres, was sold first to Joseph Bloor in 1831. Then in 1835 it was divided, the western part going to William Botsford Jarvis and the eastern part to Samuel Peters Jarvis. The latter would eventually acquire the entire western portion by 1842.

Originally the Cayley land included a small log house built by Captain Playter and located near the present intersection of Parliament and Bloor Street East. The estate had long been called "Drumsnab," a Scottish word for a long, narrow hill or ridge. The word had first been used as a nickname for a curious-looking conical hill in the Don Valley visible from the property.

Francis Cayley was born in Toronto in 1809 at Elmsley Villa and educated at Upper Canada College. On graduation he spent 15 years working at the Bank of Toronto. After that he worked mainly in the real estate business. He was a prominent and well-known figure in the expansion and development of Toronto. He never married. One brother was the Honourable William Cayley, an celebrated barrister in Toronto, who held positions as MPP, Inspector General, President of the Bank of Upper Canada and surrogate court clerk. Another brother, John, was rector of St. George's Anglican Church. The Cayley brothers were descended from one of England's oldest families.

The small one-storey house was built in 1834 on a hill facing the Don River Valley, just north of "Castle Frank." It was a simple Regency-style villa of one storey with a broad verandah. It was constructed of fieldstone and faced with stucco. Its many tall windows and bays made it bright and airy. French doors opened onto the porch, allowing in the natural light, and giving views of the garden and landscaped grounds. Its only real adornment was the flat-roofed porch that stretched the entire width of the front and along the sides. The supports were simple square posts, with decorative bases trimmed with moldings and cutout designs, the tops adorned with lacy triangular brackets.

"Drumsnab," home of Francis Cayley.
Pen and ink drawing by Walter J. Coucill, 1970, Toronto Reference Library T11174

The interior was spacious, and Francis apparently used his artistic talents to enliven his home, frescoing the living room with paintings inspired by *Faust*.[1]

In 1847 Francis Cayley's brother John married Clara Boulton, and around 1860 the house was expanded to accommodate them as well. Architect William Thomas, winner of a contest to design public schools for Toronto, was retained for the job. A second floor was added, constructed of brick covered with stucco, much in keeping with the original house. The upstairs windows were only slightly more decorative, with simple pedimented crowns, multi-paned to match the French doors. The roof was low-pitched, with wide overhanging eaves and visible rafters, but lacked decorative supports.

The addition provided the family with three more bedrooms and a lovely sitting room. The French doors of the main floor were repeated in this room, leading to an upper balcony above the main floor verandah. Later the Cayleys would put in a newfangled bathroom and beautify the spectacular grounds with gardens and fruit trees.[2]

"Drumsnab"
as it appears today.
Photograph by
Mario Angastiniotis

Francis sold off most of the estate before his death in 1874, leaving only eight acres around the house and gardens, plus an additional 26 acres in the Don Valley. The largest portion went to Samuel Peters Jarvis, but Edward Nanton bought 24 acres in 1866 for $1,000. The remaining property, including the house, were sold to Maunsell Jackson in 1874 for $15,750.

Historian Lucy Booth Martyn tells an amusing story of Maunsell Jackson and Edgar Jarvis. Jarvis constructed the Huntley Street Bridge (or the "White Bridge" as it was called) over the Rosedale ravine at a cost of $30,000, obviously an enormous sum in the 1870s. To help defray his out-of-pocket expenses, Jarvis erected a toll-booth at the entrance to the bridge. Maunsell Jackson was so outraged that he ran his coach and four through the barrier. Later, when Yorkville was annexed to the City of Toronto in 1883, the City reimbursed Jarvis for $10,000 in payment for the bridge.[3]

The Drumsnab house remained in the Jackson family until 1965. By then, however, most of the land surrounding the home had been sold off.

"Chestnut Park," home of David Lewis MacPherson, circa 1900.
Toronto Reference Library T11413

CHESTNUT PARK

Chestnut Park, the estate of David Lewis Macpherson, occupied the block bounded by Roxborough Street East (formerly Murray Street) on the south, Yonge Street on the west, and what was in the 1850s Chestnut Street (later MacPherson, now Rowanwood Avenue). Macpherson bought the property for £7,000 from William Mathers in 1855. Mathers had acquired the southern half of Township Lot 18 eight years earlier from the Joseph Price family. On the southwest corner of this land he built a sprawling and rather fanciful residence surrounded by substantial grounds. Originally, MacPherson Avenue was called Chestnut Street because of the stately chestnut trees that lined it and Yonge Street. Mathers named his estate "Chestnut Grove."[1] The city directory first listed D.L. Macpherson with the "Chestnut Grove" address in 1856.

Houses on Chestnut Park Road, circa 1915.

Toronto Reference Library T3488

Houses on Chestnut Park Road,
circa 1915.
Toronto Reference Library T14078

David Lewis Macpherson was born in 1818 into the well-to-do family of David Macpherson of Inverness, Scotland. The family immigrated to Canada in 1834 and settled in Montreal. David Jr. was educated there and married Elizabeth Sarah Molson in 1844. The young man became a railway contractor during the Canadian railway boom, which started in 1850 and spanned the remainder of the century. After moving to Toronto the young Macpherson joined Casimir Gzowski, a Polish engineer. The two men became partners, achieving not only fame but also fortune with the Grand Trunk Railway, which linked Sarnia, Toronto and Montreal. By 1862–63 Macpherson and Gzowski together had built Toronto's first large steel rolling mills to stock their railway projects with tracks, spikes and bridge work.

Macpherson, a Conservative and loyal supporter of Sir John A. Macdonald, was appointed to the Senate in 1867. He was Speaker of the House from 1880 until 1883 and Minister of the Interior in 1883.[2] During the 1870s the Honourable David Macpherson organized and was president of the Interocean Railway Company, one of the companies vying to build a railway across Canada to the Pacific Ocean. A scandal ensued over the financing of the railway; the Liberals charged that Macdonald's government had been bribed to give contracts to his supporters. While Macpherson was not involved, the affair caused the resignation of the Conservative government in 1873.

The "Chestnut Park" house was a massive dwelling spread out horizontally with many wings and additions, including a greenhouse. The mansion was obviously ample enough to accommodate the Macphersons' seven children and numerous household servants. The main house, three storeys high and constructed of brick, with a steep-pitched roof, dominant gable and inset dormers, faced west toward Yonge Street. The first major wing was two storeys, also with a front-facing gable. The third and final addition was one and a half storeys, and built much lower. This addition boasted two gables adorned with elaborate gingerbread verge boards. The roof was topped with a cupola crowned with finial. The estate included broad manicured lawns and accompanying stable, coach house and barn.

In 1875 David Lewis bought "Rosedale House" from the Jarvises, his neighbours to the south. His daughter, Christina, and her husband, Percival Ridout, lived there from 1889 until 1905. Sometime between 1884 and 1890, Macpherson began plans for subdividing the significant land accompanying his own estate. The property to the east was divided into lots, and three new north-south streets were laid out: Orchard Road, Prospect Road and View Place. This blueprint (Plan 84E) never left the drawing boards, however. The plan eventually used was Plan 233E, registered by Macpherson estate trustees William Molson Macpherson, Percival Ridout and Allen Cassels in 1902.

Architect S. Hamilton Townsend was employed to plan the layout of the suburb. While travelling widely throughout Great Britain and Europe in the 1880s Townsend witnessed the emergence of the Neo-Tudor style of architectural design. He would experiment with various features of this design in the Chestnut Park suburb. His ideas were quite novel at the time, incorporating winding streets, brick sidewalks and classic lamp posts with black iron bases and white globe-shaped lights. Wiring ran underground. Townsend obviously imagined an enchanting neighbourhood, with tree-lined streets, and handsome homes with large front lawns. There would be nothing distasteful about Chestnut Park. Clear-cut rules governed the buildings and their location on the lots.[3] A new bridge across Sherbourne Street meant that residents could easily reach the city's financial core by streetcar service along Yonge, Sherbourne, or Church Streets.

S.H. Townsend designed the Boultbee House at 35 Crescent Road in 1895, a home at 48 Crescent Road in 1901, the John J. Dixon House at 52 Cluny Drive in 1904 and numbers 24 and 49 Chestnut Park in 1905. Other architects in the Chestnut Park mini-subdivision included A.E. Boultbee, designer of 20 Chestnut Park (1905–06); Langley and Howland, who designed 22 Chestnut Park (1904) and 15 Chestnut Park (1911); Burke, Horwood and White, designers of the James Ryrie's house at 1 Chestnut Park (1915); and Curry and Sparling, who were responsible for 45ABC Chestnut Park (1915).

Sir David Lewis Macpherson died in 1896. St. Andrews College took over the grand home from 1899 until 1905, after which the boys' school moved to North Rosedale. The "Chestnut Park" house was demolished in 1906, and the 12 acres remaining of the original estate were partitioned off for residential development.

CAVERHILL 1855

*124 Park Road, home of
James Boyd Davis.*
Photograph by Bess Crawford

Caverhill, the three-storey yellow brick dwelling at 124 Park Road just south of South Drive, is probably the best loved of the original Rosedale mansions. It is also one of the oldest of the Rosedale estates, second only to the Cayley villa, "Drumsnab."

While other homes in the area may boast additional rooms, greater square footage and more ostentatious styles, none can compare with "Caverhill's" sheer elegance and simplicity of design or the serenity of its setting and the layout of its grounds. It is perched on a hill with gently sloping lawns, overlooking the Rosedale ravine to the south and the Avondale ravine to the west. The entire estate appears untouched by time.

Villa Lot XXII, Plan 103, was the first plot sold in the new Rose-Park subdivision. The original property encompassed the entire block on the west side of Park Road from the present Avondale Avenue as far north as South Drive (previously Woodland Avenue).

James Boyd Davis, a solicitor, purchased the property in 1854. The original home, built of red brick, with matching coach house at the rear, was much smaller, having only one and a half storeys. The centre hall plan, with stairs at the back, opened to a dining room on the right, living room to the left, and kitchen in the basement. The second floor, of yellow brick, was not constructed until 1863. The builder simply raised the existing roof to accommodate the additional floor.

The *Toronto Directory* of 1856 lists James Davis, barrister of York Chambers, Court Street, as owner. His address was given as Rose Park, Yorkville. Sometime between this time and publication of the 1862–63 directory, Mr. Davis had died, but his widow continued to live in the home.

John Stark bought the estate around 1874 and over the next few years made further changes, installing a white marble fireplace in the living room and the wing at the rear. It is probably around this time that a wrap-around porch was added. He also sectioned off one large lot to the immediate north (the southwest corner of Park Road and Woodland Avenue) and several lots to the south, leaving a still substantial property measuring 248 feet by 170 feet. At least two of the lots to the south were sold to men who worked in his company.

John Stark began his career as bookkeeper for the prestigious firm of Blaikie and Alexander, stockbrokers and financial agents of 10 King Street East. The *Toronto Directory* of 1875 mentions Mr. Stark as a partner of that firm. He is also listed as a partner in the William Alexander and Lawrence Buchan Company. By 1876 Blaikie had left the firm. John Stark took over as a partner and the Alexander and Stark Company was formed. By 1878 Stark had ventured out on his own, establishing John Stark and Company, stockbrokers and financial agents with offices at 28–30 Toronto Street.

The basic house, constructed primarily of yellow brick and decorated with matching brick trim on the corners and windows, is a simple Georgian design with few elaborations. Wings project to the rear. The hipped roof is of relatively low pitch with a small decorative central front gable. Three majestic chimneys stand tall above the roof line. The facade is symmetrical with five tall windows aligned horizontally and vertically in rows across the front. Belt courses separate the first and second floors. The high ceilings and tall windows give the home a lightness and delicacy lacking in the architectural styles common later in the century. The single-storey front porch, of plain design and extending the full width of the house, most likely appeared around 1907. It is supported by round columns which set off the double French doors on both sides of the front door. Doublewidth steps lead to the cobbled drive. The perfect positioning of the original red brick coach house and matching yellow brick garage (added in the 1990s) enhances the ambience of the entire property.

124 Park Road, another view.
Photograph by
Mario Angastiniotis

"Caverhill" remained the Stark family home until 1922. It was bought by Colonel "Reg." Geary, mayor of Toronto, for $36,000 in 1927. Geary was married to Montreal socialite Beatrice Caverhill. According to Donald Jones in his book *Fifty Tales of Toronto*, the property remained in the Geary family until the early 1980s.[1]

This beautiful residence stood deserted for many years but was eventually purchased in 1993 by the present owners. Extensive renovations and restorations were undertaken to the buildings and grounds. Even the landscaping reproduces the traditional gardens of the late 19th century. Orange and yellow daylilies complement the colour of the brick, and all is framed by a simple wrought-iron fence and curved cobbled drive.

124 Park Road, another view.
Photograph by Bess Crawford

IDELWOLD 1859

Walter Brown, land agent, money broker, banker and publisher of the *Toronto General Directory*, was the second man to purchase property in Rose-Park. He selected Villa Lot XI, one of the choicest, most picturesque parcels of land in the new subdivision. It monopolized the corner of Rosedale Road and Avondale Avenue, commanding an unimpeded vantage of the beautiful ravines to the south and east, just south of the Jarvis family's Rosedale estate. By 1859 Walter Brown had constructed a home on the site, which he named "Idlewold." The charming and rather informal Italianate farmhouse was strategically set into the hillside. But despite the ambience of the situation, historical records indicate that Mr. Brown only lived in his new home until 1868.

Information from the *Toronto Directories* suggests that the house was vacant until Arthur Harvey acquired the place for $6,000 in 1872. Harvey was manager and secretary of the Provincial Insurance Company of Canada and was associated with barristers Haverson and St. John of 28 Wellington Street. (Within a few years, James Haverson would construct a residence for himself only a few blocks away, on North Drive.) By 1878 Arthur Harvey became manager of the Toronto Life Assurance Company and Tontine, as well as president of the Toronto Land and Loan Company.

"Idlewold," home of Walter Brown.
Photograph by
Mario Angastiniotis

The Harveys must have thought land in Rose-Park was a good investment. A year later they purchased Villa Lots 7 and 8, a desirable land holding on the west side of Rosedale Road, also overlooking a ravine. It was just west of their own house, the approximate site of the Arbour Glen apartment building today. The couple would eventually sell these lots to James Good and Edmund Meredith.

In another development scheme, Lots 10 and 11 were subdivided into 18 smaller lots by Plan 47E, registered December 12, 1889, by Jane Harvey. This was amended in 1893 by Plan 137E, registered by Isaac Moody, another Rosedale speculator, who owned a house across the road on the east side of Rosedale Road. Avondale Place, previously Moody's Lane, was opened in 1893 to give access to potential property owners in this new mini-subdivision. Moody also owned land at the corner of Rosedale Road and North Drive, which would be developed into Cluny Avenue.

Around 1893, the Harveys moved to 78 North Drive, later renamed Crescent Road. Their estate was purchased by Henry Osborne, a stockbroker. Shortly after moving in, the Osbornes altered the house, employing architect Alfred Boultbee for the job. Boultbee himself was very familiar with Rosedale, living at number 35 Crescent Road in a house designed by Hamilton Townsend, architect of note in Chestnut Park (see page 106). His father, Member of Parliament W. Boultbee, lived a few doors down at 25 Crescent Road, just east of Yonge Street. Osborne would undertake a major expansion to the house in 1911.

"Idlewold" is clad in cream-coloured stucco. A three-storeyed house laid out in a rambling L shape, it has cottage windows and French doors, both covered with miniature horizontally sloping roofs, fronted with wrought-iron Juliet balconies and enclosed with dark green shutters. It is Rosedale's version of the Hansel and Gretel cottage, set in an enchanted forest on a hill surrounded by tall trees, overgrown shrubs and hedges, complete with a stone wall, gate and ivy. Sprawling gardens at the rear all lend a magical and delightful mood to the property.

"Idlewold,"
was later named
Rose Cottage.
Photograph by
Mario Angastiniotis

The roof is of low pitch, with wide overhanging eaves, ornamented with decorative brackets. As was common in houses of this style, it sported a lookout tower topped with a row of small arched windows.

The house was extensively renovated in the late 1980s with extreme care taken to retain the overall feeling and sentiment of the original house.

It is unknown when the name "Idlewold" was changed to "Rose Cottage." Many mistakenly believe that this was the original Jarvis homestead and that it was the roses growing wild on the hillside here that led Mary Jarvis to christen her estate Rosedale. To be sure, wild roses may have grown in abundance on these slopes, but this was not the original Jarvis house.

THE DALE 1862

The Dale, once located on the south side of Dale Avenue opposite the intersection of Maple Avenue and immediately west of McKenzie Avenue, was the ornate and rambling dwelling of John Hoskin. The property was totally endearing. The house itself, with its steep roofs, gables, dormers, turrets and fanciful front porch spindlework, reminds one of a large multi-tiered wedding cake. The position of the house amidst the expansive grounds and gardens could not have been lovelier. As G. Mercer Adam wrote in his book *Toronto Old and New*, published in 1891, "For beauty of situation, no less than for its fine sylvan setting and the rare attractions of its conservatories, 'The Dale' is well-nigh unsurpassed among Toronto homes."[1]

"The Dale,"
home of John Hoskin,
circa 1880.
Toronto Reference Library
T11275

Mr. Hoskin purchased the property in 1862. The house was constructed after his marriage in 1866 to the eldest daughter of Walter McKenzie of nearby "Castle Frank." "The Dale" was not listed in the *Toronto Directories* until 1880.

John Hoskin was born in Devonshire, England, in 1836. He was educated in Canada and called to the Bar of Upper Canada in 1863. He was created a Queen's Counsel 10 years later and was a Bencher of the Law Society of Upper Canada for 15 years.

Among his titles was that of Official Guardian of Infants. In 1889 he was awarded an honorary Doctor of Laws degree. By 1890 he held positions as President of the County of York Law Association, President of the National Investment Company, Vice-President of the Toronto General Trusts Company, Director of the Canadian Bank of Commerce, and Trustee of the University of Toronto. In an advertisement for the National Investment Company of Canada found in the *Toronto Directory* of 1890, John Hoskin is named along with William Alexander, A.R. Creelman and John Stark. Three of these four men resided in Rosedale at the time. John Hoskin is also listed as director of the Canada Landed Credit Company in 1890.

The beautiful three-storey, yellow brick house was probably best described as of Gothic Revival design. It must

have been quite a conversation piece when it was built. "The Dale" was noticeably different from the heavy Italianate homes common in Toronto at the time.

It was of typical asymmetrical design, with a dominant gable on the right front and two dormers of different sizes on the left. Projecting bay windows monopolized the right side. On this side as well, a square turret rose from ground level and extended above the roof line of the main house. The turret was topped with its own steep roof with an inset dormer and was ornamented by a finial.

The large, single-storey front entry porch was particularly fanciful. Lace-like brackets and delicate Gothic tracery decorated the porch supports and lower and upper porch railings.

The roof was steeply pitched, of particularly irregular shape, and embellished with fanciful patterned shingles. The whole was accentuated by the prominent front-facing gable, front dormers and smaller roofs over the side bay windows and turret. The widely overhanging eaves sported decorative supports, and the front gable boasted an elegant decorative truss.

The windows were of simple Gothic arch shape, the sashes single-pane, complemented by Gothic shutters and simple brick crowns. Decorative raised brick or belt-courses ran in horizontal lines around the house, the first line half-way up the first floor, the second line directly below the second-storey windows.

The *Toronto Directories* list the John Hoskin family as residents of 21 Dale Avenue until 1909. By 1910, "The Dale" was vacant, and in 1911 was inhabited by Albert E. Dyment, who lived in the home until 1939. Since no listing is given for "The Dale" after that date, it is assumed the house was torn down soon afterwards.

"The Dale" is now only a distant memory, revived by old photographs detailing its original spendour. A low-rise apartment building now occupies the beautiful parkland where the house once stood.

Gates to "The Dale," near Castle Frank and Bloor St. East.
Photograph by R. W. Anderson, Toronto Reference Library T11406

"Denbrae,"
home of William Alexander.
Photograph by Mario Angastiniotis

DENBRAE 1876

The large brick mansion on the southwest corner of Bridge/Huntley Street and Elm Avenue was built by William Alexander between 1874 and 1876. It was nearby Edgar Jarvis's own estate, "Glen Hurst," perched on a hill, peering out over the Rosedale ravine.

This part of Rosedale Plan 329 was not very accessible until after the White Bridge on Huntley Street was opened around 1872. William Alexander bought Lots 15 and 16, Plan 326, from Edgar Jarvis in 1873. He paid $2,400. Previously he had lived on Jarvis Street, Yorkville (later Bismarck Street, today Asquith Avenue), next door to his long-time business partner John Blaikie and just down the street from Edgar Jarvis's brother Frederick William Jarvis and his wife, Caroline.

In the early 1870s, the area to the north of Bloor and Yonge was still largely undeveloped. Bloor Street East was a dirt road ending at Sherbourne Street and, unlike today, was a residential street. Grand homes owned by Toronto establishment families like Robert Simpson, John Stark (later of Park Road), the Honourable William McMaster, the Honourable Frank Smith, and Thomas Thompson lined the north side. Only a few houses had been built further north near William Botsford Jarvis's original Rosedale estate.

But a spurt of development was about to begin around Edgar Jarvis's home, "Glen Hurst." William Alexander was the first to buy. William Davies and John Blaikie followed suit in 1876, the former purchasing property a bit to the north and the latter slightly to the east. Within eight years they would be joined by Joseph Cawthra, William Warren and Henry Ellis. Construction of the White Bridge on Huntley Street greatly improved access to the area, making it possible to transport materials to the building sites.

By the time William Alexander moved into his expansive new residence on Elm Avenue, John Blaikie had left the business partnership of Blaikie and Alexander, and Alexander had joined forces with John Stark to form the Alexander & Stark Company. By 1884 Alexander was President of the National Investment Company.

The fabulous residence he built was a three-storey brick structure of early Queen Anne style. It lacked the ornamentation and decorative elements like spindles and gingerbread common later in the Victorian period. As historian Lucy Booth Martyn points out, at this point in Toronto history, the rich and famous displayed their wealth by the size and magnitude of their residences; architectural style was of lesser importance. There was certainly no mistake about the size of William Alexander's house. The roof was steeply pitched and irregularly shaped, with a false gable set into the hipped roof. Another dominant front-facing gable monopolized the front, forming an L shape. Both gables were shaped and parapeted, with artistic brick inserts. Two particularly interesting chimneys with handsome patterned masonry were striking features of the asymmetrical facade.

A three-storey wing adjoins the east side and a two-storey wing the west side of the house. Its windows are relatively simple; sashes are two-pane. Surrounds are plain and unadorned, except for those on the second floor which are tall and narrow, hooded above and with simple sill below.

William Alexander only lived here until 1883, selling the house to Thomas Thompson for $17,500. In 1903 the property, including the house, was acquired by Mary Scott, founder of the Branksome Hall School, a private institute for girls. She was relocating from her original address at 92 Bloor Street East. The brick has now been painted over a pale beige colour, while the lush green lawn in front of this little compound of houses has been replaced with parking spaces. But the beautiful ravine still spreads out to the south, many areas seemingly unchanged by the passage of time.

LORNE HALL 1876

Lorne Hall, the beautiful three-storey yellow brick home at 3 Meredith Crescent was commissioned by William Davies in 1876. It is of classic Second Empire style, designed by architect Henry Langley, of the prestigious Toronto firm Langley, Langley and Burke.

William Davies, a newcomer to the city in 1854, could afford such talents to construct his private residence. Since coming to Canada he had done very well for himself. The country was enjoying rapid economic growth and Davies soon established a very profitable provisioning business by the name of Davies Pork Packing House. The Davies had lived at various addresses before moving to Rosedale. In 1859 they resided at 60 Jarvis Street, Yorkville (the present Asquith Avenue). Davies may well have known various members of the Jarvis family who were located on the same street.

Davies bought Villa Lot number XXIII, Plan 104, consisting of three acres, from Edgar Jarvis in 1876 for $3,000. Located on the southeast corner of Park Road and South Drive on a hill with superb views of the Rosedale ravine, just north and a short distance west of Edgar Jarvis's own estate, "Glen Hurst." The Davies's house was finished in the fall of 1876. Davies, an Englishman, likely christened his home "Lorne Hall" after Lord Lorne, husband of Queen Victoria's daughter Louise.[1] The royal couple were very popular and visited Toronto in 1879.

The charming, well-proportioned home built in the Second Empire style was considered quite avant-garde at the time. It has a symmetrical centre hall plan with 12-foot ceilings and multiple fireplaces. While large by normal standards, it is small compared with many of the Rosedale estates built around this time by men like William Alexander and John Blaikie.

The mansard roof is the main signature of the Second Empire style, but this house also incorporates decorative features of the Italianate style. Molded cornices complement the roof slope, above and below the eaves. The square, truncated cupola or tower was also a standard design feature. The flat-topped pitched roof was functional because it permitted use of a full third floor.

The windows of "Lorne Hall" are tall and narrow with full arched tops on the second and third floors. Its third floor dormers are trimmed with curved pediments, while those on the second floor are hooded with elaborate stone crowns in an inverted U shape. Sashes frame "one-over-one" or "two-over-two" glazings. The windows on the second floor are grouped in twos on either side of the central French doors opening onto the balcony over the front entrance porch. On the main floor, to both the right and left of the front door, stand three-window bays with segmental arch windows giving the house a very symmetrical appearance.

The front entry porch is of single-storey height, supported by square stone posts with bevelled corners. An upper balcony ornamented by a stone spindle railing complements this. The front porch design is repeated on a much larger scale on a back porch at the side and rear of the house.

In a letter home to England in 1880, Davies wrote, "We have a beautiful place in a beautiful spot. It is part table land, part hillside, a sunny slope and balance valley, it is triangular in shape and a road on two sides. We have abundance of fruit, grapes, pears, strawberries, raspberries, currants, and gooseberries, about one hundred and fifty apple, pear, plum, and cherry trees. I cut three tons of hay off my grass field this summer."[2]

"Lorne Hall," home of William Davies.
Photograph by Bess Crawford

Davies only lived in the house until 1889. The property was sold to William White, who divided the estate into a mini-subdivision, Plan 24E. A total of 18 building lots were created on the north and south sides of Kensington Crescent. Senator Lawrence Coffee bought the house itself in 1890. For some time he was the only resident on the street. Before the turn of the century Kensington Crescent was renamed Meredith Crescent after Edmund A. Meredith, husband of "Fanny" Jarvis. By 1905 "Lorne Hall" had been sold to the Honourable J. Idington. By that time, eight more houses had been constructed on the street.

In 1927 a charming home was built at the corner of Park Road and South Drive by Mrs. Harry Symons, the daughter of William Perkins Bull, who owned "Lorne Hall" after the turn of the century. It was designed by Mackenzie Waters, a well-known Toronto architect of middle- and upper-class homes.

Gone are the stately lawns and gardens descending the slope to the Rosedale ravine. Gone is the winding private drive that ushered the carriages of the Davies's visitors to the front door. Now the lot has been reduced to 87 feet by 115 feet, the front yard abuts the sidewalk and new dwellings crowd in on all sides. But the grand old home remains. A complete restoration is currently underway, both inside and out, repairing the damage wrought previously when the home was turned into apartments.

HOLLYDENE 1876–1880

Hollydene, the imposing red brick mansion positioned on the northeast corner of Elm Avenue and what was at the time Bridge Street (now Mount Pleasant Road), was built by John Lang Blaikie, a well-known businessman and financier of Toronto society during the latter half of the 19th century. The house formed part of an exclusive residential compound being built in the 1870s in this location by Edgar Jarvis, William Alexander and William Davies. They would be joined in a few years by Joseph Cawthra, Richard Brodie and William Warren.

John Blaikie, of Roxburghshire, Scotland, arrived in Canada in 1858 at the age of 35. Originally of the firm Blaikie and Alexander, accountants, brokers and estate agents with offices at Jordan and King Streets, Blaikie had left the firm by 1876 to become President of the Canada Landed Credit Company of 23 Toronto Street. He also held positions as President of Consumers Gas, Vice President of the North American Life Assurance Company, Director of the Northern Railway, and Trustee of the Toronto General Hospital. It is interesting to note that John Stark, who bought the lovely home on the west side of Park Road (later called "Caverhill"), was a bookkeeper for the Alexander and Blaikie Company in 1867–68. After John Blaikie left the company, John Stark was henceforth listed as a partner along with William Alexander and Lawrence Buchan.

"Hollydene," home of John Blaikie.
Toronto Reference Library

For many years John Blaikie and William Alexander lived next door to each other on Jarvis Street (now Asquith Avenue) in the town of Yorkville, one block north of Bloor Street, east of Yonge Street.

Mr. Blaikie and Mr. Alexander were two of the first to purchase property from Edgar Jarvis in the southern sector of the Rosedale suburb. Alexander purchased Lots 15 and 16 in 1873 for $2,400, while Blaikie bought Lots 11 and 12 of Plan 326 in 1876 for $4,300. The *Toronto Directory* lists William Alexander's home address as "Rosedale" for the first time in 1876, whereas, the residence of John Blaikie is not given as "Rosedale" until 1880. The two men remained neighbours, the Blaikie estate monopolizing the northeast corner of Elm Avenue and Bridge Street, the Alexander estate kitty-corner across the street on the southwest corner.

While Joseph Cawthra would build a large estate on the southeast corner of Bridge and Elm Avenue in 1884, for many years there were no other houses between there and

Bloor Street. The same was true further north and east, the Toronto Lacrosse Grounds at Elm Avenue and Sherbourne Street being the only development of note.

"Hollydene" itself is a massive three-storey red brick mansion. It is of High Victorian design, combining several styles popular in 1880, notably the Queen Anne style, recognized by its many flourishes of fantasy, and the more fortress-like Romanesque style just then coming into vogue.

The home is a basic centre hall plan of asymmetrical design, the front dominated by a large portico of heavy post and lintel construction, added at a later date. Carriages could sweep up to the grand entrance of the house. Of only slightly lesser dominance is the large one-storey multi-windowed conservatory with flat roof, located to the right of the front door. A definite Tudor influence is displayed by the two large gables and smaller dormers accenting the front roof. A medium-sized dormer extends to the right. Additional roofed dormers are found on the sides of the house. Most of the windows are tall and plain, the sashes of single glass panes. Generally, simple stone lintels crown the windows. The main exceptions are the front second-floor windows that are topped with intricate arched brickwork. The windows in the conservatory have simple stone frames with a stone transom above, quite a new feature of housing construction in the late 1870s. A large two-storey cutout bay distinguishes the west side of the house.

The decorative brickwork patterns incorporated on the house in the form of semi-circular caps above the second floor windows and raised belt-lines running horizontally around the home mark a visual separation between the first and second floors. The roof is steep and hipped, but lacks the large overhang and decorative supporting brackets of the earlier Italianate style.

The Blaikies did not live in the house for long. In 1886 "Hollydene" was sold for $26,000 to Hugh Ryan, a wealthy railway contractor from Limerick, Ireland. It was sold again in 1912 to Branksome Hall School and remains part of the school campus today.

"Hollydene," another view.
Photograph by Mario Angastiniotis

Home of John Highet Thom.
Photograph by Mario Angastiniotis

THE THOM HOUSE 1881

The Thom house at 54 South Drive, built in 1881, is an extraordinary example of the architecture of the first homes constructed in the Rosedale suburb. It may not be considered one of the grand Rosedale estates. Nor could it be classified as a mansion. Nonetheless, it is truly an architectural gem characteristic of the early Victorian period. It clearly belongs to an era predating most of the rest of Rosedale. At the time it was constructed, there were only eight other homes in the immediate vicinity, none of which were of this particular architectural style.

Mr. John Highet Thom, barrister, built the home on the north side of South Drive near the intersection of Park Road and what was once Woodland Avenue. Of Mr. Thom we know very little except that he was a lawyer and taxing officer in the Accountant's Office, Osgoode Hall.

Mr. Thom paid $1,500 for Lot #1, Plan 353, a subdivision registered by Benjamin Morton in 1874. It divided Villa lots 26 and 27 of Rose-Park into seven building lots. By 1880 Edgar Jarvis had acquired the mini-subdivision. The lots sold quickly and by 1884 three houses had been erected on the block. Within six years, a fourth had been added. Lot 1 belonged to Mr. Thom, Lot 2 to the Honourable David Reesor, senator, Lot 4 to Mr. Henry Hogben of Saloon 4 Court, and Lot 6 to Mr. James Henderson. By 1884, James Henderson had purchased a large block of land along the entire west side of Centre Road and continuing west on the north side of South Drive. These were Villa Lots XXVI, XXVII, XXIX, XXXI, XXXIII, XXXV, and XXXVII.

The Thom house is a three-storey dwelling constructed of yellow brick with red brick trim. It is an excellent example of the Italianate style of architecture, which dominated American houses built between 1850 and 1880. Informal Italian villas or farmhouses with their characteristic square towers inspired the style. North American examples were modified, adapted and embellished.

The popularity of the Italianate style and the closely related Second Empire style seen in "Lorne Hall," the William Davies home just south on a small street running east off Park Road (now Meredith Crescent), declined during the depression that spanned the years from 1873 to the early 1890s. When prosperity returned, and people had money to spend on increasingly lavish homes, Queen Anne became the more common style choice. Romanesque and Gothic Revival also came into vogue to some degree.

The Thom house is basically a square box with dominant tower and adjoining wing. The roof is of relatively low pitch with widely overhanging eaves, accented with large decorative brackets beneath. Windows are tall and narrow and most of the original sashes were of single or double-pane glazing. Elaborate crowns top the windows.

The front entry porch is of single-storey height and encloses an interior vestibule. The front doorway is a single door with large-pane glazing in the same shape as the windows.

The "lookout" at the top of the square tower consists of a group of tall arched windows. During the Christmas season, the present owners place a small Christmas tree adorned with hundreds of tiny white lights in the sunroom at the top of the tower. It is truly a lovely sight, reminiscent of Victorian times.

The Thom house has been painstakingly restored to its former grandeur. A brick driveway and walks have been added, along with a dark green wrought iron fence effectively completing the Victorian look.

GUISELEY HOUSE 1885

Guiseley House, an imposing red brick mansion notable for its massive square watch tower, its interesting accents and additions, its gables, dormers and irregular roof lines, stood on the southeast corner of Elm Avenue and Huntley Street (now Mount Pleasant Road). It was the home of Joseph Cawthra, a relative newcomer to upper-crust Toronto society. Arriving on the scene in 1885, the house was a late addition to the enclave of mansions already clustered at the western end of Elm Avenue. The property was commonly referred to as simply "The Cawthra Estate."

Joseph Cawthra was a successful retailer and general store owner from Newmarket, Ontario. On retiring, he moved to Toronto, becoming quite active in city affairs. By 1890 he had been appointed Director of the Bank of Toronto. In the manner of the day, Cawthra gave his house a name. In this case, as in many others, the appellation came from the birthplace of the family's ancestors in the Parish of Guiseley, England.

Joseph Cawthra purchased Lot 17 Plan 329 from Edgar Jarvis in the early 1880s. The large property was approximately three acres. John Blaikie had just finished building a substantial new home on the northeast corner of Bridge/Huntley Street and Elm Avenue. Across the street on the southwest corner was his neighbour William Alexander. To imagine what this intersection looked like in the mid–1880s, one must remember that Huntley Street was a much narrower and dramatically less travelled thoroughfare than the present Mount Pleasant Road. Moreover, it ended at South Drive just a short distance to the north. There were still no other homes on the east side of Huntley Street between Bloor and the "White Bridge." Therefore, to the south, the Cawthra Estate overlooked the Rosedale ravine. The lawns and gardens accompanying the homes were expansive, and in many cases there would have been stables and coach houses on the grounds as well. As the *Toronto Directories* of this period reveal, the coachmen and gardeners employed by these well-to-do families often had homes for themselves on the large estates.

For the most part, "Guiseley House" was of Queen Anne design—large, rambling and unique, with many interesting wings, accents, irregular roof-lines, gables and dormers. Double doors, framed by marble pillars, accentuated the main entrance and a high, square watchtower above this door dominated the asymmetrical front. The view from the tower south toward Lake Ontario must have been spectacular. Windows in the tower were tall, with rounded arches on the second floor and a dramatic palladian window at the peak of the turret, which was crowned with a railing. Square towers, quite common on Italianate homes, are rare on Queen Annes. But since so many of the rich and famous of the day had towers on their homes, Cawthra followed suit. One might say that he was merely keeping up with the Jarvises.

The left side of the house was composed of a large front-facing gable with an unusual half-rounded window in the third floor and two-storey projecting bays on the first and second floors. The right side was monopolized by a smaller secondary front-facing gable. Further to the right was a one-storey conservatory/sun room. Large third-floor gabled dormers and two-storey cutout bays distinguished the north side wall.

"Guiseley House," home of Joseph Cawthra.
Negative by J. V. Salmon, Toronto Reference Library, J. V. Salmon Collection S1-742A

Windows were tall and narrow, mainly single rectangles with simple surrounds and solitary large-pane sashes. Windows to the right of the front door, the side bays and the sunroom porch boasted a smaller horizontal rectangular window above the main window, quite a modern architectural feature for that day.

Patterned masonry, an important trademark of the Queen Anne style, is not very well seen on the photo. The roof was of relatively low pitch. It was generally only the later vintage Queen Annes that had lower-pitched roofs.

After Joseph Cawthra died, his son John J. Cawthra lived in "Guiseley House" until his own death in 1951. By then, Rosedale was passing through a period of general decline. Many of the large old homes had degenerated into states of disrepair, some having been converted to rooming houses during and immediately following World War II. Others, like the Cawthra house, were torn down to make way for the low-rise apartments that were springing up all over the neighbourhood.

Advertisement for lots in the North Rosedale Subdivision, circa 1908.
Toronto Reference Library

NORTH ROSEDALE

The area known as "North Rosedale," specifically that pocket of fine homes located north of the Glen Road bridge, east of Mount Pleasant Road and west of Bayview Avenue, was opened up somewhat later than South and West Rosedale. This was undoubtedly due to the fact that it lay just marginally farther away from the business district at King and Yonge Streets. Before the turn of the century, there were building lots in abundance in the southern parts of Rosedale, and as Edgar Jarvis well knew, these were not exactly selling rapidly. Until this land was absorbed, developers in North Rosedale could hardly hope to compete. Moreover, any full-scale development of the area was all but impossible until Glen Road was extended north and a substantial bridge was built over the ravine that lay just north of Hill Street (later renamed South Drive). Another drawback was the lack of public transportation to the city centre.

North Rosedale is comprised of land from the eastern portion of original Township Lots 19, 18, and 17 in the Second Concession from the Bay. Nothing much happened to this property prior to 1880. Essentially, it remained original forest, bordered by ravines on the west, south and east, and intersected by Silver Creek, which ran through the valley and out to the Don River. At this time it was owned by four men.

The southern portion (Township Lot 19) consisting of land in the North Rosedale ravine was owned by Thomas Helliwell, who sold to Edgar Jarvis in 1874. The middle portion (Township Lot 18) was owned by Joseph Price. His mill was located on the river in the ravine near the present intersection of Mount Pleasant Road and Roxborough Street East/Roxborough Drive. Price sold the southeastern quadrant of his property to William Mathers in 1847, but kept the northeastern quadrant for himself. Mathers held his southeastern quadrant until 1880. As for the northernmost portion of North Rosedale, between Edgar and Summerhill

The Old Belt Line, east of Mount Pleasant, 1909.
City of Toronto Archives,
SC 244-7326

*MacLennan Avenue
looking south, 1921.*
City of Toronto Archives,
SC 231-230

Avenues, Township Lot 17, this was owned first by Charles Thompson, then by George Dickson.

Around 1880, development of North Rosedale began to gather momentum. Nonetheless, while a significant amount of property did change hands and subdivision of land ensued, few houses were actually built. Any construction of homes that did take place occurred primarily in the southeastern portion, on Highland Avenue, Beaumont Road and Bin-Scarth Road. The real action, in the middle and northern portions, would be postponed until late in the first decade of the 20th century.

The first spate of changes in North Rosedale commenced in December of 1880. William Mathers sold his property in the southeastern portion of Township Lot 18 to Toronto lawyers James Edgar and Charles Ritchie for the enormous sum of $25,071. Edgar and Ritchie went on to purchase the northeastern quadrant of Township Lot 18 as well, from Sarah Price on February 8, 1881. They then had acquired most of the plateau in North Rosedale. The only land they did not own was on the extreme southern and northern boundaries.

By March 1881, Edgar Jarvis had gotten wind of the upcoming action in North Rosedale. Ever in the market for a lucrative real estate deal, he sold his ravine property north of Sylvan Towers at Hill Street and Glen Road to the Scottish Ontario and Manitoba Land Company for $24,320.

Messrs. Edgar and Ritchie, for whatever reasons, did not develop the entire North Rosedale holding themselves. By June of 1881, they had sold the southern part to the Scottish Ontario and Manitoba Land Company for $26,600, at a profit of $1,529. While in 1881 this probably would have been considered a lucrative gain in only six months, it was hardly an enormous one. The prior purchase from Edgar Jarvis had effectively secured access to the new North Rosedale Park subdivision. With this accomplished, the Scottish Ontario and Manitoba Land Company quickly registered Plan 528 of subdivision, creating 72 lots in the vicinity of Pelham Place (later renamed Highland Avenue), Beaumont Road and Bin-Scarth Road.

The first lots to sell in North Rosedale were on Beaumont Road. The going price in 1884 was $1,200. In typical Rosedale fashion, many of the first purchasers were speculators who bought several lots in hopes of capitalizing on their investments. The original buyers were not disappointed. By 1885 the market value of lots on Beaumont had skyrocketed to $2,500, and in 1887 to $2,650.

By 1887 the Scottish Ontario and Manitoba Land Company had registered their second Plan of Subdivision in North Rosedale, sectioning off 12 lots on Beaumont Road. But access to these lots was difficult at best. If rapid growth was to occur, construction of roads and bridges was needed and public transportation had to be provided for. It must be remembered that in the late 1880s, when North Rosedale was just starting to be developed, there were no roads north into this area. Sherbourne Street North travelled only as far north as Centre Road and South Drive. Mount Pleasant

109 Glen Road,
formerly Rosedale
Golf & Country Club.
Photograph by Bess Crawford

Road did not exist. By 1887 Glen Road had been extended north as far as the Gooderham estate at the corner of Hill Street (now South Drive) but did not go any farther. Beyond this, the *Toronto Directory* noted private grounds, a house, stables, then a bridge which crossed over the stream and Park Drive in the ravine. While Goad's map showed the North Iron Bridge on Glen Road in 1884, and the *Toronto Directory* first mentioned it in 1887, information obtained at the Registry Office gives the timing of the bridge later. The Scottish Ontario and Manitoba Land Company had previously obtained the land in the ravine from Edgar Jarvis, but it took until 1889 for a by-law to be registered by the Corporation of the Township of York for the extension of Glen Road north into the new subdivision that was being developed.

The extension of Glen Road and the construction of the North Iron Bridge effectively put in place the means to open up North Rosedale. The Scottish Ontario and Manitoba Land Company had even granted a right of way through their property. Now, all that was needed were people to buy the lots and build homes.

Before the turn of the century, most of the purchasers of North Rosedale lots were speculators. Only a few actually built homes in the wilds of North Rosedale. The *Toronto Directory* of 1890 listed five houses on Bin-Scarth Road, one of which was vacant, another unfinished. On the north side, east of Glen Road was Francis Despard, secretary-treasurer of the Ammonia Company of Toronto, and Julian Sale, of Julian Sale and Company, manufacturers of pocket books. On the south side, also east of Glen Road, was the the estate of Ebenezer Stovel, of Stovel and Company, merchant tailors. While the Directory mentioned no other homes in North Rosedale, Registry Office records tell us that by the end of 1890 there was also one house on the north side of Beaumont Road east of Glen Road and two on the east side of Glen Road; one was owned by Charles Davidson, of C. Davidson and Company, saddlery and carriage hardware; the other belonged to Samuel Beatty, a real estate broker. The lot at the corner of Glen and Beaumont Roads was purchased by Harton Walker, another real estate agent. Walker was a man who from this point forward would figure strongly in the residential development of North Rosedale.

Harton Walker started the Harton Walker Real Estate Company in 1889. His offices were located at 5 York Chambers, 9 Toronto Street. At the Toronto Street location, Harton came into contact with many of the developers active on the Rosedale real estate scene. Samuel Beatty, who built his own residence on the east side of Glen Road just north of the North Iron Bridge, had his real estate office in the same building as Harton Walker. Next door, in the Whittemore Building, was Edgar Jarvis. Further down the street at number 15 was Robert Jenkins of the R. and T. Jenkins Real Estate Company. Jenkins lived on Dale Avenue in South Rosedale. At 25 Toronto Street was J.W.G. Whitney, long-time real estate agent for the Jarvis family, and at 28–30 Toronto Street was Scarth Cochran and Company, real estate and land agents. William Bain Scarth was a land commissioner in the province of Ontario.

Harton Walker would eventually build his own house at 12 Edgar Avenue. His son, John Harold Walker, followed in his father's footsteps. After graduating from Harbord Collegiate, John Walker formed his own real estate company, later becoming treasurer of the Toronto Real Estate Board. He married in 1911 and built a house at 204 Glen Road on the west side, south of Summerhill Avenue.

The next step in opening up North Rosedale was the provision of public transportation. Between 1884 and 1890, the Toronto Belt Line Railway acquired rights of way from landowners Hoskin, Kingston, Jarvis, Nanton, Osler and Jackson so that a rail line could be laid in the ravine east of Rosedale, along the present Bayview Avenue. This, however, failed to generate the hoped-for development of North Rosedale. By 1900, the number of homes still totalled only fourteen, including five on Beaumont, seven on Bin-Scarth, and two on Glen Road.

Further north, the property that Messrs. Edgar and Ritchie had acquired from Sarah Price and the property north of them, owned by George Pennie Dickson and his wife, Isabella, was still undeveloped. The Dicksons had registered Plan 534 of subdivision in November of 1882, producing building lots on Edgar Avenue, Ritchie Crescent, Dickson Avenue and Summerhill, but few homes were built. Any real estate activity that did occur was purely speculative. Men like Horace Thorne, Henry Mara, Donald McDermid, James Crowther, John Herbert Hyland and James Wood bought and sold lots in hopes of making money. To be sure, land prices did escalate significantly and this in turn spurred on additional activity. In 1892 Sarah Price, James Edgar and Charles Ritchie registered Plan 1135, a block of land bounded by Morris and Scholfield

Avenues. This was granted to the Toronto Lacrosse Athletic Association for their playing field.

Not all the speculators in North Rosedale made it rich, however. James Edgar was one of the noteworthy losers. In 1889 he had signed a mortgage with the Scottish Ontario and Manitoba Land Company for $23,154. But by December 1896, the Scottish Ontario and Manitoba Land Company were forced to register a Final Order of Foreclosure for non-payment of the mortgage. The company seized the 47 acres previously held by Edgar and Ritchie. Now most of North Rosedale was in the hands of the Scottish Ontario and Manitoba Land Company.

Up until this time, fewer than 20 houses had been constructed in North Rosedale. These were generally large and impressive residences with spacious grounds—just the types of residences Edgar Jarvis had envisioned for South Rosedale. To ensure that housing design would continue in this rather exclusive vein, the Scottish Ontario and Manitoba Land Company set out detailed terms and building restrictions for new construction in the area. Such restrictions were quite common during this period. The Chestnut Park mini-suburb in West Rosedale had similar restrictions, so would the Lawrence Park and Kingsway neighbourhoods which followed 10 to 20 years later.

After the turn of the century, Toronto entered a period of rapid economic and population growth. Incomes increased considerably and a new middle-class emerged. It was within this context that the majority of development in North Rosedale took place. The success of the well-planned mini-subdivision of Chestnut Park, along with the construction of homes on the remaining lots in West and South Rosedale, must have encouraged the Scottish Ontario and Manitoba Land Company. By 1908, Harton Walker, long associated with the company, embarked on a full-scale advertising campaign to lure new residents into North Rosedale Park. The stylized map on page 126 was used for promoting the new subdivision. The advertising was quite successful, and by 1910 the number of homes in North Rosedale had jumped to 73. St. Andrews College had been relocated from the old Chestnut Park estate of David Lewis Macpherson to a new location north of the present Douglas Drive, west of Scholfield and MacLennan Avenues. The Lacrosse Grounds accompanying the school occupied the area just north of Highland Avenue, the present site of Rosedale Park. East of St. Andrews and north of Edgar Avenue were the Rosedale Golf Links. The beautiful Victorian clubhouse sat at the corner of Beaumont and Glen Roads looking south over the lush North Rosedale ravine.

While it took more than 30 years to develop North Rosedale, with fortunes gained and lost by many speculators, the ultimate result was one of the most beautiful and exclusive enclaves of homes in the City of Toronto.

RESIDENTS OF NORTH ROSEDALE IN 1910

BIN-SCARTH ROAD

North side

Highland Avenue intersects

10 Wilton, Eddis

12 Kantel, Emil

14 Richmond, Henry

16 Jackman, Harry

24 vacant house

Glen Road intersects

36 vacant house

40 vacant house

42 vacant house

44 Boyd, Lawrence

50 Martin, Arthur

52 Adams, J. Frank

56 Heron, Orlando

60 Evans, H. Pollman

64 Sale, Julian

66 vacant house

68 vacant house

72 Gordon, The Misses

76 Thomson, Alexander

84 Davies, J. Edgar

94 Trethewey, William

South side

1 Langley, John

Highland Avenue intersects

13 Rosedale Golf Club

15 vacant house

17 vacant house

Glen Road intersects

35 Daley, John

41 Meredith, John

67 Alexander, David

87 May, Charles

BEAUMONT ROAD

North side

1 Watts, George

2 Robinson, George

3 Parsons, William

4 Andrews, Walter

5 Wilson, Andrew

6 Kilgour, Robert

8 McLeod, Henry

South side

Not built on

EDGAR AVENUE

North side

12 Walker, Harton

40 Bole, William

7 Lowes, Charles

GLEN ROAD

North of North Iron Bridge

East side

111 Proctor, Albert

117 Jarvis, Herbert

119 Scott, Thomas

123 Blaikie, George

Summerhill Avenue intersects

West side

132 Sparling, William

Roxborough Drive intersects

Edgar Avenue intersects

Marks, E. Richard

Summerhill Avenue intersects

HIGHLAND AVENUE

North side

64 vacant house

66 Murray, Charles

Scholfield Avenue intersects

Roxborough Drive intersects

96 Harvey, Miss Charlotte

106 Wright, Mrs. Lillian

108 Denovan, Joshua

Morris Avenue intersects

South side

53 Dundas, Alexander

55 Gibson, Charles

59 vacant house

61 Chandler, Howard

65 vacant house

71 George, William

Bin-scarth Road intersects

81 Bowden, Frank

Scholfield Avenue intersects

Roxborough Drive

93 Dunlap, David

ROXBOROUGH DRIVE

East of ravine,

North side

312 vacant house

314 Coryell, Robert

316 vacant house

318 Mara, Frederick

360 Porter, Frederick

362 vacant house

368 vacant house

370 vacant house

South side

Not built on

WHITNEY AVENUE

East from Glen Road,

North side

Not built on

South side

3 unfinished houses

5 Jackson, Reverend George

7 Copp, William

9 Galbraith, Robert

11 White, Murray

REAL ESTATE AGENTS

L
and speculation in Toronto was rampant during the late 19th century. By 1880 few of the old family estates remained near Lake Ontario. Factories and commercial buildings crowded the original Park Lots granted by Governor Simcoe. Residential development was being pushed farther afield. The area just below Bloor Street had been subdivided, and lots were selling so fast that prices escalated. Speculators with the money to get in on the action were definitely making a lot of money buying and selling real estate.

As the city grew and commercial activity close to the lake increased, the grand homes and estates moved further north. Jarvis and Sherbourne Streets were popular addresses for Toronto's rich and famous. Robert Simpson, the Honourable Frank Smith and the Honourable William McMaster, for example, built large residences on the north side of Bloor Street east of Yonge Street.

As time progressed and urbanization continued, factories gradually took over the southern and eastern sectors of the downtown area. In the 20 years from 1871 to 1891, Toronto witnessed a phenomenal growth in industrialization. The number of factories jumped from 500 to 2,500, and employment in factory-related jobs expanded from 9,400 to 26,000.

By the late 1800s, Rosedale, with its winding streets, ravines and rural setting, along with its easy access by street rail to the financial district on King Street became the sought-after location for many of the grand homes being constructed in the city.

The significant number of builders and related companies at that time indicates the rapid pace of Toronto development. The business section of the 1884 *Toronto Directory* listed no fewer than 66 real estate agents. Many of the original purchasers of lots in the new Rosedale suburb were themselves estate agents and developers; men like James Henderson, president of the Home District Savings Bank, James Fraser, secretary and treasurer of the Metropolitan Permanent Building Society, George and Greenhow Banks of Banks Brothers, and Frank Cayley of the "Drumsnab" estate. Builders and contractors, like Alfred Allen of South Drive, George White of Rosedale Road, Jeremiah Bedford and his sons of Elm Avenue and George Elliott of Roxborough Street East, as well as architects such as Grant Helliwell, bought

Cheap Suburban Residences.
___
SALE BY AUCTION
Of Valuable Freehold Property
PLEASANTLY SITUATED IN THE VILLAGE OF
YORKVILLE,

ON FRIDAY the Thirteenth day of OCTOBER. 1854, the Office of the *FARMERS' AND MECHANIC BUILDING SOCIETY*, comprising nineteen Village Lo varying in extent from one-fi th to one-fourth of an ac situated on the Davenport Plank Road, in the Village Yorkville, and adjoining the Property of Capt. Otway.

TERMS.—One-fifth down ; balance in five years.

Pl ns can be seen at the Offices of the Farmers' and M chanics' Building Society, and of E. C. JONES, Esq., S licitor.

Sale at TWELVE o'clock, noon.

W. B. CREW,

Auctioneer.

Toronto, Sept. 29, 1854.   1393-t

The *Globe*, October 5, 1854

land in Rosedale on which to build their own homes. Some also purchased additional plots to sell, develop or subdivide further. It seemed that anyone who could scrape up the necessary down payment was buying Toronto property in the hope of striking it rich. All this occurred despite long bouts of economic recession and falling prices.

William Botsford Jarvis, Joseph Bloor, and William Cayley, among others, had been speculators in Yorkville real estate in the 1840s and 50s. It was the vision of these men that shaped the original ideas for the area north and east of Yonge and Bloor Streets. Others, such as George Duggan, David Macpherson, Henry Lamport, Edward Nanton, John Hoskin, Edmund Osler and Edgar Jarvis, enacted the details of the Rosedale suburb, proceeding to subdivide the land and lay out the streets. Edgar Jarvis was a land agent with offices located at the Whittemore Building on Toronto Street, among many of Toronto's other estate agents and architects. He had acquired much of the Rosedale property during the 1860s and 70s.

In North Rosedale and in the Chestnut Park mini-suburb, lots were divided well before actual development occurred. In both these cases, original plans were subsequently altered and street names changed once construction of the area began in earnest.

Another estate agent and land broker closely associated with the original development of Rosedale was James Henderson, President of the Home District Savings Bank. Henderson originally lived on the north side of Bloor Street East, but he became interested in the new suburb being developed by Edgar Jarvis and bought the entire west side of Centre Road and the north side of South Drive, Lots XXVII, XXIX, XXXI, XXXIII, XXXV and XXXVII. He built his own house on the northwest corner of Centre Road and South Drive. In addition to trading in real estate, his company also collected rents, managed estates and evaluated property.

The Banks Brothers—George, Greenhow, Arthur, William and Robert—were also very active in land dealings in the Rosedale suburb. The brothers bought several large pieces of property in Rose-Park subdivision Plan 103. They built their own family estate, "Heyroyd," at the corner of Sherbourne Street and Crescent Road, Lot XLVII. George Banks also owned Lot LVI, on the north side of Crescent Road near Centre Road. They were long associated with Kay and Banks Company, which later became simply Banks Brothers of 61 Church Street.

John Blaikie and William Alexander, of the Blaikie and Alexander Company, estate agents and influential financiers, built their private estates across the road from each other in Rosedale around 1880.

James Fraser, secretary and treasurer of the Metropolitan Permanent Building Society, purchased most of the ravine property on the west side of Woodland Avenue (now South Drive), including Lots XIX, XX, and XXI, just around the corner from the Blaikie and Alexander estates.

James E. Loney, of James Loney Real Estate Company, 828 Yonge Street, resided at 170 Park Road, and Robert Jenkins, of R. and T. Jenkins Company, Estate Agents of 15 Toronto Street, lived on Dale Avenue.

Francis Cayley, the original owner of "Drumsnab Farm," which included a huge parcel of land in southeast Rosedale, east of Castle Frank and north of Bloor Street East, had started his career in the banking business, but after selling off much of the family estate except for the house, dealt mainly in real estate.

Charles Ritchie and James Edgar, both lawyers, amassed most of the land eventually developed in North Rosedale. During the period from 1880 to 1908, the Scottish Ontario and Manitoba Land Company acquired the property and, with the help of real estate agent Harton Walker, developed it into one of the finest residential neighbourhoods in the city of Toronto.

Scarth, Cochran and Company, real estate and land agents of 28–30 Toronto Street, was another well-known real estate firm at the time. William Bain Scarth was a land commissioner in Ontario.

J.W.G. Whitney, of 25 Toronto Street, was yet another respected and successful Toronto land broker and estate agent. The Jarvis family used his services to rent the Rosedale House in 1870. It is unknown whether Whitney Avenue in North Rosedale was named after him or after Sir James Pliny Whitney, Premier of Ontario from 1905 to 1908.

Other real estate companies of the late 1880s included: Buchan and Company of 7 Toronto Street, Robert Beaty and Company of 53 King Street East and Samuel Beatty, of George D. Beatty and Stovel Real Estate, 64 Victoria Street, 6 York Chambers, 9 Toronto Street, residence. Samuel Beatty lived on Glen Road.

David Lewis Macpherson of "Chestnut Park," while not in the real estate business, became a key figure in the development of Rosedale. In addition to his own sizable estate, he also bought a large parcel of land in the Rose-Park subdivision. Villa Lots V and VI Plan103 encompassed most of the west side of Rosedale Road and were eventually subdivided into lots. After his death, his own estate was divided into the beautiful mini-subdivision of the same name.

TORONTO AUCTION MART.

Sale of Cottages and Lots
IN YORKVILLE.

The undersigned will sell by Auction at the above rooms,

On Saturday, April 11th,

At Twelve o'clock noon,

THREE COTTAGES AND LOT,

On the south side of Sydenham street, about 100 feet west of Yonge street. Also,

A VACANT LOT,

On the north side of Sydenham street, opposite the above.

The whole will be sold to wind up an estate.
TERMS CASH.
F. W. COATE & CO.,
8-5-6
Auctioneers.

The *Mail*, April 10, 1874

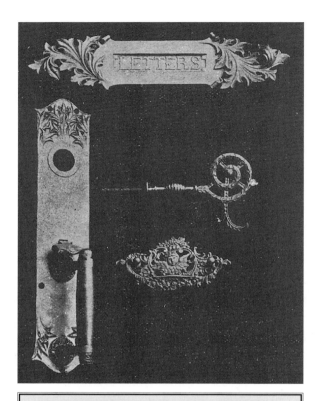

TORONTO LOCK CO., LIMITED

In the manufacture of cabinet and builder's hardware and brass and bronze castings a representative and reliable concern in the city is that known as the Toronto Lock. Co., Limited, whose salesrooms and factory are situated at 76 Esplanade street west. The prosperous industry was incorporated in 1892 under the laws of Canada, and has a liberal and influential patronage in Ontario, Quebec and Manitoba. The premises occupied comprise a spacious three-story brick building, 75 x 75 feet in dimensions, fully equipped with every convenience. The foundry and workshops are supplied with modern tools and machinery, and fifteen skilled workmen are employed. The company manufacture all kinds of cabinet and builders' hardware, easels, tables, fire screens, banner stands, window fittings, etc., and also turn out first-class bronze and brass castings for outside work and the trade at very reasonable rates. The estimates are promptly given on special work, and complete satisfaction is guaranteed patrons. Only carefully selected metals are utilized and the goods produced are unsurpassed for quality, elegance and design of workmanship, and the demand for them is steadily increasing in all sections of the country. A specialty is made in fine bronze goods in builders' hardware, and the business is both wholesale and retail.

Toronto Illustrated 1893

BUILDERS, TRADES AND MATERIALS

The *Toronto Directory* of 1884 listed 198 builders and contractors in the city. They were the largest business category, totalling even more than barristers and attorneys at 163. Also listed were 7 roofers, 8 sash and door factories, 13 brick manufacturers, 3 calcine plasterers, 9 marble dealers, 3 plate glass companies, 8 wallpaper dealers, 17 locksmiths and bell hangers, and 55 lumber merchants. Nonetheless, a surprising number of the doors, doorknobs, hinges, servants' bells, baseboards, bathroom fixtures and plaster adornments such as ceiling medallions and crown moldings are of similar design in many of the old Rosedale homes.

Alfred Allen, George White, Jeremiah Bedford, and George Elliott were all contractors and builders who lived in Rosedale during the second half of the 19th century. Many of the homes they constructed are still standing today and noted in Heritage Toronto's *Inventory of Heritage Properties* (see pages 157 to 158). The house that George Elliott built for himself in 1889 is located at 176 Roxborough Street East. Jeremiah Bedford and his sons lived on Elm Avenue in 1890. Three of the Bedford homes can be seen at 53 and 55 Elm Avenue (1888), and at 61 Elm Avenue (1890).

Other well-known Rosedale builders included: Mr. Mathers, who built "Chestnut Park"; John Howard, who renovated "Rosedale House," Sheriff Jarvis's home, in 1837; William Thomas, who built the addition to the Cayley house in 1856; and A. Coleman, who built homes at 6 and 8 Glen Road (1883) and at 10 and 12 Glen Road (1888).

Methods and styles of North American house construction changed markedly during the 1800s. The primitive log and wood dwellings of the early settlers were replaced by more permanent and durable structures that could endure the harsh weather and provide more than nominal comfort to their inhabitants. Residences of the wealthy became exceedingly large, often with many wings and additions and increasingly adorned with ornate Victorian embellishments.

Wood, the primary building material of the earlier era, was almost entirely replaced by brick or stone after 1850. This change of material considerably reduced the previously constant risk of fire. In a wooden structure, a loose ember from the cooking or heating fire, or an upset candle or oil lamp, could cause a fire which would spread quickly, engulfing many homes on a street, given the lack of sophisticated firefighting equipment. The barn and many of the outbuildings at "Rosedale House" succumbed to fire in 1849.

Many of Toronto's 13 brick manufacturing companies listed in 1880 had located operations in Yorkville since the 1840s. They used clay from "Blue Hill" skirting Davenport Road to make white and red brick. The largest brickworks included the operations of John Sheppard of 14 Beverley Street, Thomas Nightingale of 213 Yonge Street (who was associated with the F.A. Townsley brick yards of 203 Avenue Road), Mrs. Bulmer of 207 Yonge Street, John Dunn of 5 Price Street, Leo Pears of 120 Davenport Road, John Purkiss of 205 Avenue Road, and the Helliwell and Taylor family, who owned the brickworks at Todmorden Mills.

The progression of building design through the century was closely linked to advances in methods of construction and home heating. Balloon framing was the wood construction method in most common use by the 1860s. It enabled builders to design much more elaborate structures simply, quickly and inexpensively. Closely spaced two-by-fours were used for the house frame, even for homes of two- or three-storey height. Joints were simply nailed together. Upper floors were effectively hung from this frame. Corner posts, instead of being large ten-inch by ten-inch beams, were now built up with grouped two-inch by four-inch wooden planks. Some 55 lumber merchants had businesses in Toronto in 1880. Foundations were of stone or brick with eight-inch by ten-inch or ten-inch by ten-inch supporting timbers. Floor joists were two inches by twelve inches.

Contractors paid 75 cents per day for general labourers, $1.00 to $1.25 for carpenters and $1.25 to $1.50 for bricklayers. Nails cost 4 cents a pound.

Roofs of Toronto homes were generally steeply pitched to facilitate snow removal during the winter. The seven roofers and roofing materials companies operating in Toronto circa 1880 installed mainly wood shake or slate shingles. Copper roofs were used on some of the large public buildings, however, and felt roofing was also used to some degree. The ability to manufacture asphalt-type shingles was available in the late 19th century but did not gain general acceptance until well into the 20th century. Felt, cloth or paper (with granular surface) was saturated with tar to prevent it from becoming hard and brittle.

Before 1850, Toronto homes were heated almost universally by large stone or brick fireplaces placed strategically to generate maximum heat. This necessity placed limitations on housing design. Cast-iron stoves and cooking ranges were not in widespread use until the 1830s. In many of the early Rosedale homes the circular opening for the metal stovepipe can still be seen in the chimney, now bricked in. While fireplaces were retained for decorative purposes in the parlour, living room, dining room, hall and bedrooms, their requirement as a primary heating source had all but disappeared, replaced in the 1880s by central furnaces burning coal or wood, then later oil or gas. The furnace heated water for use in radiators or warm air was fed by gravity through metal ducts and ultimately through ornate vents set into floors or interior walls. The cost of coal ranged from $8 per ton for egg-sized coal to $8.50 per ton for stove-sized pieces.[1]

JAMES PELL.

THE business of manufacturing woven-wire mattresses, etc., in this city is ably represented by Mr. James Pell, successor to R. Thorne & Co., who had established it in 1881. Mr. Pell bought out the firm in 1892 and has since been doing a splendid business, which is widely diffused throughout the whole of Canada. The

building occupied is a situated at No. 33 Pearl street, is a two-story structure, 35 x 80 feet in dimensions, and steady employment is given to ten expert hands. Mr. Pell manufactures a superior quality of woven-wire mattresses, also spiral and slat beds, iron bedsteads, cots, etc., and fills orders from the wholesale trade and jobbing houses. He was born in this city, has always resided here, and is well and favorably known as an upright, honorable business man. He is an active member of the Foresters.

Toronto Illustrated 1893

E. LARTER.

ONE of the best practical steam, hot water and gas fitters in Toronto is Mr. E. Larter, who has devoted many years to the business and has had a long, valuable experience. He began business on his own account several years ago on York street, and in 1891 removed to the premises now occupied at 128 Bay street, where ten skilled hands are kept constantly employed. Every branch of steam, hot water and gas fitting is undertaken by Mr. Larter, and contracts entered into for the entire fitting up of buildings and dwellings for the introduction of heat and gas, also for repairing, etc. Mr. Larter is a native Canadian and for many years has resided in Toronto. He pays particular attention to fitting up factories with steam, and fully guarantees all his work.

Toronto Illustrated 1893

ROBB & KAY.

IN the manufacture of plumbers' copper and galvanized iron work, a reliable firm in Toronto is that of Messrs. Robb & Kay, gas fitters, tin, copper and sheet iron workers, whose store and workshops are situated at 190 King street west. This business was founded five years ago by Messrs. David Robb and Geo. Kay, who are both thoroughly practical workmen, and employ only first-class workmen. Messrs. Robb & Kay are manufacturers of the noted Canadian Automatic Air Gas Machine, which

they have placed and fitted up in many of the principal residences in Toronto and suburbs, which is perfectly safe and easily handled, while the price quoted is extremely moderate. They also line tanks with copper and galvanized iron, and manufacture ventilation pipes, expansion tanks, etc., and also deal in gasoline. Messrs. Robb & Kay were born in Canada. They are men of energy and integrity, and thoroughly reliable in all their dealings.

Toronto Illustrated 1893

Lighting for many buildings consisted of hanging lamps with whale-sperm-oil dipped tapers as well as sconces for candles. The first gas lines were laid in the city by the Toronto Gas-Light and Water Company in 1842. Main street corners were lighted by gas. The Consumers Gas Company was formed five years later in 1847. Piped or manufactured gas was used for fireplaces and lighting. In the late 1850s, coal oil lamps were introduced.

Although the lightbulb was invented in 1879, extensive use of electricity did not come until after the turn of the century. In 1883 there were 2,419 gas lamps in the city; nonetheless, gas was gradually being replaced by electricity. By the late 1880s, several hotels and steam ships had their own private electricity plants and used incandescent bulbs. Toronto manufacturers pioneered the use of electricity in the buildings of the Toronto Industrial Exhibition (now CNE) in 1882–83.[2] The following year, the first electric arc lights were installed for street lighting at King and Yonge Streets. By 1889 The Toronto Incandescent Electric Light Company was formed. Electrification of the Toronto Street Railway occurred in 1894. Shortly after the turn of the century, the Toronto Electric Light Company was charging eight cents a kilowatt-hour for domestic service. In 1903 the Hydro-Electric Power Commission of Ontario was appointed to supply power under a municipal system at prices below the reach of commercial competition. According to Jesse Edgar Middleton in his book, *Toronto's 100 Years, 1834–1934*, energy was first delivered to Toronto in 1911. The price per kilowatt-hour, when averaged among residential, commercial, and industrial users, was below one and one-half cents.[3]

Decorative cast-iron grates and fireplaces that burned coal, wood or piped gas were faced with marble or small ceramic tiles in a variety of colours, a feature frequently used by Toronto architect Eden Smith. The whole was complemented by elaborate mantelpieces, which often extended to the ceiling and incorporated large mirrors with carved wood or plaster trim.

Plaster applied over newspaper insulation, then lath, faced the interior walls of homes. Plaster was of smooth, fine and dense texture, and much given to cracking, especially in stairways and attic ceilings. Sometimes the plaster was covered with canvas to better keep it attached to the lath. Coved ceilings were common but far from universal. Ornate ceiling medallions around lighting fixtures gave artisans scope to show off their talents. Walls were often embellished with molded plaster several inches wide, featuring geometric or floral motifs in the shape of large frames. Similar matching trim incorporating ferns, flowers and the like surrounded mantelpiece mirrors. Deep crown moldings were also common.

Wallpaper was all the rage. Velvet and silver flock, rich gold, silver, oak panel and satin papers were imported from Europe. George Booth and his son, residents of Roxborough Street East, were wallpaper hangers and house painters, as was Frederick Phillips of Dunbar Road. Paint techniques, including frescoes and murals, were also the latest vogue.

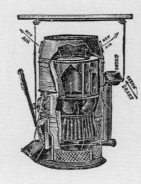
Toronto Illustrated 1893

Furniture of the Sixties and Seventies was massive—and generally walnut. The set to which this imposing bed belonged included a marble-topped washstand, a wardrobe and a bureau as large as a sideboard.

T. Eaton Company, *Golden Jubilee*, 1869–1919

Baseboards, and door and window trim manufactured by local Toronto companies varied in style, degree of detail and width. The standard width was around 10 inches, but in the larger mansions baseboards might measure two feet. Carpenters charged 15 cents an hour.

Windows tended to be large, generally composed of one or two panes of glass per sash. As the Victorian era reached its peak, their forms became more elaborate. Squared bays, circular bays, transoms, and Palladian and many-sided turrets appeared. Other styles featured perhaps a large single pane on the bottom sash with multi-panes on top, large panes surrounded by multi-coloured small panes, or a semi-circular stained-glass panel atop a large single pane on the bottom. It seems the variations were endless.

Modern conveniences for the home made their appearance gradually throughout the 19th century, picking up momentum as the century progressed. Toronto became a manufacturing centre in its own right. Skilled craftsmen and artisans were available. Architects and homeowners no longer had to order all the latest styles and conveniences from Europe. Trains brought goods from Montreal, as well as New York and other American cities.

W. B. MALCOLM'S SANITARY GOODS.

ONE of the most progressive and reliable importers and manufacturers of sanitary earthenware in Toronto is Mr. W. B. Malcolm. whose office, store and work-shops are situated at 89 and 91 Church street. Mr. Malcolm, who is a thoroughly practical sanitary engineer and expert, established this business in 1871, on Jarvis street. Eventually, in 1873, he moved to his present commodious premises. He occupies a spacious three-story building, 44 x 86 feet in area, the first floor being devoted to offices and show rooms, the second to tank room, brass factory, lathes, etc., while the third floor is utilized for storage. He imports direct the best porcelain bowls, etc., for his closets and basins, and manufactures all his own brass work, and keeps constantly in stock full lines of engineers', plumbers', gas and steam fitters' supplies, making a specialty of brass castings and brass work of every description. Mr. Malcolm manufactures the "Toilet," "Autocrat," "Merrimac" and "Pilot" water closets, which are unrivalled for utility, reliability and efficiency, and are general favorites wherever introduced. He has the finest stock of improved sanitary earthenware in Toronto. Orders are carefully filled at the lowest possible prices, and the trade of the house now extends throughout the entire Dominion. Mr. Malcolm was born in Scotland, but has resided in Toronto the greater part of his life. He is widely known for his mechanical skill and integrity, and justly merits the substantial patronage secured in this useful industry. The Telephone call of the office is 650.

Toronto Illustrated 1893

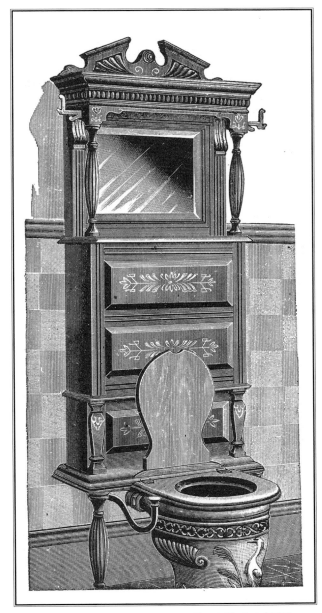

Toronto Illustrated 1893

The rich began to install indoor bathrooms between 1850 and 1870. The Cayleys, for example, added a bathroom during this period. In 1854 George Harding, plumber and manufacturer of baths, force pumps and water closets, advertised in *The Globe* a newfangled "hot water apparatus" that the homeowner could attach to the common cooking stove to heat water for bathing and laundry.

Malcolm's Sanitary Goods Company specialized in sanitary earthenware such as flush toilets, four-legged bath tubs and sinks (usually a white ceramic bowl set into a marble slab top). Showers were marble stalls equipped with a large shower-head and often a pipe in the shape of a U with small holes that shot water out over the middle body in criss-cross fashion. Bathroom floors were made from white

B. WALTON.

AMONG the many washers and wringers that have been placed on the market within the last decade it is safe to say that none have met with such universal favor as that invented, patented and manufactured by Mr. B. Walton. It is known as the " Surprise" Washer and Wringer, and sold all over Canada, and has

given better satisfaction than any other ever before brought to the notice of the public. Everybody is shouting the praise of this machine. The office and factory are located at No. 271 King street east, and every convenience is provided for manufacturing the washers and wringers on a large scale. Mr. Walton is a native of Canada, came to Toronto in 1886, and established business at 57 Jarvis street, and in 1893, owing to increasing trade, he secured the premises in which he is now located. The " Surprise " washers and wringers beat the record, and are highly recommended by the many thousands of families and laundries, hotels, etc., having them in use for 14 years, and filling the full bill of claims without one exception. His new Gatling Washer (Price $2.00) is also a marvel.

———————

Toronto Illustrated 1893

L. NAGEL.

A leading furniture house on Queen street east is that of Mr. L. Nagel, at 100 on that street. Mr. Nagel, who was born in Germany, has been in Toronto since 1886, been established in business since 1887 and has always enjoyed a large patronage. The premises have dimensions of 25 x 100 feet and in the stock will be found elegant richly upholstered parlor and bed room suites, extension tables, library furniture, chairs, rockery, hat racks, book cases, side boards; in short, everything in the line of household furniture. Goods are sold for cash on the installment plan snd the best satisfaction guaranteed purchasers. Mr Nagel also tends to upholstering in all its branches and repairing and keeps in his employ experienced workmen. He is doing a large busioness and is universally popular.

Toronto Illustrated 1893

half-inch octagonal ceramic tiles, often with pale blue or black accents. Bathroom walls were usually tongue-and-groove wainscotting. Ceramic tiles on walls came later.

Kitchens included a butler's pantry with a thick pine counter, cupboards below and windowed cupboards above. The kitchen proper boasted minimal storage space. Ice closets were constructed of closely packed hardwood tongue-and-groove with sawdust on the floor. Ice in 10-pound blocks was delivered daily by horsedrawn wagon. Ice for the season might add around $5 to the family's annual budget.[4] The maid and butler climbed the back staircase to reach their quarters on the third floor from where they could be summoned by bells located in the living and dining rooms. The services of an experienced maidservant ran at about $7 or $8 a month.[5]

There were primitive open sewers in Toronto as early as 1817, but it is unknown whether these were the first ones installed. Following its incorporation in 1834, the city borrowed money for more sewers. The first ones were laid by city engineer John G. Howard. Waste matter was dumped in fields set aside for that purpose. One such reservoir was the site of what was later the Birks, Ellis, Ryrie Store. By the late 1890s, many parts of the city still had open sewers. Outhouses were shared by many families, and public baths were still the standard.[6]

Private wells and two town pumps supplied water to residents who didn't live near springs or creeks. Carters delivered barrels of water to customers. In 1843 the Toronto Gas-Light and Water Company began to supply water from Lake Ontario, but by 1858 there were only 850 customers in a city of 7,500 houses. Waterworks at that time were under the supervision of Albert Furniss. Toronto residents constantly complained about the unsatisfactory service, especially in the Town of Yorkville, where water came from the pumping station at Cottingham Street and Poplar Plains, built at a cost of $65,000 to $75,000. The quantity and quality of the water was so poor that it is said to have caused land values to decline. The waterworks were underfunded and lacked the necessary capital for new equipment and pipe laying. Residents previously against annexation began to campaign vigorously to join Toronto just so that the city would take over the waterworks. By 1881 all wells inside the city limits were ordered closed.

In 1895 James Mansergh, an English consultant hired by the city, reported in favour of developing the existing Toronto water plant and continuing the intake of water from the south shore of Toronto Island.[7]

Important streets were not paved until 1867; elsewhere, they were dirt, strewn with manure. Sidewalks were constructed of wooden planks set lengthwise. The cost of constructing them averaged about seven shillings a rod. The first sidewalks in Toronto were laid on one side of King Street. "Granolithic," then asphalt and finally concrete began to replace the wooden planks in the late 1890s, but even in the early 1900s many of the shop owners on Yonge Street still complained vociferously about the mud and dust being tracked into their places of business due to the lack of sidewalks.[8]

Cars only made their appearance in substantial numbers in the decade after 1910. Coach houses then began to be used as garages.

Toronto Architectural Guild, 1888.
BACK ROW (LEFT TO RIGHT): *R.J. Edwards, Wm. R. Gregg, J. Gemmell, H.J. Webster.* MIDDLE ROW: *Edm. Burke,*
Wm. A. Langton, H. Langley, J.B. Gordon. FRONT ROW: *Wm. G. Storm, S.G. Curry, N.B. Dick, J. Smith*
Toronto Reference Library T31524

Rosedale Architects

E. J. Lennox
G. M. Adam, *Toronto Old & New*

Henry Langley
G. M. Adam, *Toronto Old & New*

Edmund Burke
G. M. Adam, *Toronto Old & New*

Prior to 1890, when the University of Toronto opened the Department of Architecture in the School of Practical Science, young men seeking a career in architecture were simply apprenticed to a practising architect for five years. Unlike today, they took no formal examinations. If the student had previously been educated in drafting, drawing or engineering, the training period could be reduced. Drawing classes were available at the Toronto Mechanics Institute as early as 1832. Upper Canada College also had courses in mechanical and ornamental drawing. In 1872 the Ontario Society of Artists was formed, and the Ontario School of Art was opened in 1876; Toronto architects Frank Darling and James Smith were active in the school. In 1880 the Royal Canadian Academy was begun with Henry Langley, W.F. Storm and James Smith as its original members. Then, in 1888, the Ontario Association of Architects was formed. It was within this increasingly professional environment that architects designing homes for the Toronto establishment operated. Many of these architects came from wealthy families and constructed fabulous residences not only for their clients but also for themselves. Henry Langley, for example, bought Lot 18 in Edgar Jarvis's new mini-suburb of South Rosedale in 1876. Grant Helliwell owned a house at 41 Rosedale Road.

Dictionary of Rosedale Architects and the Homes They designed

The *Toronto Directory* of 1884 listed 32 architects in the city, at least four of whom lived in Rosedale. Many of the architectural firms in the city at that time had their offices on Toronto Street. This was also the location for many of the land brokers and real estate agents. One of these agents was none other than Edgar Jarvis, located at Temple Chambers, Toronto Street. It seems that the closely knit circle of real estate agents, developers and architects was the same in the late 19th century Toronto as it is today.

ALLWARD, Hugh

3 Beaumont Road c. 1932
7 Rosedale Road 1930 (Dorothy Stevens House)

BOULTBEE, Alfred E. (1863–1928)
The son of Alfred Boultbee, MP for East York, apprenticed under William G. Storm in the 1880s, then set up his own practice.

22 Chestnut Park Road 1904–05
20 Chestnut Park Road 1905–06 (Robert Greig House)
50 Chestnut Park Road 1905–06 (S. B. Gundy House)
23 Rosedale Road 1857–58 ("Idlewold" Walter Brown House, later the Arthur Harvey House, later Henry Osborne House) altered in 1890; enlarged in 1911 by A. Boultbee

BROWN, J. Francis (1866–1942)
Born in Levis, Quebec, brought up in England between 1870 and 1882. Brown returned to Canada, receiving his architectural apprenticeship under Edwards & Webster.

79 South Drive 1902
67 South Drive 1907–08
24 Elm Avenue 1910–11 (Thomas Wilkins House)

3 Beaumont Road

7 Rosedale Road

22 Chestnut Park

20 Chestnut Park

50 Chestnut Park

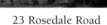
23 Rosedale Road

79 South Drive

67 South Drive

24 Elm Avenue

BURKE, Edmund (1850–1919)

Educated at Upper Canada College, trained with Thomas Gundry and Henry Langley, his uncle, from 1865 to around 1870. Formed a partnership with his cousin Edward Langley and uncle Henry Langley. They were one of the best known and successful architectural firms in Toronto. Burke left the family enterprise in 1892 to take over the business of the recently deceased W. G. Storm. In 1894 he linked up with J.C.B. Horwood. Murray White joined their firm in 1909.

3 Meredith Crescent 1876 (Wm. Davies House), Langley,
    Langley & Burke
36 Maple Avenue 1895–06, Langley & Burke
40 Maple Avenue 1897 (H.H. Fudger House), E. Burke
166 Crescent Road 1899–1900 (Fisher House), Burke & Horwood
86 Chestnut Park Road 1904–05 (James Mickleborough House),
    Burke & Horwood
116 South Drive 1905–06, Burke & Horwood
6 Hawthorn Gardens. 1910 ("Marbrae," M. White House),
    Burke, Horwood & White
1 Chestnut Park Road 1912–15 (James Ryrie House),
    Burke, Horwood & White

CALVIN & SHEPARD

4–18 Ancroft Place 1927, 21-unit housing complex

CHADWICK, (Wm. Craven), Vaux (1868–1941)

Son of Marion Chadwick, author of *Ontario Families*, studied at Upper Canada College. He originally pursued a legal career with his father, but switched to architecture, training with R.C. Windeyer. Chadwick began work in the mid-1890s and by 1900 he had formed a partnership with Samuel Beckett, a graduate of Cornell University. The firm designed mainly upper- and middle-class homes and is most remembered for its role in planning and designing the earliest homes in Lawrence Park. Beckett was killed in the First World War.

3 Meredith Crescent

36 Maple Avenue

40 Maple Avenue

166 Crescent Road

86 Chestnut Park

116 South Drive

6 Hawthorn Gardens

1 Chestnut Park

4-18 Ancroft Place

55 Glen Road 1901–02 (Oliver Adams House)
45 Rosedale Road 1905 (Charlie Niles House)
43 Castle Frank Road 1907–08
65 Castle Frank Road 1912 (Henry Kelly House)
154 Glen Road 1913–14
2 Hawthorn Gardens 1929–30 (Norman Seagram House)

CHAPMAN, A.H.

Studied at the Ecole des Beaux-Arts in Paris, then trained in New York. Chapman moved to Toronto and joined J.M. Oxley, Engineer, designing 1920s office towers. His son is architect Howard D. Chapman.

93 Roxborough Drive East 1927 (A.H. Chapman House)

CURRY, (Samuel) George (1854–1942)

Born in Port Hope, Curry started his career with Frank Darling in 1880. In 1892 he left the firm to work with Sproatt & Pearson. From 1895 to 1898 he practised with F.S. Baker, from 1906 to 1908 with Henry Sproatt and Ernest Rolph, and from 1910 to 1917 with W.F. Sparling. Curry had a large practice, specializing primarily in upper middle-class residential work.

97 Glen Road 1910–11
45 Chestnut Park Road 1915

DARLING, Frank (1850–1923)

Educated at Upper Canada College, Trinity College and apprenticed under Henry Langley. Between 1870 and 1873, Darling worked in London, England with G.E. Street. He was awarded the Royal Gold Medal for Architecture in 1915. His lucrative career centred around designing banks and upper middle-class homes.
Partnerships included: 1874–5 Macdougall & Darling; 1878–79 Darling & Edwards; 1880–91 Darling & Curry; 1892 Darling, Curry, Sproatt & Pearson; 1893–1896 Darling, Sproatt & Pearson; 1897–1923 Darling & Pearson.

55 Glen Road

45 Rosedale Road

43 Castle Frank

65 Castle Frank

154 Glen Road

2 Hawthorn Gardens

93 Roxborough Drive East

97 Glen Road

45 Chestnut Park Road

DARLING, Frank *continued*

3 Elm Avenue 1878 (Wm. Alexander House); addition 1897
   Darling, Sproat, Pearson
4 Beaumont Road 1898, Darling & Pearson
160 South Drive 1903, gates designed by Darling

GEMMELL, John (1850–1915)

Born in Ayrshire, Scotland, moved to Canada as a child and was raised in Toronto. Studied architecture with James Smith and remained in partnership with Smith for 45 years.

2 Elm Avenue 1866 ("Glen Hurst," Edgar Jarvis House);
addition Smith & Gemmell 1880

GEORGE, MOOREHOUSE & KING

A Toronto firm known for designing Georgian Revival homes for upper-class families in the 1920s. Thereafter, the George & Moorehouse partnership turned their specialty to designing commercial and institutional buildings.

8 Castle Frank Road 1926 (Gerald Larkin House)
8 May Street 1930
30 Rosedale Road 1929–30 (John Gibbons House)

GIBSON, Charles J. (1862–1935)

Born in Quebec and raised in England until 1870. Gibson studied architecture in New York City and moved to Toronto in 1885, where he set up a business with Henry Simpson during the period from 1888 to 1890. Thereafter he practised on his own, specializing mainly in upper middle-class residences. He is said to have designed some 40 homes in Rosedale.

14 Elm Avenue 1895 (Chas. Nelson House), verandah added
   by Gibson 1911
49 McKenzie Avenue 1896 (James Ramsey House)
18 Elm Avenue 1897–98 (Henry Drayton House)

3 Elm Avenue

4 Beaumont Road

2 Elm Avenue

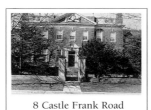
8 Castle Frank Road

8 May Street

30 Rosedale Road

14 Elm Avenue

49 McKenzie

18 Elm Avenue

16 Elm Avenue 1898 (part of 10 Elm Avenue.)

50 Elm Avenue 1898 (Henry O'Hara House)

92–94 Elm Avenue 1900

46 Hawthorn Avenue 1905–06

GORDON, Henry Bauld (1854–1951)

Born in Toronto and apprenticed with Henry Langley. In 1877 he ventured out on his own, joining up with Grant Helliwell in 1879. The two men stayed together until 1931, when both retired from business after over 50 years.

HELLIWELL, Grant (1857–1953)

Of the well-known Helliwell family of Todmorden Mills. He was educated at Jarvis Collegiate. It is thought that he trained in the offices of Langley, Langley & Burke and met Henry Gordon there. The *Toronto Directory* of 1890 lists Helliwell's address as 41 Rosedale Road.

35 Rosedale Road 1892 (Capt. Samuel Crangle House)

40 Maple Avenue 1897–98 (Harris Henry Fudger House)
   Gordon & Helliwell; additions by Burke & Horwood 1902–03

49 Elm Avenue 1901–02

181 Crescent Road 1901–02

HERBERT, F.H.

Originally from Bath, England, immigrated to Canada in 1890. Herbert designed numerous imaginative high Victorian and Edwardian houses in Toronto during the late 1890s and early 1900s.

20 Elm Avenue 1898 (Mrs. Mary Davies House)

21 Elm Avenue 1904–05 (Percival Leadlay House)

45 Elm Avenue 1905–06

23 Elm Avenue 1908–09 (Robert McLean House)

16 Elm Avenue

50 Elm Avenue

46 Hawthorn Avenue

35 Rosedale Road

40 Maple Avenue

49 Elm Avenue

181 Crescent Road

20 Elm Avenue

21 Elm Avenue

45 Elm Avenue

23 Elm Avenue

HORWOOD, John Charles Batstone (1864–1938)

Born in Newfoundland, trained under Langley, Langley & Burke between 1882 and 1887. Horwood worked in New York City in the early 1890s, but returned to Toronto in 1894, setting up a partnership with Edmund Burke. In 1909, Murray White joined the firm. By 1919 the company was called Horwood & White. Horwood retired in 1938; his son Eric Crompton continued in his place. Much of the firm's work was designing commercial buildings.

HYNES, James Patrick (1868–1953)

One of Toronto's best-known plastering companies in the 1890s was owned by James Hynes's older brothers. James was an architectural student for Kennedy & Holland, Darling & Curry, and Strickland & Symons from 1885 through 1889.

33 Maple Avenue 1903–04 probably J.P. Hynes
26 Elm Avenue 1914 (Wm. Kernohan House)

JARVIS, Edgar Beaumont (1864–1948)

The oldest son of Edgar John Jarvis, born and raised in Toronto, studied at Upper Canada College. Jarvis practised at Knox, Elliot & Jarvis from 1889 to 1890, but left to work on his own thereafter.

48 Hawthorn Avenue 1902–04
157 South Drive 1905–06 ("Evenholm" Edgar John Jarvis House)

LANGLEY, Henry (1836–1907)

Born in Toronto, apprenticed under William Hay. Langley worked in partnership with Thomas Gundry until Gundry's death in 1869, then practised on his own until 1873. At that time, his brother Edward, a builder, joined the office, as later did his nephew Edmund Burke. Edward left the company in 1884; Burke left in 1892. The company's main forte was designing churches.

2 Elm Avenue 1863–66 ("Glen Hurst" Edgar Jarvis House)
    Gundry & Langley
10 Elm Avenue 1879 (John Blaikie House) Langley & Langley

33 Maple Avenue

26 Elm Avenue

48 Hawthorn Avenue

157 South Drive

2 Elm Avenue

10 Elm Avenue

LANGLEY, Charles (1870–1951)

The first graduate of the School of Architecture at the University of Toronto in 1892. As a young man he joined his father's firm and became a very well-known architect of Victorian Toronto, designing banks and public buildings as well as Second Empire homes.

36 Maple Avenue 1895–96 Langley & Burke
84 Crescent Road 1899–1900 Langley & Langley
35 Maple Avenue 1903–04 Langley & Langley
82 Chestnut Park Road 1904 Langley & Langley
15 Chestnut Park Road 1910–11 (William Carrick House)
    Langley & Howland
95 Crescent Road 1931 Langley & Howland

LANGTON, William (1854–1933)

Born in Peterborough, attended school at Upper Canada College and qualified as an architect in 1888.

36 Dunbar Road 1899
10 McKenzie Avenue 1909 (Mrs. Eleanor Street House)

LENNOX, Edward James (1855–1933)

Born and raised in Toronto, attending grammar and model schools. He trained with William Irving and took drawing classes at the Mechanics Institute, receiving a diploma in 1874 and winning first prize. After travelling widely, Lennox became a partner with William McCaw in 1876. In 1881 he ventured out and started his own firm. His brother Charles joined him until 1915, and his son joined in 1929. Lennox became one of Toronto's best-known and most influential architects.

69 South Drive 1902
89 Elm Avenue 1902–04 (C.R. Rundle House);
    1916 addition E.J. Lennox
48 Chestnut Park Road 1903–04

36 Maple Avenue

84 Crescent Road

35 Maple Avenue

82 Chestnut Park Road

15 Chestnut Park Road

95 Cresent Road

36 Dunbar Road

10 McKenzie Avenue

69 South Drive

89 Elm Avenue

48 Chestnut Park Road

LYLE, John

2 Beaumont Road 1906–07 (George Robinson House)

19 Avondale Road 1908 (John Lyle House)

19 Rosedale Road 1913–14 (John Coulson House),
   enlarged and altered by John Lyle in 1928

MATHERS & HALDENBY

A family firm started in the early 1900s, capable of undertaking a broad spectrum of architectural projects. A second generation has continued the practice into the 1990s. Eric Haldenby is current director of the School of Architecture at the University of Waterloo.

68–70 Crescent Road 1926

61 Bin-Scarth Road 1931

52 Rosedale Road 1935 (R.R. McLaughlin House)

144 South Drive 1935 (S. Temple Blackwood House)

MILLER, George Martell (1854–1933)

Originally from Port Hope, received his education at the University of Toronto School of Practical Science. From 1883 to 1885 he worked in the offices of Charles Walton and in 1886 went into business on his own, developing an active practice with the Toronto establishment.

64 Glen Road 1894

66 Glen Road 1894

11 Lamport Avenue 1905

PAGE & STEELE, PAGE & WARRINGTON

Forsey Page started the Toronto architectural partnership Page & Steele in the 1920s, specializing primarily in residential dwellings. It is still a thriving firm.

34 Rosedale Road 1919–20 Page & Warrington

115 Park Road 1931 (Sir Ernest MacMillan House)

2 Beaumont Road

19 Avondale Road

19 Rosedale Road

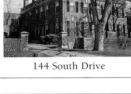
68-70 Crescent Road

61 Bin-Scarth Road

52 Rosedale Road

144 South Drive

64 Glen Road

66 Glen Road

11 Lamport Avenue

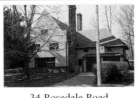
34 Rosedale Road

115 Park Road

PEARSON, John (1867–1940)

Immigrated from England in 1889 and went to work for Darling & Curry, where he became a partner three years later. Pearson is known primarily for his design of bank buildings and the reconstruction of the Parliament Buildings. (For houses designed in Rosedale, see Darling, Sproatt & Pearson.)

60 Crescent Road

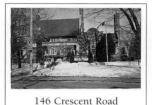

146 Crescent Road

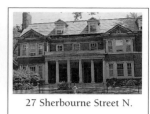

27 Sherbourne Street N.

ROLPH, Ernest (1871–1958)

The Rolph family of Toronto were well-known printers and engravers. Ernest Rolph trained under David Roberts Jr., becoming a draughtsman with Darling, Sproatt & Pearson in 1864. He formed a partnership with Henry Sproatt in 1900.

60 Crescent Road 1901
146 Crescent Road 1902–03 (Baillie House, "Mooredale")
27 Sherbourne Street North 1907–09 (E.D. Gooderham House)
48 Rosedale Road 1922–23 (Alex Gooderham House)

SIDDALL, J. Wilson (1861–1941)

Born and qualified as an architect in England. On arrival in Toronto in 1891, he joined Knox & Elliott, the latter two men later relocating to Chicago. From 1892 until 1895 Siddall partnered with Fred Baker, then later practised alone.

93 Elm Avenue

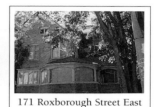

171 Roxborough Street East

93 Elm Avenue 1900–01
171 Roxborough Street East 1902–03 (Siddall House) [2]

SMITH, Eden

Born in England, came to Canada in the late 1880s. He was employed by Strickland & Symons, then partnered with Eustace Bird, and by 1900 was working alone. One of his sons joined him in practice in 1906, a second son in 1912. Eden Smith and his sons designed hundreds of English Cottage-style homes in Toronto.

48 Cluny Drive 1902–04
34 Chestnut Park Road 1904–06
20 McKenzie Avenue 1908–09 (Lewis Grant House)

SMITH, James Avon (1832–1918)

Originally from Macduff, Banffshire, Scotland, Smith immigrated to Canada in 1851, where he trained under William Thomas. In 1870 Smith hired his former student John Gemmell. The firm is best known for their design of Toronto churches. (For houses designed in Rosedale, see Gemmell.)

SPROATT, Henry (1866–1934)

Son of a civil engineer and land surveyor, Sproatt trained under A.R. Denison. On completion of his apprenticeship he went to New York City, then travelled through Europe. On returning to Toronto he went into business with Darling and Pearson. From 1893 to 1896 he partnered with Ernest Rolph. Sproatt's son Charles followed in his father's footsteps. (For houses designed in Rosedale, see Rolph, Darling and Pearson.)

SYMONS, William Limbery (c.1865–1931)

Born at Stoke, England, Symons immigrated to Canada with his parents. Research indicates that his training was probably done in Toronto under Walter Strickland. On becoming qualified as an architect he acted as consultant on the layout of Queen's University campus. Symons and his partner Rae designed many Rosedale homes. Symons lived in New York City from 1925 until 1931 and was hired by Pierpont Morgan to advise on the restoration of Trinity Church, Broadway.

41 Maple Avenue 1902
170 Crescent Road 1907–08 (Charles Boone House)

48 Cluny Avenue

34 Chestnut Park

20 McKenzie Avenue

41 Maple Avenue

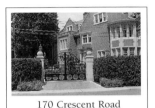
170 Crescent Road

TOWNSEND, (Samuel) Hamilton (1856–1940)

Born in Brantford, Ontario, and educated at the Toronto Model School. He apprenticed under W. G. Storm from 1874 to 1876. Townsend was a partner with Herbert Hancock for a short time after he became qualified as an architect, then travelled extensively in the United Kingdom and Europe in the 1880s. Townsend specialized in designing residential dwellings and is best remembered for his work planning the layout, the brick sidewalks and street lamps in the Chestnut Park subdivision. Townsend's designs are easily recognized. They feature the Neo-Tudor style.

35 Crescent Road 1895 (Boultbee House)
48 Crescent Road 1901
49 Cluny Avenue 1901–02
52 Cluny Avenue 1902–04 (John Dixon House)
2 McKenzie Avenue 1903–05
49 Chestnut Park Road 1905
77 Chestnut Park Road 1906–07
39 Chestnut Park Road 1906–07
4 Hawthorn Gardens 1910–11 (Wm. Gundy House)

WILKES, Hilton & WATERS, Mackenzie

11 Highland Avenue 1926 (Hilton Wilkes House)

35 Crescent Road

48 Crescent Road

49 Cluny Avenue

52 Cluny Avenue

2 McKenzie Avenue

49 Chestnut Park

77 Chestnut Park

39 Chestnut Park

4 Hawthorn Gardens

11 Highand Avenue

HERITAGE TORONTO'S
Inventory of Heritage Properties

The following is an alphabetical listing of the Rosedale houses designated by Heritage Toronto as architecturally and/or historically important.

Ancroft Place, 4-11	Row housing 1927, Shepard & Calvin
Ancroft Place, 12-18	Row housing 1927, Shepard & Calvin
Avondale Road, 19	John M. Lyle House 1908, John M. Lyle
Avondale Road, 23	"Rose Cottage"
Beaumont Road, 1	Rosedale Golf & Country Club
Beaumont Road, 2	George L. Robinson House 1906–07, John M. Lyle
Beaumont Road, 3	House c.1932, Hugh Allward
Beaumont Road, 4	House 1898, Darling & Pearson
Bin-Scarth Road, 61	House 1931, Mathers & Haldenby
Castle Frank Road, 8	Gerald Larkin House 1926, George, Moorhouse & King
Chestnut Park	Street lamps, brick sidewalks c.1905, conceived by S.H. Townsend
Chestnut Park, 1	James Ryrie House 1915, Burke, Horwood & White
Chestnut Park, 15	House 1911, Langley & Howland
Chestnut Park, 20	House 1905–06, A.E. Boultbee
Chestnut Park, 22	House 1904, A.E. Boultbee
Chestnut Park, 24	House 1905, S.H. Townsend
Chestnut Park, 45 ABC	House 1915, Curry & Sparling
Chestnut Park, 49	House 1905, S.H. Townsend
Chestnut Park, 82	House c.1905
Cluny Drive, 2	House c.1923, Eden Smith
Cluny Drive, 49	John Northway House c.1902
Cluny Drive, 52	John J. Dixon House 1904, S.H. Townsend
Crescent Road, 35	Boultbee House 1895, S.H. Townsend
Crescent Road, 48	House 1901, S.H. Townsend
Crescent Road, 75	Castlemere Apartments 1912, H. Simpson
Crescent Road, 84	House 1899, Langley & Langley
Crescent Road, 88	House 1884
Crescent Road, 146	Baillie House 1902, Sproatt & Rolph
Crescent Road, 166	Fisher House 1900, Burke & Horwood

Dale Avenue, 2	House c.1887
Dale Avenue, 12	House 1889
Dale Avenue, 15	Former gate lodge of "The Dale" c.1875-80
Drumsnab Road, 5	"Drumsnab," William Cayley 1830 Addition William Thomas 1856, addition Eden Smith 1908
Dunbar Road, 36	House 1899, W.A. Langton
Elm Avenue, 2	"Glen Hurst" 1866, addition Smith & Gemmell 1880
Elm Avenue, 10	John Blaikie House and fence 1879
Elm Avenue, 14	House and fence c.1895, part of 10 Elm Avenue
Elm Avenue, 16	House and fence 1898, C.J. Gibson, part of 10 Elm Avenue
Elm Avenue, 18	House and fence 1898, C.J. Gibson
Elm Avenue, 20	House 1898, F.H. Herbert
Elm Avenue, 24	House 1910, J.F. Brown
Elm Avenue, 26	House 1914, J.P. Hynes
Elm Avenue, 44-46	Semi-detached house c.1875
Elm Avenue, 49	House 1901, Gordon & Helliwell
Elm Avenue, 50	House c.1887
Elm Avenue, 51	House 1888, J.A. Radford
Elm Avenue, 53-55	Semi-detached house c.1888, J. Bedford builder
Elm Avenue, 61	House 1890, J. Bedford builder
Elm Avenue, 89	C.R. Rundle House 1903, addition 1916 E.J. Lennox
Elm Avenue, 93	House 1900, J.W. Siddall, porte-cochère by G.M. Miller from house on Sherbourne Street
Glen Road, 6-8	Semi-detached house 1883, A. Coleman builder
Glen Road, 9	House 1888, Eden Smith
Glen Road, 10-12	Semi-detached house 1888, A. Coleman builder
Glen Road, 14-16	Semi-detached house 1888
Glen Road, 55	House 1902, Chadwick & Beckett
Glen Road, 64	House 1894, G.M. Miller
Glen Road, 65	House 1891
Glen Road, 66	House 1894, G.M. Miller
Glen Road, 87-89	Semi-detached house 1901

Glen Road, 92-94	Semi-detached house 1900, C.J. Gibson
Glen Road, 97	House 1910–11, Curry & Sparlin
Glen Road	Rosedale Viaduct between 105 Glen Road and Beaumont Road
Glen Road, 109	Rosedale Golf & Country Club
Glen Road, 134	House 1910–11, Curry & Sparling
Glen Road, 136	C.L. Burton House c.1928, Douglas Kertland
Glen Road, 154	House 1913–14, Chadwick & Beckett
Hawthorn Avenue, 1	House 1892–93
Hawthorn Avenue, 3	House 1892–93
Hawthorn Avenue, 5	House 1892–93
Hawthorn Gardens, 2	N. Seagram House 1929–30, Vaux & Bryan Chadwick
Hawthorn Gardens, 4	House c.1910, S.H. Townsend
Highland Avenue, 11	Wilkes House 1926, Hilton Wilkes & Mackenzie Waters
Lamport Avenue, 11	G.M. Miller House c.1905, G.M. Miller
Maple Avenue, 36	House 1895–96, Langley & Burke
Maple Avenue, 40	H.H. Fudger House 1897, E. Burke
May Street, 8	House c.1930, George, Moorehouse & King
McKenzie Avenue, 20	House 1908, Eden Smith
McKenzie Avenue, 49	House 1896, C.J. Gibson
Meredith Crescent, 3	William Davies House 1876, Langley, Langley & Burke, later William Perkins Bull House
Nanton Avenue, 28	House 1894
Nanton Avenue, 30	House 1894
Nanton Avenue, 32	House 1894
Nanton Avenue, 34	House 1894
Park Road, 29	House c.1900
Park Road, 104	House 1887–88
Park Road, 108	House 1888–89
Park Road, 110	House 1887–88
Park Road, 114	Shaw House 1886
Park Road, 115	Sir Ernest MacMillan House 1931, Page & Steele
Park Road, 124	House c.1865

Pine Hill Road, 6	House 1892, D. Richards
Pine Hill Road, 10	House 1892
Pine Hill Road, 12	House 1892
Pine Hill Road, 14	House 1892
Rosedale Road, 3	House 1904
Rosedale Road, 7	Dorothy Stevens House 1930, Hugh L. Allward
Rosedale Road, 19	House 1913, John M. Lyle
Rosedale Road, 34	House 1921, Page & Warrington
Rosedale Road, 39	House 1891–92
Rosedale Road, 41-43	Semi-detached house 1883
Rosedale Road, 45	House 1889
Rosedale Road, 47	House c.1889
Roxborough Drive, 93	A.H. Chapman House 1927, A.H. Chapman
Roxborough St. E., 19-21	Semi-detached house c.1896
Roxborough St. E., 37-39	Semi-detached house c.1896
Roxborough St. E., 141-147	Row housing c.1889–90
Roxborough St. E., 143	Row housing c.1889–90
Roxborough St. E., 145	Row housing c.1889–90
Roxborough St. E., 170	House c.1889
Roxborough St. E., 171	Siddall House, c.1912, J.W. Siddall
Roxborough St. E., 172	House c.1889
Roxborough St. E., 174	House c.1890
Roxborough St. E., 176	G.A. Elliott House c.1889, G.A. Elliott builder
Sherbourne St. N., 1	Housing complex at 18 Ancroft Place
Sherbourne St. N., 9	House c.1898
Sherbourne St. N., 27	E. D. Gooderham House 1907, Sproatt & Rolph
Sherbourne St. N., 35	House
South Drive, 82	House 1888, demolished
South Drive, 86	House 1888
South Drive, 88	House 1896
South Drive, 103	House 1896
South Drive, 116	House 1905–06, Burke & Horwood
South Drive, 160	Former gate house to "Craigleigh" 1903, Darling & Pearson

ROSEDALE TODAY

T he wild roses that once blanketed the slopes of the Rosedale ravine may be gone. The original forests of maple, ash, oak, beech and basswood have been cleared and new trees have been planted in their place. The Severn Creek that flowed into Bloor's millpond is a distant memory. The rickety wooden bridges that spanned the streams have been replaced by concrete and steel structures. But the spirit of Rosedale endures, the character of this charming suburb defined by the long and interesting history of the houses and by the succession of families that have inhabited them.

This sense of history pervades the winding streets that still meander their way through Rosedale's 450 acres. A leisurely stroll through the ravines that carve the neighbourhood into distinctive sections evokes visions of what the area was like 150 years ago. One can imagine William Botsford Jarvis pushing his wagon out of the mud on the Park Road hill, or Maunsell Jackson running his coach and four through Edgar Jarvis's toll-gate on the White Bridge.

On casual observation, the houses appear remarkably unchanged by the passing years. But the roads are now paved and bordered by concrete sidewalks. Street lights provide illumination for late-night dog walkers and joggers. Cars have replaced carriages in the old coach houses. The old homes boast not only hot and cold running water, but whirlpool baths, spas, saunas, hot tubs, and the occasional fountain and swimming pool. State-of-the-art kitchens feature microwave and convection ovens, dishwashers, garbage compactors, indoor barbecues and grills, wine fridges and the like. Double-glazed windows, custom designed to replicate the originals, and high-efficiency furnaces keep inhabitants toasty warm in the winter months; air conditioning keeps residents cool in summer. Fireplaces more often than not burn fake logs. Driveways are heated to melt snow. Garbage is picked up weekly, mail is delivered daily, and courier services provide next-day delivery around the world. Intercoms have replaced the maid's bell, and security systems protect homes from break-ins. Butlers are no longer required, and the services formerly the role of the household "maid" are now provided by

Rosedale Manors, a new enclave of fine homes north of Pricefield Road.
Photograph by
Roger Crawford

*Street scene,
Rosedale today.*
Photograph by
Mario Angastiniotis

cleaning ladies, housekeepers and live-in nannies. The Rosedale and Sherbourne Street buses ferry passengers regularly to the Rosedale, Sherbourne and Castle Frank subway stations. Telephones, cable TV, satellite dishes, and computers hooked up to fax and internet service are now standard amenities.

Surprisingly enough, relatively few of the original homes have been demolished over the past 150 years. Chief Justice Draper's rural cottage, "Hazeldean," was torn down in 1890 for construction of houses on Collier Street. "Rosedale House" met with the wrecker's ball in 1905, "Chestnut Park" in 1906, "Sylvan Towers" and "Norcastle" in 1933, and "Guiseley House" around 1951. "The Dale" and "Craigleigh" are also gone. The houses closest to Yonge Street on Crescent Road, Roxborough Street East and Rowanwood were lost when the Yonge subway line went through. Several others were demolished to make room for low-rise apartment buildings in the 1950s and 1960s. But while these losses are lamented, it is remarkable that such a large number of homes have survived over so many years.

The years immediately following World War II saw a mass exodus of families from downtown residential areas into the suburbs. The dramatic increase in the Toronto population from 1946 through the mid-1960s, a result of a significant influx of immigrants and a spate of Baby Boom births, spurred construction of hundreds of thousands of new homes in the areas immediately surrounding Toronto. These new homes had all the modern conveniences of the period and were placed on large lots. Suburban neighbourhoods, which tried to create the ambience of small country towns, bragged of semi-rural settings far removed from the hustle and bustle, the traffic and crime of the city core. New schools, shopping malls, skating rinks, parks, baseball diamonds and municipal swimming pools were attractive extras to lure young families away from downtown.

The result was that Rosedale underwent a general process of decline during this period. Large old homes, many not updated since they were built, became increasingly difficult and expensive to maintain. The grounds of the largest estates were often hard to keep up, the wiring and plumbing outdated; kitchens lacked the conveniences of the new era, and bathrooms were insufficient according to today's standards for large families with numerous young children. Home renovations were far from common in the 1950s and 1960s. Consequently, more than a few Rosedale homes were converted into rooming houses or torn down to make way for the low-rise apartment buildings then sprouting up throughout the neighbourhood.

Although the majority of homes in Rosedale are single detached dwellings, there are a small number of semi-detached houses and apartment buildings. The first apartment building made its appearance in Rosedale in 1912. Located at 75 Crescent Road, "Castlemere" was designed by architect Henry Simpson. These were not the apartment units typical of today.

The building itself is only three storeys high, with enormous pillars framing the front entrance. Balconies, detailed with curlicue wrought-iron trim, adorn the front facade. There are only three apartments per floor. They are spacious, boasting hardwood floors, high ceilings, living room fireplaces, and French doors. The units were extensively renovated in the 1980s and converted into condominiums. They have current assessed values ranging from $115,000 for basement units to $262,000 for above-grade units, and in 1999 were selling, on average, in the neighbourhood of $250,000.

It was some 30 years before additional multi-unit buildings were constructed. Many of the low-rise apartment buildings of 1950s and 1960s vintage are now condominiums. They are scattered throughout the area and include 1A Dale Avenue, 21 Dale Avenue, 120 Rosedale Valley Road, 16 Rosedale Road, 5 Elm Avenue, 30 Elm Avenue, 83 Elm Avenue, 149 South Drive, 94 Crescent Road, 158 Crescent Road, 66 Roxborough Street East, 40 Glen Road, 45 Glen Road, 10 Lamport Avenue, 40 Maple Avenue, 36 Castle Frank, 40 Park Road, and 7 Thornwood Road.

The latest offerings on the apartment scene include Thornwood, (Scrivener Square) Incorporated and 2 Roxborough Street East. Both were still under construction in 1999. The former is marketed as "Rosedale's last great address." It is located just south of the Canadian Pacific Railway tracks and east of the LCBO store. Garden suites have asking prices of $150,000 to $500,000; Park suites ask $400,000 to $1,500,000. Number 2 Roxborough East, by the Diamante Development Corporation, is scheduled for completion in the summer of 2000. Price tags (1999) ranged from $293,900 for an 866-square-foot suite with one bedroom and den, to $925,000 for a 2,500-square-foot apartment with two bedrooms, a den, a family room and three baths.

Townhouses are also interspersed throughout Rosedale. The first were built at numbers 2 through 18 Ancroft Place in 1927, designed by the architectural firm of Shepard and Calvin. They are of the English Cottage Movement style. The units are two storeys in height, with hardwood floors, separate living and dining rooms, and fireplaces in the living room and master bedroom. They contain three bedrooms; the master with ensuite bath. All are set on a particularly idyllic spot overlooking the ravine at Sherbourne

Castlemere Apartments, 75 Crescent Road.
Photograph by Roger Crawford

66 Roxborough Street East apartment.
Photograph by Roger Crawford

88 Crescent Road
Photograph by
Roger Crawford

Street just north of Bloor Street East and what was once the White Bridge. Ivy climbs the exterior red brick walls, and tall trees grace the wide lawns. It seems impossible that this English countryside setting could possibly be so close to a Toronto subway station at Sherbourne and Bloor Streets or within easy walking distance of the Hudson's Bay Centre at Bloor and Yonge Streets. Even James Ryrie's grand home at 1 Chestnut Park Road, designed by Burke, Horwood and White and built in 1915, has been turned into four fabulous apartments, with price tags of a million dollars or more.

Another rambling old estate, at 88 Crescent Road, was developed into exclusive townhouse-type units in the late 1980s. Also, the charming vintage apartment building at 46 South Drive was redeveloped in 1996 by award-winning Fairmount Properties. The handsome exterior brick shell of the building was retained and the interior redesigned into three Georgian-style attached homes, with 12-foot ceilings on the main floor and all the latest accoutrements, including requisite marble baths, gourmet kitchen, finished basement and underground parking, all set on a private cobbled road christened Corrigan Close. Two sizable single detached houses were built on the property as well. They are of the same architectural style as the original apartment building. The development is an excellent example of architectural designs that truly fit into the community. The passerby would be hard pressed to guess which is the original building and which are the recently constructed ones, the finishes are so authentic.

Rosedale apartments and townhouse-style units vary in size and price, ranging from as little as $125,000 to a million dollars and up, depending on location, square-footage, number of bathrooms, modernity of kitchen and the extent and quality of architectural finishes and flourishes.

The actual number of households in Rosedale today is estimated at about 2,500. This includes families living in single detached dwellings, semi-detached homes, and multiple dwellings such as duplexes, triplexes and apartment units (both rented and owned). An exact count is impossible because so many of the large houses have apartments, rooms or coach houses that can be rented out. Sometimes these units are tenanted, sometimes not.

Information regarding the Current Value Assessment (CVA) of Rosedale properties is summarized in this section. These are the property values determined by the City of Toronto for calculating property taxes. The assessed values were based on market values at June 1996. In many cases these values do not take into consideration peculiarities of the individual properties. Often, assessments on a particular street were based on the value of a single house that sold in the spring of 1996, whether in fact that house was truly comparable to the rest of the homes on the street. Actually, many of the CVAs do not reflect the current value of a particular property any more accurately than they did in June 1996.

For analytical purposes, not all properties were included. City of Toronto properties, including schools, churches, and commercial buildings (apartments and others) were excluded, while condominium apartments were included. Assessment data for 1,663 properties in Rosedale were analyzed. For each street, the average assessed value was calculated and the lowest and highest individual property value was recorded. These average street values were then sorted in descending order.

The surprisingly wide spread between the low and the high values tells us a considerable amount about the nature of the Rosdale neighbourhood.

On any one street, we find small houses side by side with extremely large ones, detached, semi-detached, apartments, and rooming houses. We find houses built in 1855 co-existing with houses built in 1998. We find houses relatively untouched by time and houses that have been totally renovated. These are the very things that make Rosedale so unique, eclectic and interesting. This

Corrigan Close
Photograph by
Mario Angastiniotis

variety is not the exception, it is the rule. As is seen on the accompanying table, there are few streets that do not have this large spread between low and high values. Even the lengths of the streets vary dramatically throughout Rosedale. There are only four homes on Old George Place and Rachael Street, while there are 174 homes on Glen Road, the longest street.

The average assessed value for the entire Rosedale area in 1999 was $764,426 (the aggregate assessed value of all the dwellings, $1,271,240,852, divided by 1,663, the total number of dwellings). The highest assessed value was $5,253,000 on Bin-Scarth Road, the lowest was $105,000 for an apartment unit on Crescent Road.[1]

There were 255 homes assessed at between $1 million and $2 million, 26 homes assessed at between $2 million and $3 million, 10 homes assessed at between $3 million and $4 million, 1 home assessed at between $4 million and $5 million, and 1 home assessed at over $5 million.

The actual cost of purchasing a home in Rosedale varies quite markedly from the assessed values. According to Toronto Real Estate Board statistics,[2] 109 properties were sold in Rosedale in 1998, for a gross total value of $86,842,200. The average sale price was $796,717. Of this total, 83 of the sales were houses, 26 were apartment units. The average sale price of a single family dwelling was $989,015, while that of apartment units was $182,846.

During the first nine months of 1999, 107 properties were sold in Rosedale: 82 homes and 25 apartment units. The gross value was $99,107,050, the average sale price for houses was $1,147,107 and that of apartments was $201,768. The lowest priced house in 1999 was $270,000, the highest was $3,925,000. The lowest priced apartment sold for $124,900, the highest for $400,000.

METROPOLITAN
TORONTO
PROPERTY
ASSESSMENT
VALUES,
1999

Street Name	Average CVA $	Number of Houses	Aggregate CVA $	Low CVA $	High CVA $
Beaumont Road	2,091,917	12	25,103,004	551,000	3,304,000
Highland Gardens	1,627,400	7	8,137,000	724,000	2,663,000
Drumsnab Road	1,345,250	8	10,762,000	789,000	2,892,000
Highland Avenue	1,272,731	52	66,182,012	440,000	3,659,000
Old George Place	1,163,250	4	4,653,000	796,000	1,585,000
Avondale Road	1,152,857	7	8,069,999	753,000	2,184,000
Cluny Avenue	1,111,333	6	6,667,998	741,000	1,535,000
Chestnut Park Road	1,046,214	42	43,940,988	531,000	1,660,000
Park Road	1,023,667	12	12,284,004	508,000	2,422,000
Roxborough Drive	1,019,907	86	87,712,002	366,000	3,671,000
Pine Hill Road	1,017,750	8	8,142,000	546,000	1,437,000
Bin-Scarth Road	1,000,969	64	64,062,016	416,000	5,253,000
Whitney Avenue	978,455	33	32,289,015	556,000	1,935,000
May Street	967,941	17	16,454,997	591,000	4,344,000
Lamport Avenue	935,750	8	7,486,000	614,000	1,374,000
South Drive	899,536	56	50,374,016	467,000	2,346,000
Edgar Avenue	876,708	24	21,040,992	620,000	1,701,000
Castle Frank Road	860,656	64	55,081,984	390,000	3,776,000
Scarth Road	848,538	13	11,030,994	503,000	1,283,000
Scholfield Avenue	803,333	9	7,229,997	511,000	1,159,000
McKenzie Avenue	795,000	21	16,695,000	516,000	1,782,000
Elm Avenue	773,089	56	43,292,984	370,000	1,710,000
Rosedale Road	760,138	29	22,044,002	450,000	2,411,000
Sherbourne Street North	757,125	16	12,114,000	307,000	1,154,000
Douglas Drive	750,412	131	98,303,972	316,000	2,244,000
Maple Avenue	736,353	51	37,554,003	400,000	1,352,000
Crescent Road	718,239	92	66,077,988	105,000	1,558,000
Rachael Street	717,500	4	2,870,000	562,000	977,000
Meredith Crescent	711,364	11	7,825,004	525,000	1,021,000
Roxborough Street East	654,111	72	47,095,992	150,000	1,321,000
Rowanwood Avenue	650,000	35	22,750,000	380,000	1,173,000
Glen Road	640,224	174	111,398,976	194,000	2,784,000
Dunbar Road	626,900	30	8,807,000	395,000	1,019,000
Nanton Avenue	582,263	38	22,125,994	313,000	1,158,000
St. Andrews Gardens	577,627	51	29,458,977	467,000	831,000
Whitehall Road	557,847	59	32,912,973	396,000	809,000
MacLennan Avenue	541,353	17	9,203,001	449,000	857,000
Pricefield Road	506,182	33	16,704,006	372,000	793,000
Astley Avenue	474,061	49	23,228,989	235,000	1,521,000
Edgewood Crescent	408,333	27	11,024,991	277,000	566,000
Standish Avenue	363,958	48	17,469,984	251,000	549,000
Jean Street	338,583	12	4,062,996	266,000	434,000
Ancroft Place	329,765	17	5,606,005	289,000	659,000
TOTAL ROSEDALE	764,426	1,663	1,271,240,852	105,000	5,253,000

Data Source: City of Toronto Assessment Rolls and the Toronto Real Estate Board

The 1970s saw the beginnings of the rebirth of Rosedale, a rejuvenation that has continued to gain momentum during the 1980s and 1990s. An unwritten law seems to have emerged over the last 20 years that favours renovation and restoration rather than demolition and reconstruction. Rosedale residents are proud of the long history of their charming suburb and want to preserve the homes that give the neighbourhood its character. Consequently, renovation money is now flooding into Rosedale. So many of the old dowagers have received facelifts that there are few "original" houses left to redo.

Some of the more extravagant renovations in Rosedale during 1999 included those at 3 Meredith Crescent, 48 South Drive, 40 Cluny Avenue, 61 Crescent Road, and 65 Crescent Road.

The full-scale restoration of "Lorne Hall," the William Davies home at 3 Meredith Crescent, continued through 1998 and 1999. The grand Second Empire house had been converted into apartments in the 1950s, and with almost 50 years of neglect, gradually descended into a state of disrepair. The present owners purchased the house in 1994 and began the painstaking job of returning the property to its former elegance.

48 South Drive
Photograph by
Mario Angastiniotis

Another historic jewel, hiding at 48 South Drive, is also being resurrected. The former home of dentist J.B. How, built circa 1876, was concealed beneath layers of white paint. This has now been removed, revealing the beautiful details of the original brickwork. The home had last been renovated in the 1950s. At that time, a central front watch tower was removed, along with an old verandah at the side of the house. The architects responsible for the current round of renovations are taking special care to make their changes more authentic to the styles of the past century. A new wing has been added; the bricks on the addition match the old house perfectly. New windows replicate the style of those common when the residence was constructed.

The M.c.Osborne house at 40 Cluny Avenue, built around the turn of the century, has been undergoing a substantial makeover for several years now. This grand, architecturally significant residence, set on a ravine lot, is dominated by large commanding entrance pillars and an imposing second-storey verandah. Its design is one of striking originality; unique and totally endearing.

Another handsome Rosedale home, at 61 Crescent Road, vintage 1900, has also recently been revamped. The workmanship is superb. The best features of the original, including the multi-paned arched windows and stone foundation, have been accentuated and a formerly unnoticed basement window exposed. New front steps and landscaping are in perfect proportion and design to complement the front entrance.

Number 65 Crescent Road, next door to the above, has also received major attention from contractors. The interior has been restored, the exterior bricks have been cleaned, new bay windows installed and a fresh coat of grey paint applied to

61 Crescent Road
Photograph by Mario Angastiniotis

40 Cluny Avenue
Photograph by Roger Crawford

complement the slate roof. A new brick porch with wonderful wrought-iron inset now graces the entrance. Landscaping combines stone walks, a driveway and beautiful greenery. As in so many of the other recent renovations, attention has been focused on preserving the original flavour of the home.

The best way to discover the real Rosedale is to walk the streets, look at the beautiful homes, take a picnic and wander the ravines—all the time imagining the early residents and times past.

Patricia McHugh's book *Toronto Architecture: A City Guide,* (McClelland & Stewart) contains a thorough tour of Rosedale, complete with maps so you won't get lost. A general description of the area is included, along with a bit of history, and detailed architectural comments about the houses, including information about the original owners and the architects who designed them. Walk 21, through Southwest Rosedale, takes you through the original Rose-Park suburb and Chestnut Park. It is an area bounded by Rosedale Valley Road on the south, Yonge Street on the west and Chestnut Park Road on the north, and extends as far east as the western end of Maple and Elm Avenues near Sherbourne Street North. Over 50 homes are noted. Walk 22, through Southeast Rosedale, takes you through an area bounded by Mount Pleasant Road on the west, Rosedale Valley Road on the south, Castle Frank on the east, and South Drive on the north. On this excursion, more than 60 homes are listed.

Another stop of interest on a tour of Rosedale is Mooredale House, located at 146 Crescent Road. It is home to the Rosedale-Moore Park Association, a non-profit charitable organization and community centre. Membership is open to children, youths and adults, even those who do not live in the area. Classes and workshops are offered in gourmet cooking, entertaining, wine tasting, fitness, golf, biking, hockey, skating, music, dance, art, football, softball and soccer. There is a concert series, a book club, a sailing club, and a bridge club. Day camps are organized for kids during the summer holidays and March break. Swimming and tennis classes are available, as well as early childhood education for pre-schoolers. Since 1946 Mooredale has been the host of Mayfair, the annual outdoor spring fair held in Rosedale Park.

There are at least eight parks positioned throughout Rosedale. They vary in size and ambience. Severn Creek Park runs along the east side of the Yonge Subway line and is accessible from a footpath located just east of the Rosedale Subway station on Crescent Road. The path exits in the Rosedale ravine near the intersection of Rosedale Valley Road and Park Road. It is a particularly picturesque spot, perfect for dog walking, picnicking or just gazing at the backs of the gracious homes on Cluny Avenue that overlook the valley below.

From here it is just a few steps to the Lawren Harris Park, on the northwest side of Park Road and Rosedale Valley Road, and the Hazeldean Park, on the northeast side of the same intersection. A bike ride east along Rosedale Valley Road is also a lovely excursion, evoking images of the area 150 years ago. This is the former site of Bloor's mill, brewery and millpond.

Craigleigh Gardens, located east of Glen Road and the extension of South Drive and Milkmen's Road, is the old estate grounds of Edmund Osler. This is a beautiful place, enclosed by an elegant gate and a handsome wrought-iron fence. It offers a refreshing vista out over the Don River Valley. Another similar vantage point can be found further north in Chorley Park, east of Douglas Drive in North Rosedale.

Other views of the Rosedale Valley are available by walking south of St. Clair Avenue, along Avoca Avenue and following the path that leads south through the ravine that skirts the west side of Mount Pleasant Road. This is the eastern extremity of David A. Balfour Park. The path ends just north of Roxborough Street East. The trail continues on the other side of Mount Pleasant Road and travels east along the Park Drive Reservation and the old Belt Line Trail. When Rosedale was being developed, Park Drive Reservation was mapped out as a road through this part of the Rosedale ravine, meeting up with the route of the Belt Line Railway, which ran along the Don River Valley (Bayview Avenue.) It never became a well-used thoroughfare.

Mooredale, 146 Crescent Road
Photograph by Roger Crawford

128 Park Road
Photograph by Bess Crawford

Gates to Craigleigh Gardens.
Photograph by Roger Crawford

Last but not least is Rosedale Park at the northwest corner of Highland and Scholfield Avenues. This is the home of Mayfair, Mooredale's spring fair. The park is a wonderful place for small children to play. There is an outdoor skating rink in the winter and many baseball games are played on its field in the summer. At the turn of the century, the Lacrosse Grounds of St. Andrews College were located near here. Further north and to the east were the Rosedale Golf Links. The original clubhouse still stands on the corner of Beaumont and Glen Roads.

The Metropolitan Toronto Reference Library is a gold mine of information about Toronto in the last century. Many individuals have donated photographs, letters and other family records to the library. Thanks is due to all the authors who took the time to record details about this city in its early days: descriptions of the land itself, the people, the houses, the political, social and economic scenes. Without their input, this book could not have been written.

Every reasonable care has been taken to trace ownership of copyrighted material. I welcome any information that will enable me to correct in subsequent editions any erroneous credit. Acknowledgment is made to the following sources used for this book.

TITLE PAGE
1 Peter C. Newman, *The Canadian Establishment*, p. 82

THE STORY OF ROSEDALE
1 John Ross Robertson, *Landmarks of Toronto*, p. 559
2 E.C. Kyte, *Old Toronto*, p. 153
3 William Dendy and William Kilbourn, *Toronto Observed*, p. 31
4 E.C. Kyte, *Old Toronto*, p. 155

EARLY BEGINNINGS
1 Peter G. Goheen, *Victorian Toronto*, p. 92
2 D. Masters, *The Rise of Toronto*, p. 165
3 Peter G. Goheen, *Victorian Toronto*, p. 73
4 *The Daily Leader*, October 20, 1854

CHRONOLOGY OF DEVELOPMENT 1854-1890
  R. L. Polk & Company, *Toronto Directory 1890*
1 C. Pelham Mulvany, *Toronto: Past and Present. A Handbook of the City*, p. 261
2 Michael Kluckner, *Toronto The Way it Was* p. 245

ROSEDALE AND THE JARVIS FAMILY
William Botsford Jarvis
1 Alden Griffin Meredith, *Mary's Rosedale and Gossip of Little York*, p. 60
2 *Ibid.*, p. 75
3 *Ibid.*, p. 92, 93
4 *Ibid.*, p. 113
5 *Ibid.*, p. 158
6 *Ibid.*, p. 156
7 *Ibid.*, p. 157
8 *Ibid.*, p. 190
9 *Ibid.*, p. 196
10 *Ibid.*, p. 207

11 *Ibid.*, p. 220, 221
12 *Ibid.*, p. 221
13 *Ibid.*, p. 225
14 *Ibid.*, p. 229, 230
15 *Ibid.*, p. 232–234
16 *Ibid.*, p. 234
17 *Ibid.*, p. 238
18 Lucy Booth Martyn, Toronto: *100 Years of Grandeur*, p. 74, 75

Samuel Peters Jarvis
1 W. Stewart Wallace, *Dictionary of Canadian Biography* Volume VIII, p. 431
2 *Ibid.*, p. 432
3 *Ibid.*
4 *Ibid.*

Edgar John Jarvis
1 Lucy Booth Martyn, *Toronto: 100 Years of Grandeur*, p. 162
2 *Ibid.*, p. 166
3 *Ibid.*, p. 168
4 Patricia McHugh, *Toronto Architecture: A City Guide*, Second Edition, p. 246

SETTING THE SCENE
  J. E. Middleton, *Toronto's 100 Years, 1834-1934*

A BIRD'S-EYE VIEW OF ROSEDALE BY STREET, 1890
  R. L. Polk & Company, *Toronto Directory 1890*

A WHO'S WHO OF ROSEDALE'S FIRST CENTURY
  R. L. Polk & Company, *Toronto Directories 1848* through *1890*
1 Henry Scadding, *Toronto of Old*

STREET NAMES: THEIR ORIGIN AND EVOLUTION

Information for the evolution of street names was obtained primarily from maps dated 1854, 1877, 1884, 1890, 1905 and 1910. In some cases this differs from material contained in Polk's *Toronto Directories*.

Henry Scadding, *Toronto of Old*, p. 302

John Ross Robertson, *Landmarks of Toronto*, p. 517 through 528

Eric Arthur, *Toronto, No Mean City*, Appendix C, p. 274 through 293

THE FIRST ROSEDALE LANDOWNERS

R. L. Polk & Company, *Toronto Directories 1848* through *1890*

1 Peter Goheen, *Victorian Toronto, 1850 to 1900: Patterns and Process of Growth*, p. 72

ARCHITECTURE OF ROSEDALE HOMES

1 Virginia & Lee McAlester, *A Field Guide to American Houses*, p. 212

2 *Ibid.*, p. 242

3 *Ibid.*, p. 268

4 *Ibid.*, p. 263

5 *Ibid.*, p. 301

6 *Ibid.*

7 *Ibid.*, p. 321

ROSEDALE HOUSE 1824

1 Alden Griffin Meredith, *Mary's Rosedale and Gossip of Little York*, p. 60

2 *The Globe*, October 3, 1854

DRUMSNAB 1834

1 Henry Scadding, *Toronto of Old*, p. 175

2 W. Dendy and W. Kilbourn, *Toronto Observed*, p. 31

3 Lucy Booth Martyn, *Toronto: 100 Years of Grandeur*, p. 168

CHESTNUT PARK 1850-55

1 S. Hutcheson, *Yorkville in Pictures*

2 W. Stewart Wallace, *The Dictionary of Canadian Biography*, p. 682–689

3 S. Hutcheson, *Yorkville in Pictures*

CAVERHILL 1855

1 Donald Jones, *Fifty Tales of Toronto*, p. 45

THE DALE 1862

1 G. Mercer Adam, *Toronto Old & New*, p. 92

LORNE HALL 1876

1 Lucy Booth Martyn, *Aristocratic Toronto*, p. 164

2 Davies, William, *Letters of William Davies, Toronto 1854-1861*

BUILDERS, TRADES AND MATERIALS

1 T. Eaton Company, *Golden Jubilee 1869-1919*, p. 22

2 J.E. Middleton, *Toronto's 100 Years, 1834-1934*, p. 137, 138

3 *Ibid.*, p. 137, 138

4 T. Eaton Company, *Golden Jubilee 1869-1919*, p. 22

5 *Ibid.*, p. 22

6 C. Pelham Mulvany, *Toronto: Past and Present. A Handbook of the City*,
William Dendy and William Kilbourn, *Toronto Observed*, T. Eaton Company, *Golden Jubilee 1869-1919*;
J. E. Middleton, *Toronto's 100 Years, 1834-1934*, Martha Shepard, *The First Things of Toronto*

7 C. Pelham Mulvany, *Toronto: Past and Present. A Handbook of the City*,
William Dendy and William Kilbourn, *Toronto Observed*,
T. Eaton Company, *Golden Jubilee 1869-1919*,
J.E. Middleton, *Toronto's 100 Years, 1834-1934*, Martha Shepard, *The First Things of Toronto*

8 C. Pelham Mulvany, *Toronto: Past and Present. A Handbook of the City*,
William Dendy and William Kilbourn, *Toronto Observed*,
T. Eaton Company, *Golden Jubilee 1869-1919*,
J.E. Middleton, *Toronto's 100 Years, 1834-1934*,
Martha Shepard, *The First Things of Toronto*

ROSEDALE ARCHITECTS

Rosedale Architects and the Homes They Designed

1 Biographical material for the Rosedale architects was taken extensively from:

Eric Arthur, *Toronto, No Mean City*, Third Edition;

Patricia McHugh, *Toronto Architecture: A City Guide*, Second Edition;

William Dendy and William Kilbourn, *Toronto Observed*;

W. Stewart Wallace, *Dictionary of Canadian Biography*.

The list of houses and dates of construction attributed to specific architects was gathered from the above sources as well as from Heritage Toronto, *The City of Toronto's Inventory of Heritage Properties*

2 Another source suggests that 171 Roxborough Street East was built in 1912

HERITAGE TORONTO'S INVENTORY OF HERITAGE PROPERTIES

Heritage Toronto, *The City of Toronto's Inventory of Heritage Properties*

ROSEDALE TODAY

1 City of Toronto Assessment Rolls

2 Toronto Real Estate Board

The story of Rosedale could not have been adequately written without the many illustrations. Reference is given to the page number where the illustration appears in this book. Additional information that would further identify any references in future editions is welcomed.

Metropolitan Toronto Reference Library, Picture Collection: Dedication 5, 12, 15, 16, 17, 18 (all), 19, 21 (right), 22, 24, 31, 36, 41, 43, 45, 48, 50, 52, 53, 60, 62, 69, 71, 78, 88, 89, 97, 106, 107, 108, 114, 115, 120, 126, 144

Alden Griffin Meredith, *Mary's Rosedale and Gossip of Little York* (1928) and Metropolitan Toronto Reference Library, Picture Collection: 3, 39, 40, 42, 47, 102

Charles E. Goad, *The Mapping of Victorian Toronto, Atlas of the City of Toronto (1910)* and Metropolitan Toronto Reference Library, Picture Collection: 32

John Ross Robertson, *Landmarks of Toronto 1894 (1894-1914)* and Metropolitan Toronto Reference Library, Picture Collection: 13, 20, 21 (left), 55

Royal Ontario Museum and Metropolitan Toronto Reference Library, Picture Collection: 18(upper left), 40 (left and right)

T. Eaton Company Limited, *Golden Jubilee 1869-1919 (1919)* and Metropolitan Toronto Reference Library, Picture Collection: 64 (left, middle, right), 140

Salmon Collection and Metropolitan Toronto Reference Library, Picture Collection: 125

G. Mercer Adam, *Toronto Old & New (1891)* and Metropolitan Toronto Reference Library, Picture Collection: 80 (upper left, lower left, lower right), 145 (left, middle, right)

Lucy Booth Martyn, *Toronto: 100 Years of Grandeur* (1978) and Metropolitan Toronto Reference Library, Picture Collection: 58

Ontario Genealogical Society, Toronto Branch, *Toronto Illustrated 1893* (1993): 80 (upper right), 85 (left, middle, right), 136, 137, 138 (all), 139, 140, 141 (all), 142 (all

North Rosedale Ratepayers Association, Mrs. W.G. Fraser Grant and Metropolitan Toronto Reference Library, Picture Collection: 126

Toronto Department of Public Works and Metropolitan Toronto Reference Library, Picture Collection: 90

City of Toronto Archives: 127: SC 244-7326, 128: SC 231-230

Walter J. Coucill, 1970, and Metropolitan Toronto Reference Library, Picture Collection: 104

Map Art, *Downtown Toronto Explorer* and Metropolitan Toronto Reference Library, Picture Collection: 23

Mario Angastiniotis: 8, 49, 61, 92, 105, 112, 113, 116, 121, 122, 146 to 156 inclusive, 160, 163, 165, 166 (top), 167 (top),

Bess Crawford: 110, 111, 119, 129

Roger Crawford: 63 (all), 159, 161 (all), 162, 166 (bottom), 167 (bottom), 168

The Globe and Metropolitan Toronto Reference Library, Picture Collection: 133

The Leader and Metropolitan Toronto Reference Library, Picture Collection: 51 (left), 82 (top), 94

The Mail and Metropolitan Toronto Reference Library, Picture Collection: 81, 135

Toronto Mail and Metropolitan Toronto Reference Library, Picture Collection: 81, 82 (bottom)

The Daily Leader and Metropolitan Toronto Reference Library, Picture Collection: 30

BIBLIOGRAPHY

Adam, G. Mercer. *Toronto Old & New* (Toronto: The Mail Printing Company, 1891)

Arthur, Eric. *Toronto, No Mean City* Third Edition (Toronto: University of Toronto Press, 1986)

Chadwick, Edward M. *Ontarian Families 1894-98*, 2 Vols. (Toronto: Rolph & Co. 1894–1898)

Consolidated Illustrating Co. *Toronto Illustrated 1893* (Ontario Genealogical Society, Toronto Branch, 1992)

Cruxton, J. Bradley and Wilson, W. Douglas. *Flashback Canada* (Toronto: Oxford University Press, 1978)

Davies, William. *Letters of William Davies, Toronto 1854-1861* (Toronto: University of Toronto Press, 1945)

Dendy, William and Kilbourn, William. *Toronto Observed* (Toronto: Oxford University Press, 1986)

Duff, J. Clarence. *Pen Sketches of Historic Toronto* (Toronto: J. Clarence Duff, 1967)

Englehardt, George W. *Toronto Board of Trade* (Toronto: George W. Englehardt, 1898)

Firth, Edith E. *Toronto in Art, 150 Years Through Artists' Eyes* (Markham: Fitzhenry & Whiteside in cooperation with The City of Toronto, 1983)

Goad, Charles E. *The Mapping of Victorian Toronto* (Toronto: Paget Press, 1984)

Goheen, Peter G. *Victorian Toronto, 1850 to 1900: Patterns and Process of Growth* (Chicago: University of Chicago Dept. of Geography, 1970)

Guillet, Edwin C. *Toronto Illustrated, From Trading Post to Great City* (Toronto: The Ontario Publishing Co., 1939)

Hacker, A. E., Wemp, B. S., Stewart, E. P. *Toronto Diamond Jubilee (1867-1927)* (Toronto: The Stewart Printing Service, 1927)

Heritage Toronto. *The City of Toronto's Inventory of Heritage Properties* (Toronto: Heritage Toronto, 1984)

Hutcheson, Stephanie. *Yorkville: in Pictures 1853-1883* (Toronto: Public Library Board, 1978)

Jones, Donald. *Fifty Tales of Toronto* (Toronto: University of Toronto Press, 1992)

Kluckner, Michael. *Toronto The Way It Was* (Toronto: Whitecap Books, 1988)

Kyte, E.C. *Old Toronto; A selection of excerpts from Landmarks of Toronto by John Ross Robertson* (Toronto: Macmillan, 1954)

Martyn, Lucy Booth. *Aristocratic Toronto: 19th Century Grandeur* (Toronto: Gage, 1980)

Martyn, Lucy Booth. *Toronto: 100 Years of Grandeur* (Toronto: Pagurian Press, 1978)

Masters, D. *The Rise of Toronto 1850-1890* (Toronto: University of Toronto Press, 1947)

McAlester, Virginia & Lee. *A Field Guide to American Houses* (New York: Alfred A. Knopf, 1997)

McHugh, Patricia. *Toronto Architecture: A City Guide*, Second Edition (Toronto: McCelland & Stewart, 1989)

Meredith, Alden Griffin. *Mary's Rosedale and Gossip of Little York* (Ottawa: Graphic Publishers, 1928)

Middleton, Jesse Edgar. *The Municipality of Toronto: A History*, Vols. 1 & 2 (Toronto: The Dominion Publishing Co., 1923)

Middleton, Jesse Edgar. *Toronto's 100 Years, 1834-1934* (Toronto: Centennial Committee, 1934)

Morgan, Henry. *Canadian Men and Women of the Time* (Toronto: W. Biggs, 1898)

Mulvany, C. Pelham. *Toronto: Past and Present. A Handbook of the City* (Toronto: W. E. Daiger, 1884)

Newman, Peter C. *The Canadian Establishment* (Agincourt: Methuen Publications, 1983)

Pearson, W. H. *Recollections and Records of Toronto of Old* (Toronto: William Briggs, 1914)

Polk, R. L. & Company. *Toronto Directory 1890*, Vol. 1 (Toronto: R. L. Polk & Co., 1890)

Pursley, Louis H. *Street Railways of Toronto 1861-1921* (Los Angeles: Interurbans, 1958)

Reed, T. A. *Royal Architectural Institute of Canada Journal, Toronto's Early Architects, The Story of Toronto* (Toronto: Royal Architectural Institute of Canada, February 1950)

Robertson, John Ross. *Landmarks of Toronto 1894* (Toronto: J. Ross Robertson, 1894–1914)

Robson, Mary E. *The Origins of Street Names in Toronto's Ward 5* (Toronto: Community History Project, 1987)

Scadding, Henry. *Toronto of Old* (Toronto: Oxford University Press, 1966)

Scadding and Dent. *Toronto Past and Present* (Toronto: Hunter Rose & Co., 1884)

Shepard, Martha. *The First Things of Toronto* (Toronto: Martha Shepard, 1938)

The Scribe, T. Eaton Company Ltd., *Golden Jubilee, 1869–1919* (Toronto: T. Eaton, 1919)

Wallace, W. Stewart. *The Dictionary of Canadian Biography* (Toronto: Macmillan, 1926)

West, Bruce. *Toronto* (Toronto: Doubleday Canada, 1967)

Adam, G. Mercer 114
Adam, James 72
Adam, John 82
Adams, J. Frank 132
Adams, Oliver 148
Adelaide Street 66, 83-84
Aldbury Lodge 83
Alexander & Lawrence Buchan 87, 111, 120
Alexander & Stark Company 111, 117
Alexander, David 72, 82, 132
Alexander, William 82, 95, 98, 111, 114, 114, 116-118, 120, 124, 134
Allen, Alfred 82, 133, 136
Allen, John 72, 82
Allward, Hugh 140, 157, 158
Ammonia Company of Toronto 83, 130
Ancroft Place 37, 70, 88, 90, 146, 156, 158, 161, 164
Anderson, Captain 42-43
Anderson, James 79, 82
Andrews, Walter 132
Annex 100
Apostolic Church 84
Arbour Glen Apartments 112
Architecture, Department of 145
Asquith Avenue 31, 81, 116, 118, 120
Astley Avenue 23, 37, 70, 90, 164
Avenue Road 137
Avoca Avenue 167
Avondale Avenue 33-34, 37, 93, 95, 110, 112
Avondale Place 112
Avondale Road 14, 71, 96, 152, 156, 164
Ayrshire 148

Baillie House 154, 157
Baker, Frederick 148, 154
Baldwin, John 43
Baldwin, Robert 40
balloon frame construction 98, 137
Bank of Montreal 83
Bank of Toronto 82, 104, 124
Bank of Upper Canada 16, 43, 56-57
Banks Brothers 30, 82, 133-134
Banks, Arthur 83
Banks, George 82, 133-134
Banks, Greenhow 76, 80, 82, 95, 133-134
Banks, Robert 82, 95, 134
Banks, William 82, 134
Bath, England 150
Bay Street 13, 83-84, 100
Bayview Avenue 123, 127, 130, 167
Beatty & Stovel Real Estate 82, 135
Beatty, Samuel 73, 82, 130, 134
Beatty, W. H. 82

Beaty, Hamilton & Cassels 84
Beaty, Robert & Company 135
Beau Street 23, 25, 57, 59, 75-76, 79, 88, 92
Beaumont Road 24, 27, 57, 79, 121, 124-125, 140, 143, 147, 151-152, 160, 164
Beaumont, Charlotte 79
Beaux Arts 92
Beckett, Samuel 141
Bedford, J. & Sons 59, 71
Bedford, Jeremiah 71, 127, 129, 152
Bell Telephone Company 53
Bellingham 31
Belmont Street 97
Belt Line: Railway 30; 34, 127, 130, 167 Trail 160
Beverley Street 137
Bin-Scarth Road 25, 27, 57, 59, 61, 65, 72, 76-77, 79, 121, 124-125, 147, 151, 159-160
Bird, Eustace 148
Birks, Ellis, Ryrie 52, 133
Birrell, Charles 65, 71
Bismarck Street 110
Blackwood, Arthur 71
Blackwood, Charles 71
Blackwood, S. Temple 147
Blackwood, Thomas 59, 71
Blaikie & Alexander Company 82, 87, 98, 111, 117, 120, 134,
Blaikie, George 132
Blaikie, John 31, 61, 80, 82, 98, 111, 116-118, 120, 124, 134, 151, 157
Blake, Samuel 44
block house 16, 18, 46
Bloor Street 13-14, 16, 19, 23, 27, 29, 39, 41, 45, 53, 57, 60, 75, 79, 84, 85-88, 94, 120-121, 133-134, 162; Bloor Street East 13, 17, 19, 23, 33, 35, 91, 93, 104, 117, 162
Bloor, Joseph 16, 18-19, 21, 27, 41, 95, 104, 134; brewery 16, 18, 19, 27, 95, 167
Blue Hill 23, 137
Board of Trade 67
Bole, William 132
Bolton, Henry 47
Bond Head, Governor Sir Francis 16, 42-43, 57
Boone, Charles 155
Booth & Son 83
Booth, Arthur 83
Booth, George 78, 83, 139
Boswell, Robertson & Eddis 83
Boultbee, Alfred 109, 113, 146, 156-157
Boulton, Clara 105
Boulton, Henry 54
Bowden, Frank 132

Boyd, Lawrence 132
Branksome Hall School 117, 121
Bridge Street 33, 35, 88, 91, 95-96, 126, British North America Act 66
Briton Medical & General Life Association 84
Brock 42
Brodie, Johanna 72, 83
Brodie, Richard 120
Brown, George 66
Brown, J. Francis 146, 157
Brown, Walter 60, 95, 98, 112, 146
Buchan, Lawrence 120
Buckler, Frederick 75, 83
Bull, William Perkins 119, 158
Bulmer, Mrs. 137
Burgess, Ralph 72, 83
Burke & Horwood 147, 150, 157-158
Burke, Edmund 144-145, 147, 151, 158
Burke, Horwood & White 109, 147, 150, 157-158, 162
Burton, C. L. 158

Caer Howell 48
Calvin & Shepard 147
Canada Landed Credit Company 82, 114
Canadian Bank of Commerce 83, 86, 114
Canadian Pacific Railway 17, 23, 67
Canadian Sportsman & Livestock Journal 83
Canadian Yacht Club 40, 66
Carlton Street 30
Carpmael, Charles 72, ,83
Carroll, John 679, 83
Carruthers, Frederick 19, 26, 33, 48, 59, 103
Cassels, Allen 109
Castle Frank 13, 23, 31, 104, 114, 134, 160-161, 166; Avenue 37, 71, 84, 88, 91-92; Road 23, 148-149, 157, 164
Castlemere Apartments 157, 160-161
Caverhill 60. 95, 98, 110-111, 120, 170
Caverhill, Beatrice 111
Cawthra Estate 118-119
Cawthra, Joseph 72, 83, 87, 96, 98, 117, 120, 125
Cayley, Francis 19, 27, 33, 41, 50, 57, 80, 83, 89, 95, 97, 104, 110, 133-134, 136
Cayley, John 83, 104-105
Cayley, William 134, 157
Centre Road 33, ,35, 37, 71, 77, 79, 91-92, 96, 122, 129, 134
Chadwick & Beckett 157-158
Chadwick, (Wm. Craven), Vaux 147
Chadwick, Marion 147
Chadwick, Vaux & Bryan 158

Chandler, Howard 132
Chapman & Company 83
Chapman, A. H. 148, 158
Chapman, George 75, 83, 96
Chapman, Howard 148
Charlottetown Conference 66
Chestnut Grove 7, 26, 106
Chestnut Park 20, 22, 26, 29, 35, 37, 60, 63, 75, 78, 86, 89-90, 95, 97, 99, 101, 106-109, 113, 131, 134-136, 156-157, 160, 166, 170; Road 37, 71, 93, 146-148, 152, 155-156, 162, 164, 166
Chestnut Street 106
Chorley Park 23, 37, 167
Church Street 30, 86, 109, 134
Clarewood Avenue 37, 91
Cluny Avenue 37, 69, 71, 91-93, 96, 102, 112, 156, 164-167
Cluny Crescent 71
Cluny Drive 103, 109, 155, 157
CNE 67, 139
Coatsworth, Hodgens & Company 84
Coffee & Co. & Thomas F. Flynn Grain Commission 83
Coffee, John 83
Coffee, Lawrence 75, 83, 119
Colborne Lodge 103
Colborne Street 83
Colborne, Sir John 44
Coleman, A. 136, 157
College Street 54
Collier Street 160
Colonial Revival 101
Common Pleas Division 84
Confederation 65-66
Connecticut 39, 53
Consumers Gas Company 66, 120, 138
Copp, William 132
Cornell University 147
Corrigan Close 162-163
Coryell, Robert 132
Cottingham Street 17, 143
Coulson, John 153
Court of Chancery 54, 57
Court Street 110
Cox, Arthur 79, 83
Craigleigh 61, 63, 86, 95, 158; Gardens 167-168
Crangle, Samuel 77, 83, 150
Creelman, A. R. 114
Crescent Road 9, 13, 17, 19, 31, 33, 35, 37, 51, 69, 71, 75, 79, 86, 88-89, 91-92, 95-96, 101, 109, 113, 134, 147, 151-152, 154-156, 160-167
Croft & Sons 83
Croft, William 72, 83

Crowther, James 130
Current Value Assessment 162
Curry & Sparling 109, 148, 157-158
Curry, (Samuel) George 144, 148

Dale Avenue 33-35, 72, 75, 83-85, 88-89, 92, 95-96, 114-115, 130, 134, 157, 161
Dale, The 31, 95, 114-115, 157, 160, 170
Daley, John 132
Daniels, Walter 75
Darling & Curry 148, 151, 154
Darling & Edwards 148
Darling & Pearson 148-149, 157-158
Darling, Curry, Sproatt & Pearson 148
Darling, Frank 145, 148
Darling, Henry 62, 73, 83, 96
Darling, Robert 72
Darling, Sproatt & Pearson 148, 154
Davenport Road 16, 23, 42, 103, 137
David A. Balfour Park 167
Davidson & Company 83, 130
Davidson, Charles 73, 83, 130
Davies Pork Packing House 118
Davies, J. Edgar 125
Davies, Mary 150
Davies, Reverend Henry 77, 79
Davies, William 31, 83, 95, 98, 100, 117-120, 123, 147, 158, 165
Davis, James 60, 83, 95-96, 110, 132
Deancroft 62, 96
Denbrae 82, 95, 116-117
Denison, A. R. 155
Denovan, Joshua 132
Despard, Francis 71, 83, 130
Diamante Development Corporation 161
Dick, N. B. 139, 144
Dick, William 777, 83
Dickson & Company 72
Dickson Avenue 37, 89, 91, 130
Dickson, George 89, 128, 130
Dickson, Isabella 34, 130
Dickson, James 79, 83
Dinnick, Wilfred 25
Dixon, John 109, 156-157
Dixon, W. E. 34
Dodds, Edward K. 79, 83
Dominion Bank of Canada 86
Don River 19, 30, 104, 127
Don Valley 61, 97, 104, 167
Dorset, 90
Douglas Drive 92, 131, 164, 167
Draper, Chief Justice 14, 16, 26, 95, 160
Drayton, Henry 149
Drumsnab 19, 82-84, 89, 97, 104-105, 110, 133, 157, 171; Farm 89, 134; Road 72, 157, 164

Duggan, Edmund 61
Duggan, George 19, 26, 29, 33, 48, 59, 94, 103, 134
Dunbar Road 34, 37, 72, 8286, 91, 139, 152, 157, 164
Dundas, Alexander 132
Dunlap, David 132
Dunn, John 137
Dyment, Albert 115

Easton, Alexander 29
Eaton, T. & Company 65-66, 94
Ecole des Beaux-Arts 148
Eddis, E. H. 83
Eddis, H. W. 79, 83
Edgar Avenue 37, 72, 89, 91, 13-132, 164
Edgar, James 121, 124
Edgewood Crescent 72, 164
Edwardian 99, 150
Edwards & Webster 146
Edwards, R. J. 144
Elizabethan 100
Elliott, G. A. 79, 83, 133, 136, 158
Elliott, George 133
Ellis, Eliza 59, 72
Ellis, Henry 84, 117
Ellis, John 61, 73
Elm Avenue 33, 61, 63, 71-73, 75, 79, 82-91, 95-96, 98, 116-117, 120-121, 124, 133, 136, 146, 149-150, 152, 154, 157, 160, 164
Elmsley Villa 104
Elwell, Reverend Joseph 77, 79, 84
English Cottage Movement 161
English Cottage Style 99, 154
Esplanade 47, 79
Evans, H. Pollman 132
Evenholm 63, 151
Ewart, John 54
Exeter 91

Fairmount Properties 162
Family Compact 54
Fenian Raid 66
Fermoy Lodge 84
Fifty Tales of Toronto 111
Fisher House 147, 157
Fisker, J. K. 34
Fitzgibbon, Colonel 42
Fletcher, Angus 27
Foster & Co. 86
Foy & Sons 84
Foy, J.J. 84, 96
Foy, Tupper & Macdonell 84
Fraser, James 31, 84, 133-134
Fredericton, New Brunswick 39
Freeland, Edward 77, 84
Front Street 13-14, 26, 42-43, 46-47, 67, 82-83, 85-87
Fudger, Harris Henry 147, 150, 158
Furniss, Albert 143

Galbraith, Robert 132
Gallows Hill 44
Garden City Movement 25
Geary, Col. Reg 111
Gemmell, John 144, 149, 155
George, Moorehouse & King 149, 158
George, William 132
Georgian: architecture 101, 111; Revival 149
Gibbons, John 149
Gibson, Charles J. 132, 149, 157-158
Gilbert, Elisha 57
Giles & Son 84
Giles, James 77, 84
Glen Hurst 60, 62, 95-96, 116-118, 149, 151, 157
Glen Road 123, 33-35, 61-63, 71-72, 75, 77, 82-84, 86, 91, 95-98, 127-128, 130-132, 135-136, 148, 153, 157-158, 161, 163-164, 167-168
Gloucester 87
Glover, Amelia 39
GNW Telegraph Company 83
Golden Age of Laurier 63, 67, 99
Good & Company 84
Good, James 77, 84-85, 112
Gooderham estate 129
Gooderham, E. D. 154, 158
Gordon & Helliwell 84, 150, 157
Gordon Avenue 72, 91
Gordon, Henry Bauld 150
Gordon, J. B. 144
Gordon, The Misses 132
Gordon, William (Jr.) 67; (Sr.) 73
Gothic Revival 114, 123
Grammar School 54
Grand Trunk Railway 66, 108
Granite Club 66
Gray & Company 84
Gray, Robert 72, 84
Gregg, William R. 144
Gregory Avenue 75
Grenville Street 86
Guiseley House 96, 124-125, 160
Guiseley, Parish of 124
Gull, Charles 77, 84
Gundry & Langley 60, 151
Gundry, Thomas 147, 151
Gwynne Street 14, 16, 19, 60, 77
Gwynne, Dr. William 16, 26, 43, 48, 59
Gzowski, Casimir 50, 108

Haldenby, Eric 153
Hallam, John 37
Hamilton, Hannah Owen 54
Hamilton, J. Cleland 73, 84
Hamilton, James 103
Hancock, Herbert 156
Harding, George 133
Harton Walker Real Estate Company 130, 132, 135

Harvey, Arthur 77, 84, 95, 112, 146
Harvey, Jane 34, 37, 112
Harvey, Miss Charlotte 132
Haverson & St. John 84, 112
Haverson, James 71, 84, 112
Hawthorn: Avenue 37, 72, 74, 91, 150-151, 158; Gardens 147-148, 156, 158
Hay, William 151
Hazel Burn 54
Hazeldean 14, 16, 96, 160; Park 167
Hazelton 86
Hees, Anderson & Company 82
Helliwell, Grant 77, 84, 133, 137, 145, 150
Helliwell, Thomas 19, 127
Helliwell, William 21
Henderson, Elmer 33
Henderson, James 31, 79, 96, 123, 133-134
Henderson, James D. & Company 84
Herbert, F. H. 150, 157
Heron, Orlando 132
Heyroyd 82, 92, 95, 134
High Park 103
High Victorian 61, 98, 121, 150
Highland: Avenue 37, 89, 92, 128, 131, 132, 156, 158, 164, 168; Crescent 75, 91; Gardens 75, 93, 164
Hill Street 33, 35, 62, 71-75, 79, 83-84, 86, 91, 98, 127-129
Hillcrest 62, 96
Hirschfelder, Charles 84
Hirschfelder, Jacob 73, 84
Historic Illustrated Map of York 15
Hodgens, Francis 72, 84
Hodgens, John 31
Hogben, Henry 79, 84, 123
Hogg, William 72, 84
Hollydene 96, 120-121
Home District Savings Bank 84, 133-134
Hooper, Captain Henry 75, 84, 96
Hope, William 57
Horne, Dr. Robert 16, 27, 40, 43, 103
Horwood & White 151
Horwood, John Charles Batstone 147, 151; Eric Crompton 151
Hoskin, John 31, 33-35, 72, 80, 84, 95, 114-115, 130, 134
How, James B. 79, 84, 103, 136, 142
Howard Street 72, 89; Bridge 78
Howard, John 14, 57
Howland & Sons & Company 82
Hudson's Bay Centre 162
Hughes Brothers 84
Hughes, Bernard B. 84
Huntley Street 16, 33, 37, 72, 74-79, 85, 86, 89, 91, 96, 105, 116-117, 124; Bridge 16, 105
Hydro-Electric Power Commission of Ontario 139
Hyland, John Herbert 89, 130
Hynes, James Patrick 151, 157

Idington, Hon. J. 119
Idlewold 60, 95, 98, 112-113, 146
Imperial Bank 82, 84; Building 86
Ince, Thomas Henry 56
Indian Affairs 56
Internal Revenue Department 83
Interocean Railway Company 108
Inventory of Buildings of Architectural and Historical Importance 136, 157
Irving, William 146152
Isolated Risk Fire Insurance Company 82
Italianate 98-99, 112, 115, 118, 121, 123-124

Jackes, Franklin 27
Jackman, Harry 132
Jackson, Maunsell 27, 34, 84, 105, 130
Jackson, Reverend George 132
Jackson, Walter 75, 84
Jacobean 100
Jacobethan 63, 101
Jamieson, Philip 71, 85
Jarvis Collegiate 150
Jarvis Street 30-31, 35, 43, 54, 57, 75, 79, 81, 85, 94, 118, 120, 133
Jarvis, Beaumont 8
Jarvis, Caroline 33
Jarvis, Charles 51, 85
Jarvis, Charlotte Beaumont 88, 90
Jarvis, Col. Stephen 39
Jarvis, Colborne 40
Jarvis, Edgar 30-31, 33, 39, 57-63, 82, 85, 88-90, 95, 98, 103, 105, 116-118, 120, 123-124, 127-131, 134, 145-146, 149, 151, 159
Jarvis, Edgar Beaumont 63, 151
Jarvis family 38
Jarvis, Fanny 48-50, 89, 119
Jarvis, Frederick Starr 59
Jarvis, Frederick William 26, 31, 48, 59, 61, 85, 116
Jarvis, Hanna Peters 52, 54
Jarvis, Herbert 132
Jarvis, Louisa 31, 40, 46, 48-50, 87, 89
Jarvis, Mary 9, 14, 46-49
Jarvis, Mary Boyles 27, 33, 40-42, 60, 103, 113
Jarvis, Mary Caroline 33
Jarvis, Samuel Jr. 33
Jarvis, Samuel Peters 26-27, 33, 39, 40-42, 53-55, 59, 85, 90, 104-105
Jarvis, Sarah 40, 47-48, 50-51, 56-57
Jarvis, Stephen 39, 53, 90, 103
Jarvis, William Botsford 12, 14, 17, 19, 26, 31, 35, 39-44, 47, 51, 53, 56-57, 59-60, 85, 89-90, 95, 97, 102, 104, 117, 134
Jean Street 164
Jenkins, R. & T. Estate Agents 85, 130, 134, 136, 159
Jenkins, Robert 72, 85, 130, 134

Jones, Donald 111
Jordan Street 120
Julian Sale and Company 71, 86, 134

Kantel, Emil 132
Kay & Banks Company 82, 134
Kennedy & Holland 151
Kensington Crescent 34, 37, 75
Kernohan, William 151
Kertland, Douglas 158
Kilgour, Robert 132
King Street 13, 29-30, 38, 66-67, 69, 83-84, 87, 94, 111, 120, 127, 133, 135, 139, 143
Kingston, Professor 103
Kingsway 25, 131
Kirk, Ferrier 85
Kirk, James 79, 85
Knox & Elliott 154
Knox, Elliot & Jarvis 151

Labatt's Ale & Porter 7384
Lamport Avenue 71, 75, 89, 153, 158, 160, 164
Lamport Street 34, 37, 86, 91
Lamport, Henry 31, 34, 89, 134
Land & Loan Company 84
Landed Credit Company 82, 114
Langley & Burke 147, 152, 158
Langley & Howland 109, 152
Langley & Langley 151, 152, 157
Langley, Charles 152
Langley, Edward 147
Langley, Henry 118, 144-145, 147-148, 149-150,
Langley, John 132
Langley, Langley & Burke 147, 150-152, 158
Langton, William 144, 152
Lansdowne Place 37, 92
Larkin, Gerald 149, 157
Lauraway, Abraham 26
Laurier, Sir Wilfred 67
Law Society of Upper Canada 114
Lawren Harris Park 167
Lawrence Park 25, 30, 131, 147
Leadlay, Percival 150
Lennox, Charles 152
Lennox, Edward James 138, 145-146, 152
Liverpool & London & Globe Insurance Company 84
Livingstone, F. W. 85, 96
Livingstone, John 72, 85
London & Canada Loan & Assurance Company 85
London & Canadian Loan Agency 85
Loney, James 77, 85, 134
Lorne Hall 95, 100, 118-119
Lorne, Marquis of 67
Lot Street 53
Lount, Colonel Samuel 43-44, 103

Lowes, Charles 132
Loyalist 39, 40, 43
Lunatic Asylum 44
Lundy's Lane 54
Lyle, John 153, 157-158

Macaulay, James 56
Macdonald, James Grant 90
Macdonald, Sir John A. 66, 108
MacDonald, Warfinger 42
Macdougall & Darling 148
Macduff, Banffshire 155
Mackenzie, Alexander PM 66
Mackenzie, William Lyon 16, 17, 30, 42-43, 56, 103
Macklem, Reverend T. C. Street 72, 85
MacLennan Avenue 75, 91, 128, 131, 164
MacMillan, Sir Ernest 153, 158
MacPherson Avenue 37, 71, 92, 95; East 75, 77, 92
Macpherson, Christina 51
Macpherson, Sir David Lewis 17, 22, 26, 31, 34-35, 37, 51, 60, 75, 79, 86-87, 89, 90, 95, 97, 103, 106, 108-109, 131, 134-135
Macpherson, William Molson 109
Malcolm's Sanitary Goods Company 141
Mammoth House Dry Goods 85
Manning Avenue 86
Mansergh, James 143
Maple Avenue 33,-34, 72-73, 77, 83, 85-86, 89-90-92, 95-96, 114, 146, 150, 152, 154, 158, 161, 164, 166
Mara, Frederick 130
Mara, Henry 130
Marbrae 147
Marks, E. Richard 132
Martin, Arthur 132
Martin, James 85
Martin, Thomas 77
Martyn, Lucy Booth 51, 62, 105, 117
Mary's Rosedale and Gossip of Little York 41, 46
Massey Hall 67
Massey, John 75, 86
Mathers & Haldenby 153, 157
Mathers, William 17, 22, 26, 35, 37, 106, 127-128, 136
Matthews & Company 86
Matthews, Wilmot 86
May Street 33, 35, 74, 75, 86, 89, 92, 149, 158, 164
May, Charles 132
Mayfair 167
McCaw, William 152
McDermid, Donald 130
McDermid, P. 34
McDonald, Helen 75, 86
McDougal, Peter 27
McDunnough, James 77, 85
McHugh, Patricia 166

McKenzie Avenue 34, 37, 72, 77, 89, 92, 114, 148, 152, 155-156, 158, 164
McKenzie, Walter 31, 89, 114
McLaughlin, R. R. 153
McLean, Robert 150
McLeod, Henry 132
McMaster, Hon. William 117, 133
McNab, James 75, 86
McPhail, Robert 79, 86
Mechanics Institute 59, 145, 152
Meredith Crescent 237, 59, 77, 89, 91, 95, 98, 100, 147, 158, 164-165
Meredith, Alden Griffin 41, 46
Meredith, Edmund 45, 48, 50, 51, 86, 89, 112, 118-119, 123
Meredith, John 132
Merigold, Susan 59
Metcalfe, James 57
Metropolitan Church 66
Metropolitan Permanent Building Society 84, 133-134
Meyer, George 77, 86
Mickleborough, James 147
Middleton, Jesse Edgar 139
Milkmen's Road 77, 167
Miller & Richard 86
Miller, George Martell 153, 157
Minister of the Interior 108
Model School, Ryerson 156
Molson, Elizabeth Sarah 108
Montgomery, Robert 72, 86
Montgomery's Tavern 42-43
Moody, Isaac 33, 37, 77, 80, 86, 96, 112
Moody's Lane 77, 112
Moore Park 101
Mooredale 154, 166-167
Morgan, Pierpont 155
Morris Avenue 37, 89, 92, 130, 132
Morton, Benjamin 31, 33, 35, 123
Mount Pleasant Road 20, 22, 30, 51, 59, 91-92, 120, 124, 127, 129, 166-167
Murray Street 31, 60, 86, 89
Murray, Charles 132
Murray, George 86, 96
Mutual Street 53

Nanton: Avenue 89, 91, 158, 164; Crescent 37, 77, 91, 92
Nanton, Augustus 31, 49, 50, 89, 103
Nanton, Edward 27, 33, 35, 89, 105, 134
National Investment Company of Canada 82, 84, 114, 117
National Trades and Labour Congress of Canada 67
Nelson & Son 86
Nelson, Charles 73, 86, 148
Neo-Georgian 99
Neo-Tudor 99, 109, 156
Newark (Niagara-on-the-Lake) 39, 53-54
Newmarket 83, 124
Niagara Street 30

Nightingale, Thomas 17, 31, 79, 81
Niles, Charles 148
Norcastle 62, 63, 83, 96
Normal School 83
North American Life Assurance Company 120
North Drive 33-34, 37, 71, 77, 79, 84-86, 89-90, 92-93, 96, 112-113
North Iron Bridge 32, 36, 91, 130, 132
North Rosedale 20, 22, 26, 29-30, 35, 37, 59, 89-91, 99, 101, 109, 127-131, 134-135, 167
North Rosedale Park 30, 126, 128, 131
Northern Railway 120
Northway, John 157
Norwich 90

Oakville 45
Official Guardian of Infants 114
O'Hara, Henry 150
Old City Hall 100
Old George Place 77, 163
Ontario Association of Architects 145
Ontario School of Art 145
Ontario Society of Artists 145
Ontario, Lake 13, 19, 25, 29, 124, 133, 143
Orchard Road 34, 37, 109
Ord, Lewis 49, 51, 71
Orkney Islands 88
Osborne, Henry 112, 146
Osborne, M. C. 165
Osgoode Hall 49, 66, 87, 122
Osler, Edmund 31, 34, 61, 71, 86, 95, 134, 167
Osler, Henry 78
Oxley, J. M. 148

Page & Steele 153, 158
Page & Warrington 153, 158
Page, Forsey 153
Paris Exhibition 99
Park Drive 73, 129; Reservation 167
Park Road 33-37, 59-60, 71, 75, 77, 79, 83,-84, 87-89, 91-93, 95-96, 103, 110, 115, 118-120, 122123, 134, 146, 148, 152, 156, 158, 161-162, 164, 167
Parker, Thomas 79, 86
Parliament Buildings 86, 154
Parliament Street 19, 30, 104
Parsons, William 132
Patrick, Rachel 90
Patterson, Beaty & Hamilton 84
Patterson, Robert 79, 86
Pears, Leo 137
Pearson, John 154
Pelham Place 37, 71, 77, 90, 92, 128
Pelham, George 90
Pelham, John Thomas 90
Pellatt & Osler 86
Pender, David 77, 86

Percy Street 33-35, 91-92
Permanent Building Society 84
Philbrick, Dr. 86
Phillips, Frederick 72, 86
Pine Hill Road 14, 37, 51, 77, 92, 158, 164
Playter, Captain George 19, 27, 104
Polk, R. L. & Company 69, 81
Port Hope 142, 147
Porter & Son 86
Porter, Frederick 132
Porter, George 26
Potters Field 14
Powell: Avenue 33, 77, 93, 96; Street 75, 91
Powell, John 42-43
Powell, Mary Boyles 14, 40, 54, 90, 103
Powell, William Dummer Chief Justice 14, 40-41, 54, 89-90,
Prairie School 99
Pratt, Alfred 77, 86
Price Family 17, 20, 26; mill 20
Price Street 90, 137
Price, James Hervey 17, 43
Price, Joseph 17, 20, 26, 90, 95, 103, 106, 127
Price, Miss Sarah 17, 60, 86, 90, 128, 130
Pricefield Road 23, 77, 90, 159, 164; Estate 36
Princess Louise 67, 118
Proctor, Albert 132
Prospect Road 37, 93, 109
Provincial Insurance Company of Canada 84, 112
Purkiss, John 137

Queen Anne 98, 100-101, 117, 121, 123-125
Queen Street 30, 39, 44, 66-67, 100
Queen Victoria 66-67, 118
Queen's University 155
Queen's Park 83, 100
Queen's Plate 66
Queenston 54; Heights 52

Rachael Street 33, 77, 79, 90, 163-164
Radford, J. A. 157
Rae, William 155
Ramsden Park 17
Ramsey, James 149
Ravensmount 83, 96
Rebellion of 1837 16-17, 42
Red Lion Inn (Hotel) 14, 17
Reesor, Hon. David 79, 86, 123
Regency 97, 104
Richards, D. 158
Richardsonian Romanesque 98, 100
Richmond, Henry 132
Ridout, John 54
Ridout, Percival 51, 77, 86, 103, 109
Ridout, Tom 54, 90

Riel Rebellion 67
Ritchie Crescent 36, 71, 72, 77, 90-91, 93, 130
Ritchie, Charles 22, 89-90, 128, 130-131, 135
Roberts, David 154
Robinson, George 132, 153, 157
Robinson, Robert 26
Robinson, William 42, 48
Roddy, Charles 75, 86
Rolph, Ernest 148, 154
Romanesque 60, 100, 121, 123
Rome, David 79, 86
Rose Cottage 60, 98, 113, 157
Rose Park 85, 110
Rose, John 19
Rosedale Golf & Country Club 129, 132, 157-158; Golf Links 131, 168
Rosedale House 13, 19, 26, 40, 43, 46, 48, 50-51, 59-60, 88, 95, 97, 102-103, 109, 135-136, 160
Rosedale Lane 37
Rosedale Lodge 87
Rosedale Manors 154
Rosedale Park 73, 131, 167-168
Rosedale Ravine 5, 16, 18, 23, 27, 33, 59-60, 88, 95, 105, 110, 116, 118-119, 124, 159, 167; Drive 37, 92
Rosedale Road 14, 33-35, 37, 51, 60, 76-77, 83-87, 93, 95-96, 102, 112, 133, 145-146, 149-150, 153-154, 158
Rosedale Valley 30, 167; Road 19, 23, 37, 59, 93, 161, 166
Rosedale Viaduct 158
Rosedale-Moore Park Association 166
Rose-Park 19, 25, 28, 30, 34, 61, 63, 89-90, 99, 112, 123, 134-135, 166
Rowanwood Avenue 37, 77, 90, 92
Roxborough 75, 77, 82-83; Avenue 34, 73, 92; Drive 20, 79, 127, 132, 158, 164; Street 92; Street East 30, 35, 37, 60-61, 77, 89, 90-91, 93, 106, 127, 133, 136, 139, 142, 148, 154, 159-161, 164, 166
Roxburghshire 120
Royal Canadian Academy 145
Royal Canadian Yacht Club 40, 67
Royal Insurance Building 84
Rundle, C. R. 152, 157
Ryan, Hugh 72, 86, 121
Ryrie, James 109, 147, 157, 162

St. Andrews College 109, 131
St. Andrews Gardens 79, 90
St. Clair Avenue 44, 167
St. George's Church 83, 104
St. James Cathedral 66
St. Lawrence Hall 30, 66
St. Paul's Anglican Church 45, 66
St. Simon's Anglican Church 85
Sale & Company 86
Sale, Julian 71, 86, 130, 132

Saloon 4 Court 84, 123
Savings Bank 84
Scadding, Henry 10, 16, 81, 88
Scarth Cochran & Company 130, 135
Scarth Road 37, 79, 90-91, 93
Scarth, William Bain 88, 90, 130, 135
Scholfield Avenue 37, 79, 90-91, 93, 130-132, 164, 168
Scholfield, Alexandra 90
School of Architecture 152-153
School of Practical Science 145, 153
Scott Street 84
Scott, Alexander 75, 86
Scott, Mary 117
Scott, Thomas 132
Scottish Ontario & Manitoba Land Company 22, 26, 30, 33-35, 90, 128-129131, 135
Seagram, Norman 148, 158
Second Concession from the Bay 14, 17, 25, 102, 127
Second Empire 98-99, 118, 123, 164
Severn Brothers 103; Brewery 18, 86
Severn Creek 16, 95-96, 159; Park 167
Severn River 27, 60
Severn Street 35
Severn, George 86, 95
Severn, Henry 87
Severn, William 86
Shaw, Frederick 77, 87
Shaw, Richard Norman 100
Shepard & Calvin 157, 161
Sheppard, John 137
Sherborne 88
Sherbourne Street 16-17, 19, 30, 33, 35, 39, 45, 57, 72, 75, 77-79, 82-84, 86, 88, 90, 93, 95-96, 109, 121, 133-134, 157, 160, 162; North 129, 154, 164, 166
Shuter Street 54
Siddall, J. Wilson 154, 157-158
sidewalks 65, 109, 143, 156, 159
Silver Creek 127
Simcoe, Governor 25, 53, 88, 133
Simcoe, Lake 40
Simpson, Henry 149, 157, 160
Simpson, Robert 66, 84, 117, 133
Skinner, Isaiah 26
Small, James 54

Small, John 13, 26, 102
Smith & Gemmell 149, 157
Smith, Charles 79, 87
Smith, Eden 139, 154, 157-158
Smith, Hon. Frank 117, 133
Smith, James Avon 155, 157
Smith, James F. 75, 87, 144-145, 149
Smith, Robert Home 25
Smith, Smith & Greer 87
South Drive 9, 17, 31, 33, 35, 37, 62-63, 71, 75, 77, 79, 82, 84, 86-91, 93, 95-96, 98-99, 110, 118-119, 1322-124, 126, 128, 133-134, 146, 149, 151-152, 158, 161-162, 164-167
South Rosedale 17, 27, 29-30, 35, 37, 53, 57, 59-61, 63, 69, 91, 99, 130-131, 145
Sparling, W. F. 148
Sparling, William 132
Sproatt & Pearson 148
Sproatt & Rolph 157-158
Sproatt, Charles 155
Sproatt, Henry 148, 154-155
Standish Avenue 37, 79, 93, 164
Stanley, William 57
Stark, John 31, 77, 84, 87, 110-111
Stark, John & Company 84, 87
Starr, Rachel 90
Stevens, Dorothy 146, 158
Storm, William 144-147, 156
Stovel & Company 87, 130
Stovel, Ebenezer 71, 76, 130
Strachan, Bishop 42
Strachan, John 40, 54
Strathy, John 57
Street, Eleanor 152
Street, G. E. 148
Strickland & Symons 151, 154
Strickland, Walter 155
Summerhill Avenue 23, 33, 35, 37, 79, 90-91, 127, 130, 132
Sylvan Towers 61-63, 95, 128, 160
Symons, Mrs. Harry 119
Symons, William Limbery 155

Taylor, John 35, 37, 87, 96
Temple Chambers 146
The Globe 30, 41, 51, 103
The Daily Leader 30, 51

Thom House 96, 98, 122-123
Thom, John 79, 87, 96, 99
Thomas, William 104, 136, 155, 157
Thompson Avenue 35, 37, 93
Thompson, Allen 78, 87
Thompson, Charles 90, 128
Thompson, Thomas 72, 85, 87, 117
Thomson, Alexander 132
Thorne, Horace 130
Thornwood 17, 90, 95, 103, 161; Road 37, 79, 161
Thornwood, Essex, England 90
Todmorden Mills 19-20, 137, 150
Todmorden, England 19
Toronto Architecture: A City Guide 166
Toronto Athletic Grounds 71, 72, 79
Toronto Belt Line Railway Company 34, 130
Toronto City Hall 67
Toronto Corn Exchange 67
Toronto Electric Light Company 139
Toronto Gas-Light & Water Company 139, 151
Toronto General Hospital 120
Toronto General Trusts Company 87, 114
Toronto Incandescent Electric Light Company 86, 139
Toronto Industrial Exhibition (CNE) 67, 139
Toronto Island 67, 143
Toronto Lacrosse Athletic Association 131
Toronto Lacrosse Grounds 121, 131, 168
Toronto Land and Loan Company 112
Toronto Life Assurance Company & Tontine 84, 112
Toronto Mechanics Institute 145
Toronto Old and New 114
Toronto Real Estate Board 130, 163
Toronto Rolling Mill 86
Toronto Stock Exchange 67
Toronto Street 29, 31, 59, 66-67, 81-82, 85, 87, 90, 111, 120, 130, 134-135, 146
Toronto Street Railway Company 29, 94, 139
Toronto Telephone Dispatch Company Limited 67
Toronto Turf Club 40, 66
Toronto's 100 Years, 1834-1934 139

Townsend, S. Hamilton 63, 109, 113, 156
Township of York 12
Township Lot 17 34, 128
Township Lot 18 20, 26, 33-34, 90, 102, 106, 127-128
Township Lot 19 14, 19, 26, 33, 127
Township Lot 20 17, 19, 27, 33, 57
Townsley, F. A. 137
Townsley, William 17
Treasury Department 86
Trethewey, William 132
Trinity Church, Broadway 155
Trinity College 148
Tudor 101, 121

Union Station 66-67
University of Toronto 114, 144, 152
University of Waterloo 153
Upper Canada College 104, 145, 147-148, 151-152

Vair, George 79
Vankoughnet, Philip 26, 48, 59
Vardon, George 56
Victoria Street 82, 135
Victorian era 99, 140
View Place 37, 93, 109

Walker & Sons 86
Walker, Harton 130, 132, 135
War of 1812 51, 54
Warren & Sons 87
Warren Brothers (Charles D. & William A.) 72, 87, 96; & Henry Boomer 87
Warren, William 117, 120
Waters, Mackenzie 119, 156, 158
Watts, George 132
Waycott, Charles 79, 87
Webster, H. J. 139, 144
Wellington Street 83-84, 112
West Rosedale 19, 35, 37, 69, 101, 127, 151
Western Canadian Loan & Savings Company 86
Whaley, Eli 89
White Bridge 83, 195, 116-117, 124, 159, 162
White House 86, 96, 142

White, George 87, 95, 133, 136
White, Mrs. Louisa 87
White, Murray 132, 147, 151
White, William 34, 119
Whitehall Road 79, 89
Whitney Avenue 79, 90, 93, 132, 135, 164
Whitney, J. W. G. 90, 130, 135
Whitney, Sir James Pliny 90, 135
Whittemore Building 59, 85, 130, 134
Wilkes, Hilton 156, 158
Wilkins, Thomas 146
Williams, Greene & Rome Company 86
Wilson & McPhail Company 86
Wilson, Andrew 132
Wilton, Eddis 132
Winchester Street 30; School 86
Windeyer, R. C. 147
Wood, James 130
Woodbine Cottage 17, 26, 60, 86, 90
Woodbine Race Track 67
Woodland Avenue 33, 35, 37, 77, 79, 84-88, 90, 93, 95-96, 110, 122, 134
Wrentham Place 79
Wright, George 75
Wright, Mrs. Lillian 132
Wyld, Brock & Darling 83

Yonge Street 13-14, 16, 19-23, 29-31, 33-35, 37, 40-42, 46, 54, 57, 60, 66-67, 755, 77, 84-86, 90, 92, 94-95, 102-103, 106, 109, 113, 117, 120, 126, 133-134, 137, 139, 143, 160, 162, 166-167; Highway 16, 35, 40, 102
York Chambers 82, 85, 110, 130, 135
York Street 47, 67
Yorkville 14, 16-17, 24, 27, 29-31, 35, 41, 57, 59, 81, 84-85, 94, 105, 110, 116, 118, 120, 134, 137, 143